The Hoarders

THE HOARDERS

MATERIAL DEVIANCE IN MODERN AMERICAN CULTURE

SCOTT HERRING

UNIVERSITY OF CHICAGO PRESS Chicago and London

SCOTT HERRING is associate professor in the
Department of English at Indiana University. He is the
author of Another Country: Queer Anti-Urbanism and
Queering the Underworld: Slumming, Literature,
and the Undoing of Lesbian and Gay History, also
published by the University of Chicago Press.

The University of Chicago Press, Chicago 60637
The University of Chicago Press, Ltd., London
© 2014 by The University of Chicago
All rights reserved. Published 2014.
Printed in the United States of America

23 22 21 20 19 18 17 16 15 14   1 2 3 4 5

ISBN-13: 978-0-226-17168-5   (cloth)
ISBN-13: 978-0-226-17171-5   (paper)
ISBN-13: 978-0-226-17185-2   (e-book)
DOI: 10.7208/chicago/9780226171852.001.0001

Library of Congress Cataloging-in-Publication Data

Herring, Scott, 1976– author.
   The hoarders : material deviance in modern
American culture / Scott Herring.
       pages cm
   Includes bibliographical references and index.
   ISBN 978-0-226-17168-5 (cloth : alkaline
paper) — ISBN 978-0-226-17171-5 (paperback :
alkaline paper) — ISBN 978-0-226-17185-2 (e-book)
1. Compulsive hoarding—Popular works.
2. Compulsive hoarding—Patients—Public
opinion.   I. Title.
   RC569.5.H63H47 2014
   616.85'84—dc23

                                        2014013969

♾ This paper meets the requirements of
ANSI/NISO Z39.48–1992 (Permanence of Paper).

For Marty Dowling

CONTENTS

PREFACE AND ACKNOWLEDGMENTS

When I was a child, some afternoons my mother would drive us out to a small neighborhood community—nothing more than a street of compact houses—called Wilkes Circle. Here she grew up on the edge of poverty, her bricklayer father dead before her thirteenth birthday, her unemployed mother killed by cancer four months after her marriage to my father at the age of twenty. She sorely missed this childhood home, a site of pleasure as much as trauma. She would park the car in front of her old address. She would reminisce. We would slowly pull away. Though it felt like visiting a personal shrine, I had dim awareness of her incalculable losses.

On our way to Wilkes Circle we would often pass a house unlike others from my mother's formative years. Google Maps tells me it was 1027 Woodward Road in the town of Midfield, Alabama. This residence was large—a "mansion," my mother recalls—but far from impressive. A tiny yet dense forest of magnolias and pines shielded most of the house from public viewing. A chain-link fence laced with weeds surrounded the property. Litter covered its grounds. The neighborhood children, my mother remembers when I ask years later for details, spun wild tales of the home's owner as they marveled at the things strewn about his lawn. They fantasized about his riches, his solitude, his craziness, his squalor on the inside. Kids being kids, they would sometimes toss a rock at the house hoping that someone would rush out the front door and yell them off. They named this unseen spectacle the Rat Man.

Over repeated trips back to Wilkes Circle, my mother's Rat Man became my own. I too grew enthralled by this person. He inspired fascination, dread, and no small amount of revulsion. His house was far different from my suburban home, which was vacuumed regularly and dusted weekly. A photograph of our smiling family hung in the hallway. The living room harbored an antique curio cabinet filled with keepsakes: framed wedding photos, bronze-dipped baby shoes, a Hallmark holiday ornament. The only clutter in sight was a pile of magazines or some overdue self-help books checked out from the downtown library. My house read normal; the Rat Man's cracked.

I never once saw anyone enter or exit the Rat Man's home, even though I spied intently from our moving car. When I imagined the owner, I thought only of a lonely male draped in black with a white bandage wrapped around his head.

Thinking back, I see now that my six-year-old self had confused the Rat Man with the lead actor in *The Elephant Man*, David Lynch's 1980 cinematic rendering of John (Joseph Carey) Merrick, a disabled Victorian male known largely for his cranial irregularities. This makes historical sense. If they are to be trusted, YouTube posts of promotional advertisements show that the cable television channel Home Box Office (HBO) broadcast the film in January 1982. The promotion voice-over describes Merrick as a "hooded, shambling curiosity in a Victorian freak show." I vaguely remember watching clips of this film during one of the channel's occasional free trials. The trepidation that the "Elephant Man" inspired easily transferred onto the material and human contents of 1027 Woodward Road.

I open with this vignette for a good reason: in the midst of my research I realized that my mother's childhood name for this local curiosity was an abbreviation for Pack Rat Man. In her recollection she had dropped half of the popular term for those who collect many things. When she described the house, she was not quoting Sigmund Freud's classic 1909 essay on obsessional neurosis, a mental illness whose parameters the Austrian psychoanalyst refined through a case history he referred to as the "Rat Man." My mother was simply repeating neighborhood lore of the American South's working poor. It is nevertheless clear to me that I aimed my childhood terror at someone that many today would consider a compulsive hoarder. I had turned this pack rat into a one-man freak show, but I was not the only one then, nor am I the only one now. While it can be an unreliable resource, *Wikipedia* fittingly lists Merrick's occupations before his untimely death as "sideshow performer" and "Medical Research Subject."

How did I come at such a young age to think of the Pack Rat Man and his residence as a wrongful aberration and my domestic life as an ordinary ideal? Who put this idea into my head? If I learned from my parents, then who taught them? Why were fear and disgust my default emotional responses to someone I had never met, let alone sighted? It is not inconceivable that this man lived a wonderful life with a wonderful family, each content on their lot and happy amidst their things. Or that a solitary woman lived there in lieu of a solitary male. It is feasible that I could have been inspired by the example of this house rather than repelled by it.

One initial answer to these questions is that I made sense of the Pack Rat Man thanks to a fictive version of a sideshow performer on cable TV, one that anticipated a later rash of shows medicalizing real-life hoarders as walking pathologies. Even at my early age, I was learning that it is difficult to fathom hoarders without appreciating the extensive cultural systems that aid their identification: this is the main argument of my book. Many of us are aware that hoarding can cause pain. We know that hoarding can hurt. We know firsthand, by word of mouth, or by flipping on the television that pack rats, like everyone else, can be depressed, anxious, traumatized, and grief-stricken. During and after their lives, their emotional difficulties and their piles of stuff can lead to unjustifiable stress on loved ones and neighbors. These are unremarkable, irrefutable claims, and my comments to come reflect no desire to discount anyone's lived reality. But what else might there be for us to know? How did common sense about hoarders and their hardships—my knowledge about them as a child, for instance, or my perception of them as an adult—come to be?

These are delicate questions to mull over, especially if we want to avoid sensationalizing this topic. Patience is not always my strongest suit, but I remain someone trained to take a topic and worry it for years at a time. Luckily, I am employed by a public research university to wonder about things, where they come from, how they make sense of our worlds. This book tries hard to think about what my six-year-old self did not already know about hoarders. Given that a certain line of thinking about such persons has hardened in conversations inside and outside psycho-medical institutions, the time feels ripe to reassess our knowledge of pack rats, extreme accumulators, and clutter addicts. The Hoarders thus offers my petrified childhood a different way of grasping its heightened response to the Pack Rat Man.

I haven't made it back to Wilkes Circle in some time. When I visited it last, I was not surprised to see the Rat Man's house demolished. In one of many ironies that often circulate around these individuals, row after row of storage units called Fairfield Discount Self Storage replaced the dwelling. Little trace remains of this individual save for memories that my mother and I now share when we muse over my youth spent watching her mourn her own. Given a few of the stories I am about to tell you, this vanishing is terribly fitting.

I offer my appreciation to the many librarians, curators, and archivists who assisted this book. The New York Public Library held the core of chapter 1. Columbia University's Rare Book and Manuscript Library and Government Information, Maps and Microform Services, at Indiana University in Bloomington (IU) also provided useful documents. About half of chapter 2's claims were made after reviewing files and slides at the Andy Warhol Museum, as well as supplemental materials at the Herron Art Library of Indiana University–Purdue University Indianapolis, the Lilly Library, and the Special Collections of IU's Fine Arts Library. Chapter 4's theses on late life material culture were facilitated by holdings at the Kinsey Institute for Research in Sex, Gender, and Reproduction. Alongside these institutional archives, individuals such as Terry Kovel kindly mailed me artifacts from their personal collections. A 2010 fellowship and two 2013 grants from the IU Office of the Vice Provost for Research facilitated the book's completion, as did a subvention from the Department of English with Paul Gutjahr as chairperson. I also thank the College Arts and Humanities Institute for a 2011 Research Grant.

Portions of this book have been read and reviewed by Russell Belk, Ed Comentale, Denise Cruz, Diana Fuss, Susan Gubar, Matt Guterl, John Howard, Patrick Moran, Regina Smyth, Siobhan Somerville, Maureen Stanton, Shane Vogel, and members of the Global Moral Panics reading group led by Micol Seigel. Kent Bartram, Steven Bluttal, Tim Edensor, Christoph Irmscher, Matthew Tinkcom, Matt Wrbican, and a blogger who goes by the name Buster the Raccoon offered essential leads. Chats with David Bleecker, Martin Manalansan, Debra Moddelmog, Rochelle Rives, and Jess Waggoner were also useful, as were the proofreading skills of Whitney Sperrazza and Amanda Zoch.

I thank Rachel Adams and Jonathan Flatley, respectively, for their incisive engagements with the manuscript.

Doug Mitchell was, once again, indefatigable in his support of my findings. It means something when an editor has your back.

This book is for my mother before she became my mother.

INTRODUCTION

The year 2013 was hoarding's *annus mirabilis*. As lilacs bloomed and trumpet vines unfurled, the month of May saw the American Psychiatric Association release its fifth edition of *Diagnostic and Statistical Manual of Mental Disorders* (DSM-5). First published in 1952, this compendium had long considered itself to be one of the world's preeminent authorities on the categorization of mental illness. Members of its task force and work groups had last undertaken major revisions in 1994 with DSM-IV, and readers who glanced over its latest incarnation discovered something new. Alongside older, equally questionable mental diseases such as dissociative identity disorder, DSM-5 pathologized those who hold on to their stuff for too long, who clutter their homes too much, who do not clean that often, and who harbor too many things. The manual labeled these activities "hoarding disorder" (HD, as it is sometimes called) and gave them an International Classification of Diseases (ICD-9-CM, to be precise) code of 300.3. Legitimized as a psychiatric disease and categorized under Obsessive-Compulsive and Related Disorders, this diagnosis rendered unsound certain relations to certain personal property. Hoarding, it seems, had arrived.

The American Psychiatric Association cannot, however, take sole credit for advancing this mental disorder. Of late, a profitable entertainment industry that dramatizes hoarding (reality television shows such as *Hoarders*) and a lucrative service industry that sanitizes it (professional organizers such as Practical Solutions) have joined forces with psychologists, psychiatrists, and social workers. Together they disseminate, popularize, and often sensationalize knowledge about hoarding for specialized and mass audiences. While not the first to do so, they have been the most successful. Though HD has not yet been fully assimilated into everyday life, millions will be diagnosed with this illness, as millions are now thought to suffer from it. According to one expert, hoarders constitute "between 2 and 5 percent of the population" in the twenty-first-century United States alone.[1] To put this mind-boggling number into perspective: as many hoarders may exist in America as citizens in Vermont, New Hampshire, Connecticut, Rhode Island, West Virginia, Maine, Kentucky, and Montana combined.

I guess that you have some sense of this topic, if not these figures or my quick overview of DSM-5. Maybe you have been curious about that friend of yours who never reciprocates the dinner invite. Maybe you Googled some pictures. Maybe your parents fed you fictions of Homer and Langley Collyer, two New York City recluses who occupied a dilapidated mansion filled with more than one hundred tons of matter in the 1930s and 1940s. Prior to the HD diagnosis, instances of hoarding have also been referred to as Collyer Brothers syndrome, chronic disorganization, pack rat syndrome, messy house syndrome, pathological collecting, clutter addiction, Diogenes syndrome, squalor syndrome, senile recluse syndrome, and syllogomania (stockpiling rubbish). Some of these terms remain in use. Before HD became the predominant classification, members of the medical establishment embraced many of them; others only cropped up in casual speech. Some such as *syllogomania* and *chronic disorganization* have been incorporated into scientific discourses; others have fallen out of fashion.

From one vantage point, reducing much of this extensive lexicon into a DSM diagnosis is a cause for celebration. Hoarding disorder, some believe, is a significant medical breakthrough that alleviates the mental anguish of accumulators and their intimates on a historically unprecedented scale. We attribute part of this innovation to a coterie of American-based psychologists and social workers who collaborated on studies of HD for the past two decades. The claim about population percentage was, in fact, made by Randy Frost, a professor of psychology often credited with "the first systematic study of hoarding."[2] After an undergraduate in his 1991 Abnormal Psychology class inquired into hoarding's prevalence among the general population of obsessive-compulsive disorder sufferers, Frost and his student placed advertisements in their local newspapers calling for "PACK RATS—CHRONIC SAVERS."[3] A couple of years later, the two published an article, "The Hoarding of Possessions." While several evaluations existed prior to this moment, this watershed piece authenticated the study of hoarding as a worthy research enterprise.

So influential was this essay that psychiatrists, bloggers, daytime talk-show hosts, and DSM-5 now share what was previously a working definition of extreme accumulation: "the acquisition of, and failure to discard, possessions which appear to be useless or of limited value."[4] All approach hoarding as a psychopathology of object relations. All agree that a messy house may be a sign of mental imbalance. Many depict hoarders and their environments as "behavioral oddities," community nuisances, hygienic nightmares, domestic disasters.[5] They call for cleanup crews, television specials, and self-help guides. They pinpoint hoarding in functional magnetic resonance imaging (fMRI) scans of the brain; measure it with clutter scales; tame it with cognitive-behavioral therapy (CBT); and confirm it with an ever-expanding body of knowledge that bleeds back and forth into popular cultures.

Yet from an alternate perspective that I endorse, this triumph of hoarding disorder is also a misfortune: millions will find their personal effects to be evidence of a sick head. The following pages question a general consensus that hoarding is a mental illness. While this book does not underestimate the gains of science or satellite television, it complicates the official record. It counters hoarding's formula as an individualized mental disorder, and it concentrates less on the mind of the accumulator and more on those who have characterized hoarding as an aberration in the first place. To do so this book attends to the fairly recent history of how persons now identified as hoarders incite unease with their atypical use of things. I approach the extensive literature on hoarding with as much curiosity as it approaches the hoarder, and I contend that we cannot comprehend hoarding without appreciating the unlikely confluence of psychiatrists, newspaper reporters, sociologists, social workers, professional organizers, online journalists, and novelists who foster representations of this supposed mental disease. I argue that these individuals—sometimes in dialogue, sometimes not—facilitated an ongoing panic over personal possessions, one that emerged in the first half of the twentieth century only to snowball into its second. Contra DSM-5, *The Hoarders* finds hoarding to be less an inherent disease in the head and more a decades-spanning concatenation of medico-legal expertise and popular lore.

This thesis is admittedly counterintuitive, given that my argument places much of hoarding's burden on the specialists rather than their patient-clients. I do not refine the diagnosis; I do not read a hoarder's brain scan; I claim no empirical knowledge of hoarding. This book is not a defense of hoarding but an attempt to understand what made possible the condition of defending or condemning hoarding in the first place. Intrigued by how people became intrigued by this topic, *The Hoarders* is a book about how some people's things unsettle some accepted conceptions of material culture, why documentaries, articles, and websites dedicate themselves to eradicating this activity. While debates over this topic hover around its relation to other anxiety disorders, likelihood of cure, and genetic origins, I trace different causal chains such as fears over urban disorder, unseemly collecting, poor housekeeping, and old age. My sole task is to defamiliarize hoarding by placing it in a largely unknown cultural and historical context. By the time you finish this book, I would like for you to pause before you identify a pack rat, or at least think more about why American cultures have done so in the first place.

To accomplish this goal, I unearth what sociologist Loïc J. D. Wacquant calls the "collective scientific unconscious"—in this instance, a few forgotten cultural histories that paved the way for hoarding's entry in DSM-5.[6] I query the reduction of complex material connections into an updated checklist of psychopathology, and I am curious about what omissions occurred for this diagnosis to become common sense. While from one vantage point HD happened lightning-fast following "The Hoarding of Possessions," from another it has taken at least eleven decades. I explore some moments that got us to where we are now, and I discuss a few of these buried links. In this retelling, hoarding is as much a story about sensational journalists, scientific housekeepers, collectibles enthusiasts (Ralph Kovel and his wife Terry Kovel), Christian housecleaners (Sandra Felton), well-meaning social workers (Gail Steketee), psychologists (Frost), and auction houses (Sotheby's) as it is about the hoarders (Homer and Langley Collyer, Andy Warhol, Big Edie and Little Edie Beale, that house at the end of your street).

This book is also a reckoning with how everyday objects go strange and suspicious in the wake of modern materiality and material modernity. Over the seven years that I chipped away at this topic, I found hoarding to be a historically intricate lattice of worry about the unsuitable roles that household furnishings, mass-produced whatnots, curiosa, keepsakes, and clutter play in our daily lives. The majority of these apprehensions over the stuff of normal life originated in the twentieth century, and they are not so far removed from other cultural anxieties. As much as a hoard might be about depression and impulsivity and loss and misplaced stacks of paper, it is also about fears of working-class blacks in 1930s Harlem, post-1960s New Christian Right literatures, and emerging models of appropriate aging in the 1940s and 1950s. Though neglected in the current rhetoric of chronic savers, these unlikely sources each fed into definitions of HD. In my account they move center stage.

These findings may initially appear ludicrous. What on earth do a full house and an unbalanced head in the twenty-first century have to do with the rise of antiquing nine decades ago? What relation could possibly exist between the pathologization of the aged in midcentury America and the pathologization of hoarding in the present? Or links between contemporary clutter addicts and turn-of-the-nineteenth-century hysterias over immigrant bodies? Quite a bit, I was surprised to discover. The backstories of hoarding in America are far, far stranger than the activity itself.

FOLK DEVILS AND OBJECT PANICS

What critical tools let us begin to situate hoarding within these material histories of deviance rather than embed the disease further inside an individual's cranium? This task appears a tall order, especially since scientific discourses now rely on neurological evidence to justify the empirical existence of hoarding disorder. Take but one example: in anticipation of DSM-5, a smattering of experts released a 2012 article that argued one could identify extreme accumulators by irregularities in their brain's anterior cingulate cortex. Supported by fMRI scans and published in *Archives of General Psychiatry*, these findings were then splashed across Internet websites such as *Yahoo!News* with the headline "Brain Scans of 'Hoarders' Show Unique Abnormalities."[7] The essay's conclusions went viral in a fine example of the interdependent relationship between hard science and popular journalism that repeats itself time and again.

This truism that hoarding could be located in headspace caught fire, I sense, because it lent an aura of reassuring irrefutability to an activity that can seem outlandish, unhygienic, and downright disgusting. It likewise pinpointed a cause for a behavior difficult to define as it rendered moot questions that the scientific community had debated for years. What counts as too much stuff? When do overflowing cardboard boxes spill into insanity? What is useless trash and what is valuable treasure? These queries do not need quick answers. We remind ourselves that, as sociologist and DSM critic Allan V. Horwitz theorizes, "socially deviant actions in themselves—whether murder, collecting trash, or going naked—are not signs of mental disorder."[8] Though current scientific literature overlooks his useful claim, one essay paradoxically confirmed Horwitz in its attempt to empirically verify hoarding. Half a decade after Frost and Gross's "The Hoarding of Possessions," an article in *Comprehensive Psychiatry* found that "the disorder belongs to a similar category of social deviance as homelessness, which does not necessarily represent mental illness."[9] In their efforts to puzzle out the phenomenon, the authors approached hoarding as less of a mental illness located in the brain and more of a socialized phenomenon located in the world-at-large—the inverse of its current reception.

These days a claim like Horwitz's does not receive as much attention as a brain scan. This is perfectly reasonable since it undermines hoarding's validity as a transhistorical matter of an irregular mind rather than a contestable phenomenon mired in social conditions. During DSM-5's publicized revisions, a well-placed 2010 study by international experts quelled the deviance thesis to insist that "the syndrome is not solely a result of social deviance or conflicts in society."[10] Yet attempts to purify hoarding as a neurobiological glitch have not been a complete success, and rhetorical remnants of the social pockmark recent scientific literature. With Wacquant's "scientific unconscious" in mind, you might say they haunt it. One attempt to apply CBT to hoarders finds that the disorder is a "social disruption," an illness "associated with a number of indices of social maladjustment such as low marriage rates, social anxiety and withdrawal, and dependent personality traits."[11] Here hoarding is identified by living single or bad nerves. The same essay that denounces the social deviance thesis finds that although "people with hoarding are not distressed by their behavior," "society may be concerned about health hazards or other negative consequences of hoarding."[12] Here hoarding is in the heads of those who fret over the disease as much as the individual herself. Still another finds that "in some extreme cases, hoarding may pose dangerous emotional and physical risks to individuals, as well as to entire communities."[13] Here hoarding is something out of the book of Revelation, coming soon to a suburb near you.

All joking aside, observe how scientific explanations of hoarding jump track from a psyche to an assault on society.[14] In each of these selected sentences, the disease polyps from an individual anxiety disorder to a vague communal menace. Hoarders are no longer unfortunate victims of gray matter gone awry; they are unsafe threats to self, family, marriage, community, and public health. But what if we were to read these objective claims less as indicators and more as instigators? What if the documents and their dissemination across popular media were themselves a cause for concern? We do not typically think of prestigious scientific journals as anxiety stokers, but this may be the case. The ramped-up rhetoric leads me to approach hoarding as a discomfort over how we interact with things rather than a constitutional aberration. Instead of refining HD as a mental illness liberated from social conflict, the chapters to come embed it further into the complex cultural systems that experts try to disavow.

It is a pleasure to admit that I am not the first to promenade down this avenue of thought. Alongside the singular scientific essay cited above, others before me have also suggested that hoarding is more social apprehension than neurological irregularity. Since the late 1990s, scholars in disciplines as diverse as literary studies, anthropology, sociology, museum studies, and marketing have raised collective eyebrows at hoarding's pathologization. Together they concentrate on the diagnostic politics of *material deviance*, the social constructions of an aberrant relationship with your things. One finds extreme accumulation to be "a psychiatric concern with deviance in terms of material culture."[15] Tracking the "form of deviance" found in media accounts of hoarding, another likewise finds that "the value of these stories comes from their ability to raise questions and doubts about the social order rather than from their celebration of society's triumph over deviance and disorder."[16] And a prominent museum studies scholar notes that when we think about inappropriate accumulating, "we are left with those areas of collecting around which cling uncomfortable feelings, areas we are likely to use words like 'perverted' or 'deviant' to describe."[17]

These are useful correctives to the dominant neuro-thesis. Yet while this idea that hoarding is material deviance is not breaking news, how it became so may be. Identifying something as a deviant construct is the beginning rather than the end of my account, and I am curious what historical preconditions enabled hoarding discourses to emerge in modern America. Hence I am interested in tracing how what goes by "hoarding disorder" came to be cast as a social threat and a perplexing activity. A quick scratch at its diagnostic surface, for example, finds that these associations between hoarding and social deviance exceed the 1990s and push back into the 1960s. Notes one *New York Times* journalist: "Social scientists disagree as to exactly what causes obsessive hoarding. In its December 1960 issue, the *Journal of Chronic Diseases* branded recluses like the Collyers 'deviants who are often surrounded by mystery and violence.'"[18]

We extend this periodization even further when my first chapter details the pivotal roles that Homer and Langley Collyer played in hoarding's popularization starting in the late 1930s. For now I note that we have strong theoretical models for tracking representations of hoarding as mysterious forms of deviance, disorder, and perversion. With repeated references to danger and risk—what one researcher calls a "serious and even life-threatening pathology"—hoarding specialists contribute to a slow-simmering hysteria over personal belongings.[19] Stated otherwise, the hoarder's material deviance is best viewed as a moral panic over stuff.

With "moral panic" I reference criminologist Stanley Cohen's classic *Folk Devils and Moral Panics: The Creation of the Mods and Rockers*. First published in 1972, Cohen's work questioned the social anxieties sparked by the supposed delinquencies of youth subcultures in the United Kingdom. He found that a moral panic occurs when "a condition, episode, person or group emerges to become defined as a threat to societal values and interests."[20] Expanding his thesis to other populations, he then argued that these panics revolve around *folk devils* or "visible reminders of what we should not be" (10). While their targets are clearly identifiable, the panic that they incite often exists along a continuum. There can be "*noisy* constructions—where moral panics appear (usually at an early stage) and may be associated with a single sensational case—and *quiet* constructions, where claims-makers are professionals, experts or bureaucrats."[21] Intriguingly, Cohen also mentioned how such panics reproduce fears of imagined disasters where there is "loss of cherished values and material objects resulting in death or injury or destruction to property" (22). Things, we infer, incite alarm as much as their owners.

In a prediction that came to pass, Cohen concluded his observations with a prophecy: "More moral panics will be generated and other, as yet nameless, folk devils will be created" (204). On the American scene, at least, such panics have involved lesbians and gays, undocumented immigrants, the homeless, Muslims, recreational drug users, and hoarders. Building on Cohen, I find it useful to approach hoarding as a unique moral panic over material goods, or an *object panic* whereby forms of social deviance attach not only to interpersonal behaviors but also to material ones. I do not think, however, that this panic is especially new given that anxieties over hoarding stem from the mid-twentieth century and earlier. It is better to say that this particular object panic is recurrent even as sound-bite discourses such as "Brain Scans of 'Hoarders' Show Unique Abnormalities" think themselves cutting edge. Moral panics, Cohen suggests, "are *new* (lying dormant perhaps, but hard to recognize; deceptively ordinary and routine, but invisibly creeping up the moral horizon)—but also old (camouflaged versions of traditional and well-known evils)."[22] His observation allows us to argue that individuals identified as "life-threatening" pack rats have inspired object panics for decades, that they too reside on a continuum of noisy and quiet constructions that range from a singular case such as the Collyers to widespread DSM-5 diagnostics. As we soon discover, whether the focus is two elderly brothers in Harlem (chapter 1), Andy Warhol's accumulations (chapter 2), or Big Edie Beale's squalor-ridden mansion in East Hampton (chapter 4), the cord that runs through all of these so-called hoarder cases is eerily similar: they function as visible reminders of how we should not engage with things.

Given that a cluttered home and grubby living conditions often identify a hoarder's residence, this ongoing object panic is also not far removed from British anthropologist Mary Douglas's theses on dirt and disorder in her 1966 *Purity and Danger*. Cohen says as much near the end of his 2002 introduction to *Folk Devils*'s third edition. In a suggestive link between deviance, moral panic, and dirty things, he observes that "the drawing and reinforcement of moral boundaries is as similar as Mary Douglas's comparison between physical and moral pollution."[23] Though he does not quote from *Purity and Danger*, I think Cohen may have in mind that book's famous formulation of "dirt as matter out of place."[24] For Douglas, dirt and one of its synonyms, social disorder, are culturally specific concerns. This observation seems appropriate as we confirm that mental and material disorganization come from somewhere other than brain fluid. "There is no such thing as absolute dirt," she informs her readers. "It exists in the eye of the beholder" rather than a lobe of the brain (2). And certain individuals like, say, a messy hoarder come to exemplify moralized forms of disorder vilified by the social body, and "which persons may set off knowingly or unknowingly, which are not part of the psyche and which are not to be bought or learned by initiation and training" (140). In a nice parallel to Cohen's concept of moral panic, Douglas treats dirty deeds as lightning rods of moral pollution and cultural threat. Little wonder that hoarders seem dangerous when their residences are thought to reek of "unsanitary deviancy," and little surprise that they inspire cleanup crews that take the form of companies such as Disaster Masters or psychiatrists who diagnose them with what one journalist terms a "disorder disorder."[25]

This last observation returns us to the integral role played by popularized science. When psychiatrists and social workers study hoarding, it is not hard to see how their findings inspire icky feelings that incite some to castigate accumulators as deviant or perverted. Hasn't this been one of the medical establishment's raisons d'être years before DSM? In the words of another expert on abnormalities, French philosopher Michel Foucault, psychiatry historically colludes with other policing systems to reproduce these discourses of "perversity and danger."[26] In a course taught in 1975 and published in English under the title *Abnormal* in 2003, the philosopher found that psychiatry specialized in stoking fears over the "dangerous individual," or what he defines as a socially perverse personage who inspires curiosity, apprehension, and a need for social control:

> In expert psychiatric opinion . . . the individual whom the expert has to diagnose and with whom he has to struggle, in his questioning, analysis, and diagnosis, is the potentially dangerous individual. So that in the end we have two notions that can immediately be seen to be both close to and distant from each other: on the one hand, there is the notion of "perversion" that will enable the series of medical concepts and the series of juridical concepts to be stitched together and, on the other, there is the notion of "danger," of the "dangerous individual," which will make possible the justification and theoretical foundation of an uninterrupted chain of medico-judicial institutions. Danger and perversion constitute, I think, the essential theoretical core of expert medico-legal opinion.[27]

The *Archives of General Psychiatry* article fits into this schema, as do other pieces on clutter addiction that depict hoarders as life-threatening communal risks in need of intervention. I also appreciate that Foucault gives us a deep history of this "potentially dangerous individual," one that he dates back to "the second half of the nineteenth century."[28] For better and for worse, his findings let us begin to historically track hoarders as material perverts and as dangerous persons engaged in equally dangerous object relations.

Braiding Cohen, Douglas, and Foucault together, we gain a sturdier sense of how hoarding functions as an abnormal social phenomenon to which a brain scan contributes rather than deflects. These thinkers allow us to comprehend how certain forms of object culture incite certain kinds of object panic over a certain kind of person.[29] "Underneath Every Hoarder," one newspaper headline puts it, "Is a Normal Person Waiting to Be Dug Out."[30] Its report then excoriates the "abject horror" of "people who treasure their expired tuna cans more than they do their children."[31] In the pages that follow I look forward to providing several accounts of how such awfulness came to be.

ROOT CAUSES

The aim of these tales? To transcribe into history Jill from Milwaukee, a recalcitrant featured on the show *Hoarders*.

Launched in 2009 on the American cable network A&E, the reality television series typically contrasts the biographies of two individuals castigated as hoarders and spends a good hour with their difficulty discarding stuff. The show introduces its main subjects at its start, then a psychiatrist who assesses their psychologies, then a certified professional organizer who assesses their clutter, then befuddled cleanup crews who try to haul it all away. From its opening frames, Jill's episode plays into this formula as she makes a mess of the domestic material culture that fills up her living spaces.[32] When *Hoarders* first features her rental home, camera shots spotlight piled-high countertops, overflowing shelves, fly strips more fly than strip, and the contents of a basement refrigerator that has seen better days. An epic fail at housekeeping, Jill is pretty nonchalant about all of this. "I've been a messy person all my life," she states. "I hoard food."[33] After some coaching she admits that "the mess that I live in now has reached a critical mass," yet she resists throwing out the eggs, the jars of green olives, the ground buffalo meat, and other semi-refrigerated goods whose expiration dates have long since passed.

As *Hoarders* is wont to do, the situation comes to a head once Jill finds herself having to part ways with a rotting pumpkin, an object whose cultural cross-purposes include seasonal bric-a-brac, Halloween showpiece, and domestic floor covering, as indigenous peoples once braided dried squashes into mats. Jill bypasses these traditional object uses. Noting later that Jill is "pretty sick," her sister opines that "the food in Jill's house is really scary because it is everywhere. I went into her home and I was shocked. I was just shocked." Detailing his mother's propensities, her son Aidan tells the camera that "she gets pumpkins from the church sometimes so that she can make pumpkin pies." Jill, however, has a different take. When asked to discard the decomposed pumpkin, she treats it like a treasure and offers it a requiem: "It was a very nice pumpkin when it was fresh," she reminisces. Once the cleanup starts, she states that "it was a beauty when it was alive" and then switches to direct address: "I enjoyed you while you were here. Thank you. Good-bye." After these last rites, a member of the cleanup crew assigned to her home attempts to throw it out, and Jill halts the process. "Let me just look and see if there are a few seeds in here . . . because this is an odd pumpkin. I've never seen one quite like this before, and if I can grow some that would be neat." As opposed to seeing her relation to the putrid squash as a sign of mental illness, she approaches it as a wide-eyed seed keeper.

Moments such as this jolt her relatives and her assigned therapist, David

Tolin, an advocate of DSM-5 diagnoses and a coauthor of several scientific essays cited throughout this book. Tolin tells the camera that "you have to have a certain amount of denial to allow this kind of problem to build up." And later: "Clutter is the symptom, but hoarding is the disease." And later to Jill: "Are your perceptions of food completely accurate? Or might there be something irrational?" And later: "Something is off. Your old way of doing things, your old way of thinking, [is] self-destructive as hell." Yet Jill remains fairly incorrigible from the start of the episode to its finish as she turns rotten purchases into personal treasures.

These observations and those to come do not, I hope, cheapen the distress of Jill's sister, her son, or anyone familiar with a "messy person." A heap of things can wreck lives and harm interpersonal relations. A store can come between children and parents. A hoard can index an unfathomable amount of emotional pain. But despite my own revulsion at a kitchen full of rotten food, I have come to wonder if this is the same "problem" for me as it is for Jill as it is for Jill's family as it is for her landlord (especially if Jill now chooses to embrace the DSM-5 diagnostic, since she may be protected by the Fair Housing Act, which requires property owners to reasonably accommodate individuals with mental disability). While some accumulators cause pain and suffering, I have to admit a family can be as damaged by one object as by a multitude of them, and that objects destroy interpersonal relations all the time. Sit outside your local courthouse one afternoon and listen to the squabbles over estates or injuries to property.

And why so often harm to the family? For different reasons, it is clear to me and to another psychologist featured on *Hoarders*, Suzanne A. Chabaud, that hoarding disrupts "normal family life." She says as much in a *Psychiatric Times* article, "The Hidden Lives of Children of Hoarders": "While parents acquire objects, their children fail to live a normal family life—a huge cost for a parent's distorted relationship with objects. Children of hoarders witness their parents and family slipping away, one object at a time."[34] It only gets worse down the line: "Adult children may also be resentful of the parent for the condition in which they were forced to live as a child. As these children marry and have children of their own, they are most likely resistant to ever bringing their children over to their parent's home."[35] This is tragic and no doubt true, but we should think about how experts use rhetoric of "family" and "children" given the baggage of social norms that often comes with these words. Why are hoarders presumed to be a threat to reproductive heterosexuals who have created offspring? Could it be that hoarding rattles our ideas of the normal family or the material cultures thought to inform this fantasy of domestic life? Is it conceivable that a child in this scenario might feel something other than negative emotion about the stuff that surrounds her or him?

When I read a textbook hoarding case like Jill's in this manner, I am trying to think otherwise about these acts, with awareness that they certainly strain normal family life. I just want to consider an alternative to the knee-jerk reaction that reduces this activity to an insurance-friendly diagnostic category or a damnable bizarro world. I agree that this activity can be disconcerting, but I also feel that we can comprehend this behavior beyond hypermedicalization or psychopathology. What if, as a thought experiment, we respected Jill's squash as an intimate whose company she thoroughly enjoyed rather than treat it as a red flag of an unsound mind? What if she liked hanging out with pumpkins more than with her sister?

This book does not address such alternatives at any significant length. My modus operandi for seeing hoarding disorder differently is instead to trace how several of its definitional components came to be, to search for root causes other than a wayward chromosome. I thus attend to the historical specifics that established some of the groundwork for the ire and sensationalism that accumulators such as Jill provoke. This approach tracks how representations of hoarding reinforce an ongoing "rule of the normal and the pathological" when it comes to modern things, but please do not presume that my readings of this binary signal my allegiance to it.[36] I gamble that an extended survey of how hoarding became a psychopathology paradoxically offers us an exit route for approaching this topic in a nonpathologizing light. One payoff for historicizing the hoarding-is-a-psychopathology thesis is, then, a deeper appreciation for the disease's cultural complexities even as these personal encounters with things—like many personal encounters with things—cause misery for some. Your view of it changes depending on the critical light. In my version, hoarding is the sum total of several recent material improprieties: cluttered entryways; domiciles overstuffed with knickknacks great and small; the stubborn faith that a clamshell container is as priceless as a Picasso. Across four chapters I detail representations of these worrisome behaviors from their cultural onset in the late 1930s to the present day, and each chapter concentrates on one of the diagnosis's rich nomenclatures—Collyer Brothers syndrome, pathological collecting, hoard and clutter syndrome, and senile squalor syndrome—to move us along.[37]

On one level, these writings fall traditionally within a genre of criticism that publishers term "the biography of disease." Over recent decades, numerous scholars have traced the historical developments of maladies such as posttraumatic stress disorder, obsessive-compulsive disorder, bipolar disorder, multiple personality disorder, and a slew of other mental illnesses.[38] These thorough accounts of how diseases historically came to be query scientific progress by dragging the diagnosis back into the cultural causes that led to its medical standardization in the first place. Hoarding disorder, I detail, follows a similar trajectory as we watch the word *hoarding* etymologically evolve from a sign of immoral greed into an accepted psychopathological diagnosis.

On another level, the book belongs to a genre that scholars of material culture term "the cultural biography of things," or historical accounts of our connections to stuff like farm implements, beauty products, clothing, toys, tech gadgets, home appliances, accessories, and so forth.[39] In a not unrelated vein, this genre has also produced popular works such as 2011's *Stuck Up! 100 Objects Inserted and Ingested in Places They Shouldn't Be.* I too tell several cultural biographies of inappropriately placed things, but I tell them slant. I trace how hoarders disturb what two sociologists usefully shorthand as "material social relations" as pack rats fail established modes of *object conduct,* the manner by which individuals socially and personally engage with matter.[40] My chapters discuss, among other things, how a brownstone full of curiosa became one of the more infamous hoarding cases in America; how a collection of cookie jars went mad thanks to a Sotheby's auction; how the mental disease of clutter addiction fostered nationwide recovery groups such as Messies Anonymous; and how possessions poorly cherished by the elderly (some call this squalor) became the benchmark of late-onset hoarding.

In so doing, I offer four genealogies that contributed to the cultural makeup of hoarding disorder. Each chapter traces a different backstory of the disease, a different vector of material deviance. These disease nomenclatures bleed through each other, but they do have unique histories. Collyer Brothers syndrome, chapter 1 argues, advanced what experts now call chronic disorganization, which is often considered a sign of material illness. Chapter 2 reveals pathological collecting to be a staple of DSM diagnostic. Chapter 3 does the same for hoard and clutter syndrome. Senile squalor syndrome, chapter 4 details, established stereotypes of the aged as hoarders. Not one of these genealogies was more influential than the other, and we could add others to this list. My book does not offer a clear-cut chronology. I am most interested in tracing a few of hoarding's preexisting conditions as this muddle of discourses worked its way into a bona fide mental disease. The guiding thread is that these genealogies interweave to create an object panic.

For all of this thick history, my core archives fit into a knapsack: a reel of newspaper clippings about the Collyers, a six-volume auction catalog of Warhol's posthumous effects, some Christian bookstore paperbacks about ungodly housekeeping, a documentary film about two aging women. You will learn that three of these four different genealogies are now considered famous hoarding cases. The *New York Times* prominently featured Homer and Langley Collyer; the contents of Warhol's townhouse retain their fascination years after the artist's untimely death; Edith Ewing Bouvier Beale and her daughter were the focus of a 1975 documentary and a 2009 television movie. The primary subject of chapter 3, professional organizer Sandra Felton, is likewise well known in cleaning-crew circles and was once featured in *People* magazine. As I detail, these HD lineages crisscross each other in unexpected ways. After his death Warhol was compared to the Collyers. The reclusive and aging Beales were treated as being as socially disorganized as Homer and Langley. Popular takes on the Beales feature them as senior recluses akin to the Collyers. All five have been cast as clutter-holics in need of better organization by the likes of someone such as Felton.

When arranging these genealogies I made several decisions that limit the scope of this book. My archive focuses on hoarding formations in the United States rather than considering their global reach, even as some insist that the disease "has been reported throughout the world on every continent but Antarctica."[41] *The Hoarders* acknowledges the findings of international scientific communities, yet it notes that HD's standardization rests largely on the shoulders of American-based scientists and social workers. Experts from Israel, the United Kingdom, Ireland, Germany, Taiwan, New Zealand, Australia, and elsewhere have, however, contributed to discourses regarding hoarding's psychopathology, and I cite them accordingly.[42] Likewise, some moments spin off a national frame and into the regional (chapter 2's emphasis on antiquing in New England) and the international (chapter 3's leap from messy house syndrome in the United States to *das Messie-Syndrom* in Germany). The globalization of hoarding's standardized diagnosis is, however, for another book.

I also bracket consumerism as my default interpretive rubric. This decision distinguishes itself from studies that approach hoarding as a mirror reflection of hyperconsumer commodity cultures. For some, the activity looks like a spectacle of overconsumption, or what the author of *Let Go of Clutter* terms "*redundabundance*: the unrestricted desire and ability to obtain more and more of what you already have too much of. In the past, redundabundance was a rich-person's disease, like dyspepsia. . . . Much has already been written about this peculiar syndrome (called *affluenza* by other witty researchers)."[43] I agree with this finding, given the rapid expansions of consumer culture that occurred well into the twentieth century across every socioeconomic divide. Forthcoming chapters address components of this culture such as antiquing, the collectibles industry, post–World War II spikes in mass production, links between mental health and increased demands on housekeeping, the hygiene of home decoration, and widened access to inexpensive goods such as trinkets and knickknacks.

Yet I believe that overconsumption is but one facet of hoarding's cultural legibility. Hoarding could just as well be the freakish spectacle of underconsumption—the material indecency of what sociologist Zygmunt Bauman terms *failed consumers* who disrupt standard modes of purchase, ownership, and removal.[44] While hoarding is certainly unfathomable without modern forms of consumption, a main emphasis on excessive consumerism overlooks other contributing factors that I am more engrossed in tracing. Note how the definition of *redundabundance* relies upon rhetoric of psychopathology with words such as *syndrome* and *disease*. It also historicizes the phenomenon with its reference to *affluenza* epidemics of the past. It is this narrative of deviant object relations that I am keen to tell.

In the same manner that the book backburners consumerism, it minimally engages with neuroscience or the cultural emergence of CBT's dominance across the latter half of the twentieth century.[45] Chapters to come do cite the pathological collecting featured in scientific journals such as *Brain*, the CBT therapies of bad housekeeping, and the glucose levels of hoarders. But part of my argument is that hoarding is not solely a matter for brain science to explain.

Finally, this study does not address the distinct but related topic of animal hoarding. Since my readings attend most closely to nomenclatures that enabled the current DSM discourse, animal hoarding—a phrase devised in 1997 by the Boston-based Hoarding of Animals Research Consortium—fell outside my purview. This topic occurs here and there in the scientific literature, but the APA has not incorporated it into its standard definition of HD.[46] While representations of those now called animal hoarders appear in popular cultures, the accumulation of living or dead animals is not an official component of hoarding disorder. DSM-5 equivocates: "Animal hoarding may be a special manifestation of hoarding disorder. Most individuals who hoard animals also hoard inanimate objects."[47] In essays that led up to this observation, hoarding specialists discuss this subject as one "based on limited or anecdotal information," and they call for "more substantial work" as they acknowledge similarities and differences between animal hoarders and those diagnosed with HD.[48] This book distinguishes between animal hoarding and object hoarding, given the conventional status of animals as living things and objects as insentient. Even as some theories of hoarding may argue that animals are turned into objects, I maintain the dissimilarity.

UNSTANDARDIZING MATERIAL LIFE

What are the larger ethics of *The Hoarders*? It should be clear from my preceding comments that I do not always see *these people* as unquestionably disturbed or a danger to self and others. I have no right to judge, with my own house made of most brittle glass. With so much ink spilled over the damage that hoarders do, I also think that we rarely mention the hurt of those who foster the discourse. Under the guise of abatement, they promote in earnest a better quality of life.

"But at the point where severe disorganization begins to impinge on quality of life," find two HD proponents, "the detriments outweigh the benefits and may qualify as a disorder."[49] Behind their expressed good intentions are some nagging questions with presumed answers: What counts for a full material life? Who decides "the point"? Why is "quality of life" the pivot between a normal and a pathological bond with things, or even a desired condition? Discourses of material deviance, I mean to say, not only rest upon an imaginary counterpart of cleanliness, sanity, and domestic order that my third chapter details. They often assume that the hoarder herself wants to return to this state and recover "the Normal Person Waiting to Be Dug Out." They imagine that a pack rat can and should get this life back, but they never really ask why anyone would want to do so to begin with.

The choice phrase *material life* was addressed at length by French historian Fernand Braudel in his *Capitalism and Material Life, 1400–1800* ([1967] 1973). Braudel meant this expansive concept to refer to "repeated actions, empirical processes, old methods and solutions handed down from time immemorial, like money or the separation of town and country."[50] Let's historicize the historian's definition of timeless material life for the task at hand. With their emphasis on the mental and emotional well-being afforded by personal goods, hoarding discourses continue a modern update of material life that goes by the name "standard of living"—as in the phrase "restore your standard of living." Middle-class Americans popularized this judgmental concept starting in the early twentieth century, and it now saturates self-understanding.[51] From its cultural beginnings, an appropriate standard of living applied not only to persons and their interpersonal relations but also to the quality of their objects: the home furnishings and the suitable eating utensils thought to "raise the quality of life for many Americans."[52] As much as they promote the psychopathology of object relations, hoarding experts across specialist and popular discourses reproduce and update this criterion when they endorse an ordinary standard of material life.

What is wrong with this impulse, you ask? Recall that old epigram by poet W. H. Auden: "The friends of the born nurse / Are always getting worse."[53] Scientists, social workers, and cleanup crews may do more harm than good as they attempt to sanitize the hoarder by returning her to a sound state of mind, body, and matter. To be fair, this is often an unintentional consequence. I do not deny that hoarding specialists are well-meaning, nor do I refute that some individuals find succor in their analyses. I also do not always see HD advocates as barkers asking us to step right up and gawk at scenes of material freakery. "Pollution," Douglas notes, "can be committed intentionally, but intention is irrelevant to its effect—it is more likely to happen inadvertently" (140). Douglas speaks of those thought to defile social orders, but we can widen her frame of reference and include those who promulgate pollution discourses, such as hoarding specialists. Intentionally or not, these individuals confirm an ideal of how we should go about our daily material lives and, to return us to Cohen, what our lives should not become.[54]

One aim of The Hoarders is to unstandardize these pervasive versions of material life that now inform hoarding. This book ethically maintains that there is no natural relation to our objects. One can be troubled by a single object as much as by a thousand of them, and while what looks like hoarding may be depression, so too could be a clean house. Though popularized science asks of hoarders, "Why do such people keep things?," the following might be some better questions: What counts as an acceptable material life? Who decides? Why is one material life commended while another is reviled? Who calls these shots? Under what historical circumstances? And an often unaddressed question: what if a so-called hoarder takes a liking to her possessions? Accounts of hoarding tend to rely upon the presumption of deep anguish. Less is made of the fondness for particular accumulations that may at the same time appear revolting to some.

For these reasons I made a calculated decision to concentrate on the developments of hoarding—as historical discourse, as culturally conditioned disease, as normalizing plot—rather than detailed biographies or oral histories of self-identified hoarders. I do not include many personal stories of individuals diagnosed with hoarding disorder within these pages. While I remain mostly quiet on this matter, I do not want this choice to translate into a silencing of others' experiences. I do not want to sell short anyone whose material life is informed by these discourses for better and for worse, and my sympathies reveal themselves in the gradual accumulation of my sentences. Some may sensibly consider HD diagnosis a relief to start recovery, but I still believe that it can be a lasting mark of intense shame that entangles one in degrees of social and civic punishment ranging from mortification to incarceration. In a moving personal memoir, theater scholar William Davies King reflects on his "telltale evidence of hoarding," and he confesses that "I have seen people—friends—visibly repelled by it, as if it were a monstrosity, a huge boil or wen, gruesomely fascinating but still disgusting. I wonder if those guys who save string on enormous balls have a similar experience, or the hoarders who save every newspaper, every piece of junk mail, every oily rag and unused bus transfer."[55] I think they do. For those interested, numerous other first-person accounts are out there. My hope is that this book helps readers in a different manner by giving them some knowledge about the cultural origins of their loved one's "condition" beyond a universalized diagnostic—that knowing some of this history might soothe as much as presuming that HD comes from chromosome 14.

To deindividuate hoarding, to see it as something potentially more than a solitary psychopathology, was the end of my interpretive line. I aim to see hoarders, as Foucault puts it in *Abnormal*, as but one chapter in "the multitude of incorrigible individuals caught in the apparatus of rectification" (328). Being an upstanding participant in the ongoing project of material modernity means not only embedding yourself within a calculus of mass production, technological advancement, and transnational commercial interaction. It also means having a suitable relation to the management of your objects. Some weirdness is tolerated, but don't wander too far into those woods. You otherwise run the risk of becoming socially damaged goods, morally faulty, a risk to self and others. To depathologize these suspect material social relations is my primary ethical task.

When all is said and done, I harbor few fantasies that this book will declassify DSM-5's diagnostic criteria. In scientific-journal lingo, it will have a low impact factor. Hoarding as a psychopathology will likely become more entrenched even as reconsiderations of the diagnosis abound. "This isn't weird to me," observes Kerrylea from Washington on one episode of *Hoarders*. "This is normal."[56] Linda from Virginia: "I never knew that hoarding was a disorder. Collecting things just seemed to happen."[57] This book may not alter the diagnosis of compulsive hoarding with which many struggle, but by telling several of its genealogies it introduces the historical possibility that things could have turned out otherwise, even as it accepts the historical fact that they did not.

This last paragraph strikes too pessimistic a close to my introduction, so here is another. I have the faintest hope that *The Hoarders* contributes to a future when HD's days are numbered. "Witches," Mary Douglas once commented, "are social equivalents of beetles and spiders who live in the cracks of the walls and wainscoting. They attract the fears and dislikes which other ambiguities and contradictions attract in other thought structures" (127). May the day come when we talk about hoarders as many of us now talk about witches: as dubious relics of a faded material civilization. Other, as yet nameless, folk devils will no doubt appear in their stead. That day remains fanciful, but I am content to wait-and-see. For the time being, the following pages count backwards to cross off the thousands of weeks and the hundreds of months that led up to the cultural diagnosis some now call HD. I claimed at my start that the year 2013 was momentous. In retrospect, so too was 1947. Let's begin again by exhuming two bodies—Homer and Langley Collyer—who first put hoarding into the minds of too many.

COLLYER CURIOSA

It is the stuff of legend and the legend of stuff. With a front-page headline trumpeting "Homer Collyer, Harlem Recluse, Found Dead at 70," the *New York Times* reported on March 22, 1947, that "the circumstances surrounding the death of 70-year-old Homer, blind as the poet he was named for, were as mysterious as the life the two eccentric brothers lived on the unfashionable upper reaches of Fifth Avenue, in the middle of Harlem."[1] Tipped off by a phone call, police had found Collyer's wasted corpse in his Harlem brownstone located on the corner of Fifth Avenue and 128th Street. Days later, officers located the rotting body of his brother, Langley, lying several feet from where Homer had died. Langley had been buried alive by fallen stacks of bundled newspapers, one of the many booby traps that he had rigged to ward off priers. Their bodies included, over one hundred tons of material ranging from several grand pianos to scads of pinup posters were excavated from the mansion. Deemed unsafe by the city's public administrator, the house was razed, the lot later dedicated as the Collyer Brothers Park (figure 1.1).

This sensational tale of two elderly white men living and dying in a predominantly black neighborhood has sparked fascination from the mid-1930s to the twenty-first century, and this chapter argues that the Collyers enabled a cultural shift in a curious identity category—the hoarder—that proved inextricable from their "mysterious" household effects as well as from the "unfashionable" district of Harlem. I detail these unlikely confluences in a few pages. For now I note that these two men have also lent their names to Collyer Brothers syndrome, a psychological disorder that would evolve into what is today known as hoarding disorder (HD). In a less than obvious debt, they have likewise contributed to the diagnosis of chronic disorganization, a "euphemism" that functions as both a synonym and a descriptor for those now identified as hoarders.[2] Prior to the 2013 release of DSM-5, for instance, a *New York Times* journalist noted a half-decade earlier that "at its most extreme, chronic disorganization is called hoarding, a condition many experts believe is a mental illness in its own right, although psychiatrists have yet to formally recognize it."[3] In one of their many successful attempts to standardize inappropriate accumulating into HD, Randy

FIGURE 1.1 Policeman inspecting Collyer mansion, 1947.
Courtesy of Getty Images.

Frost, a psychologist, and Gail Steketee, a social worker, likewise maintained that "clutter in the homes of people with hoarding problems is extremely disorganized; valuable objects (and sometimes money) are commonly mixed in with trash. Even in cases where the volume of possessions is not large, considerable dysfunction can result from the gross disorganization."[4] Disorganized goods, we might say, are but one hallmark of hoarding as a psychopathology, and even DSM-5 finds that hoarders have "objects piled together in a disorganized fashion."[5] The Collyers and their possessions prove no exception to this classificatory rule. In fact, they helped conceive it.

It will take me several moves to support the claims of the last paragraph above, so let's start by noting that Steketee and Frost's reference to "valuable objects (and sometimes money)" signals how markedly different contemporary descriptions of hoarding are from earlier historical formations. Before the twentieth century, *hoarding* referred primarily to the accumulation of wealth rather than trash. Dismayed at "tight-fisted" clergy, Dante Alighieri assigned hoarders to the fourth circle of Hell in his fourteenth-century *The Divine Comedy*.[6] Citing Shakespeare's late-sixteenth-century play *Henry VI, Part 3*, the *Oxford English Dictionary* defines hoarding "in modern use" as "the accumulation and hiding of money."[7] Silas Marner, a Victorian protohoarder, stockpiled bags of guineas in George Eliot's 1861 novel of the same name. Signaling this definitional fault, one recent medical expert writes that "unfortunately, Langley Collyer lived in an era when problems such as compulsive hoarding were regarded as eccentricities; something to be laughed at or ridiculed."[8] Casting hoarders as "public nuisances or even health risks," his description is revealing because it foregrounds a cultural break in how hoarders have been historically perceived. While previous centuries viewed the act as a sign of financial greed, it now functions as a psychopathological diagnosis that treats someone like the Collyers and their attachment to goods as suffering from a mental aberration.

Such being the case, late modern accounts of Collyer Brothers syndrome, chronic disorganization, and HD are far removed from fictive accounts of Silas Marner in the 1860s, even as many scientists insist upon transhistorical continuity.[9] Yet in so doing, their accounts represent "problems such as compulsive hoarding" not as questionable constructions under strain but as kinks of gray matter that lead to "considerable dysfunction" beyond a well-stocked house. Quoted in "The Genetics of Compulsive Hoarding," one psychiatrist claims that hoarders harbor "distinct susceptibility genes," in a report that also finds that hoarders "have a different pattern of glucose metabolism in the brain."[10] Another psychologist improbably states that "something at chromosome 14 may be associated with hoarding."[11] Yet another stresses that unchecked hoarding results in sanitation crises and a "substantial social burden," including "lower rates of marriage and higher rates of divorce" and what is vaguely listed as "social, marital, and recreational impairment."[12] Here hoarding is not just a quirk of genetic code or the disintegration of a particular household but a societal pathology of the brain as well.

In several instances, these findings shore up their claims with references that date back to psychoanalysts such as Sigmund Freud, Karl Abraham, and Ernest

Jones—even though these early-twentieth-century thinkers refuted causal links between disorganization and accumulation.[13] In his "Anal-Erotic Character Traits" (1918), Jones stresses that "all collectors are anal-erotics, and the objects collected are nearly always typical copro-symbols: thus, money, coins (apart from current ones), stamps, eggs, butterflies—these two being associated with the idea of babies—books, even worthless things like pins, old newspapers, etc."[14] But Jones also insists that these individuals express "intolerance for disorder."[15] Freud earlier noted in his "Character and Anal Eroticism" (1908) that "the people I am about to describe are noteworthy for a regular combination of the three following characteristics. They are especially *orderly, parsimonious* and *obstinate.*"[16] Emphasizing that "dirt is matter in the wrong place" for such tidy persons, he, like Jones, approaches individuals who accumulate things as too clean, not too messy.[17]

But if glucose, poor genetics, and a nod to some founders of Western psychoanalysis fail to make sense out of those who really, really, really like their possessions, then what does? Perhaps another allusion to Freud—that by Mary Douglas—can be of some help. As noted in this book's introduction, Douglas's famous formulation of "dirt as matter out of place" alerts us that mental and material disorganization comes from somewhere other than timeless brain fluid, and it returns us to the importance that a place like, say, Harlem plays in defining dirt.[18] Her useful theory lets us consider the historical confluences that enabled one aspect of hoarding syndrome to emerge in the twentieth century as a disorder about disorganization, an aspect that recent medical experts elide when they present hoarding as a neurobiological ill. What follows thus refutes the notion of the disease as a biochemical imbalance and instead treats stories about hoarding as one chapter in the unfinished cultural history of disorder and "gross disorganization." Taking a cue from cultural critic Jani Scandura, who argues that "in the late 1930s, when the Collyer brothers gained notoriety in newspapers, they seemed to embody a threat more culturally resonant than what might be dismissed as individual eccentricity," I detail how and why the dangerous Collyers and their disorderly matter-out-of-place resonated in midcentury Harlem and the decades thereafter.[19]

This is a brief history, then, of how a few truckloads of stuff and the two people who owned them became deviant. My genealogy of Collyer Brothers syndrome argues that representations of the Collyers facilitated a paradigm shift in hoarding as a curious abnormality—a shift that helped make chronic the gradual psychopathology of gross disorganization. While there were others whose object relations had sparked suspicion before them (I have in mind the "mentally deranged persons" whose "hoarding is usually directed to money; but it also includes almost anything besides" in a volume of William James's

1890 *The Principles of Psychology*), discourses of the Collyers were nevertheless elemental to the dissemination of hoarding as a mental illness across the nation and, eventually, the globe.[20]

To support these claims, I first turn to their mansion and explore how Harlem and its residents became stand-ins for a social disordering that the Collyers would personify in the press. I then look inside the brownstone to track how this narrative of disorganization converged with complementary tales that cast the Collyers and their personal belongings as oddities. I finally address the afterlife of this curiosa as these two interlocking narratives further aligned and as the brothers became synonymous with a narrative of insane hoarding. Throughout, this chapter contends that representations of these men shifted from eccentric and reclusive New Yorkers to pathological hoarders. In essence, depictions of the two reconfigured anxieties of social and material disorganization that, for far too long, wound not around the strands of DNA but rather a few streets north of Central Park.

HARLEMITIS

It is, following Douglas, difficult to understand the emergence of the modern hoarder without entertaining the role that place plays in accounts of chronic disorganization. Given the frequent emphasis on "unfashionable" Harlem in accounts of the Collyers, it is equally difficult not to attend to the role played by race. As much as these two men are now linked to the psychopathology of compulsive hoarding, they were once wedded to the supposed social and racial pathologies of Harlem. While connections between the neighborhood, the brothers, and their eponymous disorder are not transparent, this section teases out these relationships since they are a neglected link in the history of chronic disorganization as a mental disorder.[21]

We grasp a few of these connections in a 2006 online newspaper that ponders why the brothers "descended into madness" and diagnoses them with the unfortunate neologism "Harlemitis":

> Homer and Langley Collyer were written about in medical journals and even had a disease (Collyer Brothers Syndrome) named in their honor to account for this neurotic inability to dispose of things. Perhaps there should be a corollary to this disease as it applies to their stubborn refusal to leave Harlem, even as it descended into an entropic urban wasteland. Perhaps we can call it Harlemitis.[22]

With these two hesitant "perhaps"es, the journalist acknowledges the significant role Harlem played in the Collyers' history, yet the pat formula raises some questions. First, why would a white body take ill for holding on to some things in black Harlem in the 1930s and 1940s? Second, why is the Collyers' desire to stay in this neighborhood a "stubborn refusal" or, ratcheting up the rhetoric, an act of madness? Third, why is Harlem an "entropic urban wasteland"?

The answer to these questions lies in the journalist's derogatory juxtaposition of "Harlem" and the suffix -itis, the latter translated as an inflammatory disease of a bodily organ. While it may be difficult to trace the Collyers and their attachment to personal property as a symptomatic dysfunction, it is too easy to find representations of twentieth-century Harlem (the district, the houses, the apartments, its working-class residents) as a descent into pathology: sociologists, historians, and journalists did so for several decades prior to the Collyers' demise. Originally a haven for middle-class and upper-class whites such as the Collyer family in the late nineteenth and early twentieth centuries, Harlem witnessed surges of black migration that spiked in the 1920s and continued well into the 1930s and 1940s. Following panicked white countermigrations into the suburbs as a response to this population shift, the neighborhood became a largely black vicinity that many derided as an "entropic urban wasteland," a slum replete with "deteriorating" houses and "immoral" bodies.[23]

Presenting the district, its properties, and its working-class inhabitants as a locus of psychic, moral, and material impairment, these disease tropes painted parts of black Harlem as sites of social decay, and such skewed portraits were often inseparable from what was referred to as "urban maladjustment." The sociologist Robert E. Park, for example, stressed in 1925 that "disturbances in metabolism" and "abnormalities in social metabolism" coincided with "the great influx of southern Negroes into northern cities since the war."[24] Other sociologists in the 1930s and 1940s traced the "disturbed social relationships" and "the growth of definitely anti-social attitudes" in metropolitan "race colonies," "disorganized Negro districts" such as Harlem, and the slum, which "has always been known as the breeding-place for vice, crime, and demoralization of all kinds."[25] Yet another stated in 1939 that "disorganization and apparent lack of direction" defined Harlem's denizens.[26] For these experts, the neighborhood brimmed with "social and economic disorders," immorality, and anomaly.[27] The district was, to rephrase Douglas, a deviant outbreak of city-based social pollution, a prime instance of metropolitan matter out of place.

Harlem, stated otherwise, was cast as chronically disorganized throughout the 1930s and 1940s, and as two quotes from the previous paragraph typify, these modern tropes of urban pathology were frequently referred to as *social disorganization*, a term coined around the same time that the neighborhood witnessed initial waves of black migration. Similar in kind, if not degree, to earlier conflations of African American populations and urban disorder, the term was advanced by sociologists William I. Thomas and Florian Znaniecki in their five-volume *The Polish Peasant in Europe and America* (1918–20), and while this term did not originally signify pathologized African Americans or the Collyers, it soon would.[28] Thomas and Znaniecki—both affiliated with the University of Chicago's School of Sociology—studied the cultural flux prompted by the migration of millions from the Old World to the United States at the turn of the twentieth century. Across their fourth volume, *Disorganization and Reorganization in Poland*, and their fifth, *Organization and Disorganization in America*, they characterized the moral disruptions caused by these transnational relocations as *social disorganization*, a term that originally referred to the waning of marriages between first-generation immigrants. "We can define social disorganization briefly," Thomas and Znaniecki write, "as a *decrease of the influence of existing social rules of behavior upon individual members of the group*. This decrease may present innumerable degrees, ranging from a single break of some particular rule by one individual up to a general decay of all the institutions of the group."[29] In shelves of case studies, subsequent sociologists and other thinkers adopted this influential concept of social disorganization and applied it to the seemingly foreign bodies—other immigrant and black populations—in towns and cities across America.

Despite its objective-seeming approach to ethnic immigration, that is to say, *The Polish Peasant* also theorized social disorganization as an urban maladjustment wedded to nonwhite bodies, as a moral panic that advanced marital, familial, and social pathologies. While Thomas and Znaniecki intended *social disorganization* to be "a neutral term that could lead toward greater individual autonomy [and] new forms of the family," it signified a deviance that was soon applied to urban "abnormalities," including places such as Harlem.[30] With their passing reference to general decay, for example, the sociologists embedded themes of moral decline that overshadowed their original definition. *The Polish Peasant* deemed social disorganization a "social evil" (192) and suggested that "demoralization is the decay of the personal life organization of an individual member of a social group" (256). As much as the book used sociological science to rationalize the plights of working-class Poles at a moment of national insecurity regarding Eastern European immigrations, it thus helped render disorganization both deviance and disease. Academics, artists, and laypeople soon embraced the term to disparage Harlem as an abnormal "breeding-place" for "disorganized" and usually working-class black bodies.

And, paradoxically, the Collyers. Despite its implicit contrast to organized Anglo-Saxons, disorganization and its deviant connections to upper Manhattan were useful for describing some of the seemingly odd behaviors of the neighborhood's more famous white residents—even though one of the brothers denied this association. Like many, the Collyers seemed to have bought into racist discourses regarding their neighborhood. As one of the "marooned white families" who did not make a suburban migration in the 1920s or 1930s, they would have had little issue with questionable caricatures of Harlem as an entropic urban wasteland.[31] In a summer 1938 interview with Helen Worden (Erskine), a journalist who vaulted the brothers into local and national prominence before and after their deaths with her newspaper exposés and her 1953 *Out of This World: A Collection of Hermits and Recluses, Their Ways of Life, and the Stories behind Their Retreats*, Langley denounced his fellow black residents:

> "These terrible children. They called me the spook. They say I drag dead bodies into the house after dark and string them up from our old elm tree." He waved his fist in the general direction of Harlem. "They break my windows. They make my life miserable. They even put a sign on my door saying, 'This is a ghost house!'" . . . "My brother Homer and I were born in E. 35th St., on Murray Hill. We came here in 1909. This was a beautiful neighborhood then. We feared Murray Hill was growing commercial. When there was talk of the Triboro Bridge, Homer bought this house—2077 [the townhouse across from the one where their bodies were found]. We thought that the section would pick up again. Look at it now!" . . . His voice rose to its hysterical pitch, then subsided to its monotone as he switched to a happier topic. "Our family is one of the oldest in New York. Our ancestors came to America on the *Speedwell*, which had a better passenger list than the *Mayflower*."

With his mournful self-representation that they arrived in Harlem when it was "a beautiful neighborhood," Collyer presents a biased summary of the migratory changes in a section of Manhattan that many had begun to dismiss as a disorganized slum. Describing himself as a well-to-do and implicitly white member of New York's finest society, he contrasts himself and his family members with the predominantly black residents who surround him, and he impresses on Worden that he and Homer are not affiliated with the neighbors who allegedly taunt him. He thus confirms historian Gilbert Osofsky's claim that "it seemed unbelievable to some that theirs, one of the most exclusive sections in the entire city, should become the center of New York's most depressed and traditionally worst-housed people."[32] Noting that his family name is "one of the oldest," Collyer endorses this line of thought as he depicts himself as a bastion of Old New York, and his brother's former occupation as a Columbia University–trained lawyer and his father's as a renowned physician across several of the five boroughs cement this claim.

Langley's suspicions of his neighbors may have been mutual, given that some black residents of Harlem saw the two brothers as a "neighborhood curiosity." Yet despite associations between the Collyers and an elite whiteness, local newspapers just as often presented the two recluses as strange "objects of great curiosity," as a disorganized mess in contrast to these self-presentations as cultured gentlemen. Collyer, in fact, seems to protest too much in his interview with Worden, and this may be because the disordered representations that he personally disavowed were ones with which he and his brother had become closely associated. Ironically, the more he publicly cultivated rhetorical reserve ("Look at it now!") and privately cultivated domestic distance (the booby traps placed inside the house) from the perceived black disorder he saw around him, the more he, his brother, and their home came to represent the disorganization held by many to inhere in the neighborhood—a disorganization that would later apply to their mental states and their supposed inability to let go of their stuff.

One instance of this conflation occurs in the same interview where Collyer denigrates his neighbors. In the midst of his rant, Worden informs readers, Collyer "drew his ragged coat together, fastened it with a safety pin. 'I have to dress this way. They would rob me if I didn't. We make our home look as if no one lived in it. We would be murdered otherwise.'" Later in their discussion Worden adds that "Langley's body was clad in a weird assortment of filthy, tattered garments." Under the auspices of trying to protect himself from the perceived threat of the neighborhood's black inhabitants, Collyer's tattered self-presentation here is a symbol of the neighborhood's supposed disorder, the "decay of the personal life" revealed in personal attire. Hence his anxiety over racial pollution in his interview with Worden: his furious exclamations at Harlem signal that narratives of deviant disorganization had intercepted his biography of "old-stock" whiteness, and at such a moment Collyer embodied the discourses of disorganization that he sought to deflect. That is, the further he tried to disentangle himself from the pathologies of social disorganization, the less he appeared a carryover from the *Speedwell* and more an exemplar of slumdom.

Unwittingly and unknowingly, the Collyers began to personify pathological stories of Harlemitis. As interest in their mysterious lives coincided with the cultural emergence of Harlem as a disorganized slum across popular and academic discourses, one gradually became a corollary for the other.[33] A few days after their deaths, in an article titled "Mystery of Collyer Brothers Made Big News for a Decade," a reporter forged this connection when he observed that "in some mysterious manner—for he later declared that he never looked at newspapers—Langley knew of the grotesque picture being painted, and he resented it." This "grotesque picture" refers to the ghost house that the neighborhood children allegedly mocked, but it also references the abnormalities thought to haunt Harlem (Langley's reference to the racial slur "spook" is telling in this regard). Though the brothers attempted to avoid this guilt by association, they did not sidestep the disorganization thesis of early-century to midcentury

Harlemitis. Hence another way to approach his interview with Worden: as much as he attempted to manage his public image as an elite white male removed from working-class blacks, he also tried to neutralize the "abnormalities" of Harlem's social metabolism by presenting himself as an upstanding New Yorker of fine Puritan stock.

Hysterical rhetoric, torn clothes, and decrepit housing told a different story, however, and the brownstone they inherited only furthered this deviant narrative—especially since the two "make our home look as if no one lived in it." It is important to note that nowhere in Collyer's statement about trashing his "'ghost house'" does he refer to or have awareness of what some now call hoarding tendencies. This diagnosis, the next section reveals, would be imposed on them shortly after their deaths. Collyer insists instead that his home's exterior appears disorganized so that he can stave off the imagined threat of Harlem's disorder. Despite his paranoid fears of blackness, though, this home, much like his verbal protests and his "tattered" attire, only strengthened links among deviance, disorder, and the eccentrics. Just as disorganization discourses derided Harlem bodies as "abnormalities," so too did they frequently deride Harlem's homes as "breeding-place[s] for vice," and the press likewise depicted the facade of 2078 as a hovel.[34] Worden's interview, for instance, begins by noting that the house's "doors were barred, its wooden shutters drawn . . . and its basement gate wired together. The stone balustrade which guarded the crumbling stoop had collapsed." Calling attention to the brothers' "eccentric existence," another reported "no effort to keep the house in shape." Another states that "the mysterious old brownstone mansion . . . looked just as it has for the last five years: windows broken, storm doors shut, decaying front stoop with its balustrades lopped off and rubbish piled high in the basement entrance." Soon after police found their bodies, the mansion appears in scare quotes: "Today the Collyer 'mansion' is just another dirty, abandoned building." If Harlem's homes were treated like metonymies of urban social disorder, then the Collyers' "Harlem mystery house" became an exemplar of this cliché.

As a result, newspapers emphasized the brothers *of* Harlem rather than the brothers *in* Harlem. Nicknaming them "Harlem Mystery Men," journalists began to repetitively associate the Collyers with the neighborhood with phrases such as "Harlem's greatest mystery," "the Hermits of Harlem," the "hermit brothers of Harlem," and "the recluse brothers of Harlem." Despite Collyer's professed distance from his black neighbors, newspaper photographs published before his death featured him in close proximity with his fellow residents (see figure 1.2). Announcements that the Collyers were on familiar if not always pleasant terms with their neighbors, as well as notices that the brothers in their "once fashionable house" resided in a "virtually all-Negro district," complemented these

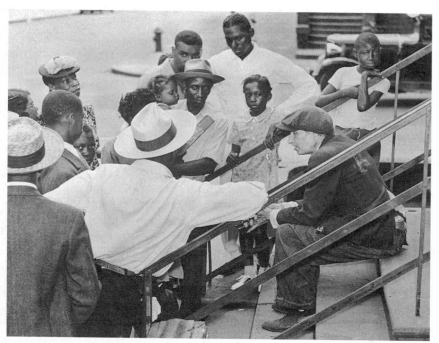

FIGURE 1.2 "Langley Collyer Chatting with Neighbors Outside," ca. 1943.
Courtesy of Corbis Images.

visual and rhetorical conjunctions. Although the Collyers may have professed to elite whiteness, they became rather intimate with Harlemites and disorderly decline. Investigations into the city's abnormalities coincided with investigations into the Collyers' eccentricities, and each made good on Scandura's intuitive hypothesis that "the hoarder, disorder and mess, these facets of modern urban culture are inextricably linked" via Harlem's most famous recluses.[35] The modern discourse of social disorganization hastened these connections as the two brothers became the neighborhood's greatest mystery, and, eventually, one of the most mysterious compulsive hoarding cases of all time.

A letter to the editor of the *New York Sun* published two days after their deaths made explicit these connections. Titled "Junk in Old Slums: Collyer Case Brings back Memories of Hazardous Living," the anonymous letter opined,

> Sir: The junk-packed Collyer mansion brings back recollections of this writer, who was born and raised in the Hell's Kitchen section of New York City some fifty years ago where tenements filled with human beings were also the scenes of congested junk piles. Yet they were not quite so bad as the

Collyer condition. Tenement streets were often crowded with ten or more loaded garbage cans.

What is striking is that the letter's reference to the Collyers' Harlem mansion makes an even earlier connection between the brothers and the "hazardous" conditions of urban immigrant life. The commentary does not compare the "junk-packed" house to *The Polish Peasant*, but it does situate the mansion alongside residences of Hell's Kitchen, a neighborhood composed mainly of working-class Irish immigrants "some fifty years ago." Tracing what the author later terms "the slum days of years gone by, with dark and dreary tenement hallways," the letter explicitly compares seemingly dirty tenements ("ten or more loaded garbage cans") and the Collyer house. To rephrase this last point: a connection emerges between the social disorganization of quasi-white Irish migrants and the tenement-identified Collyers.[36] Yet the letter nevertheless notes that the Collyer house—with historical ties to threats of urban immigrant disorder—is disorganization run even more amok: "[T]hey were not quite so bad as the Collyer condition."

The letter does so because the Collyers turned the "social abnormalities" of Harlemitis into what curious readers and social commentators began to diagnose as a personalized condition with historical antecedents. According to the OED, a new definition of *condition* emerged in 1920s America: "a state of health; esp. one that is poor or abnormal; a malady or sickness."[37] As much as the Collyers personified social disorganization in general and Harlem's disorganization in particular, their representations tweaked the neighborhood's supposed pathologies into this novel condition of a personalized abnormality. While these depictions were not alone in this shift—sociologists by the 1930s and 1940s stressed that "social disorganization is an extension of individual disorganization in that it is a projection of the neurotic traits of disorganized individuals into the field of interpersonal relations"[38]—grotesque accounts of the brothers nevertheless reified social disorganization into a chronic condition, something that would look more like the derisive malady of a hoarder and less like a quaint "gentleman of the 1880's."[39] In so doing, they enabled modern disorganization discourses surrounding immigrants and African Americans to mutate from pointing to a social pathology into identifying a psychological one.

Across overlapping public registers, the signifiers of clothing, rhetoric, housing, and reportage gradually cast the Collyers' extreme eccentricity as "a descent into madness." Some journalists prior to and after their deaths, for example, cited the brothers for being as "mad as [their] eccentric habits might indicate." Thus, it is not simply that the brothers seemed crazy for staying in Harlem— one problematic definition of Harlemitis—but that they seemed neurotic for their intimate associations with the neighborhood disorder that they abjured. In their refusal to depart, they became unconditional members of a fictive communal pathology, and they augmented social disorganization theories with an unexpected corollary: the personal neurosis of chronic disorganization. As their cultural deviance became indistinguishable from their individual disorganization, their personae laid down track for scores of future hoarders once the Collyer condition gradually became HD.

If Harlem was too often figured as a disease, the Collyers were its extended metaphor. Despite the brothers' protests, a queer picture emerged in the years immediately preceding and immediately following their deaths, and this was one step well on the way to pathologizing hoarding as a unique form of modern disorganization tied to two aging loners and their rotting brownstone. It may also be one reason why hoarding in the elderly has sometimes been referred to as social breakdown syndrome (recall that Homer was "Found Dead at 70" by the police), and I take up this link between hoarding and the aged in chapter 4. It is certainly one possible explanation that "gross disorganization" defines individuals who seem like the Collyers as well as those who later find their mental states hailed by this societal pathology. "There was widespread agreement," one commentator put it, "that the Collyers' minds had been as disordered as their home."[40]

Neurobiologists, psychiatrists, and social workers may forget these historical links when they invoke the "substantial social burden" that hoarders are thought to create with their fourteenth chromosome and their overflowing digs. But when the experts present HD as a social impairment or as a public nuisance that leads to possible health risks for the social body, they give an unknowing nod to how disorganization theories of Harlem enabled a representational shift from hoarding as eccentric greediness to hoarding as a diseased pathology with racial and ethnic roots. This is half the story that hoarding's modern emergence can tell us when we attend to the Collyers. Focusing now on the flip side of Harlemitis, I trace how their deviant possessions further expedited their eventual descent into the madness of medicine, given Homer and Langley's "neurotic inability to dispose of things."

FILTHY RICHES

This genealogy of the modern hoarder has linked the Collyers with social deviance and theories of racial and immigrant disorganization. Yet as we intuit from the New York Sun letter to the editor, this emergent narrative relied not only on two persons and their unfashionable home address but also on their ruined things—their "junk-packed" home and its similarities to "scenes of congested junk piles" and "loaded garbage cans." Such explicit associations between the brothers and disorganized rubbish were not unique to this reminiscence. Just as popular and academic discourses of Harlemitis facilitated the pathologization of the Collyers, other narratives surrounding the contents of their house also enabled the portrait of an entropic domestic wasteland. Sensational photographs and tales of these strange possessions enthralled the public, and they proved a complementary step in reconfiguring definitions of hoarding as an abnormal condition that conflated mental and material disorganization—particularly given that the term's original definition emphasized immoral stockpiles of money.

I noted earlier that Langley Collyer tried to portray himself and his brother as rich and reclusive eccentrics while they became enmeshed in discourses of Harlem-centric disorganization. Companion pieces to this story were tales of their rich and reclusive things as rumors circulated throughout the late 1930s and the 1940s about the Collyers' wealth. Newspapers reported that the brothers "were wealthy beyond the dreams of a Croesus [a king of Lydia]" and that the mystery men of Harlem secretly owned "half of [the] Waterfront." Riffing on earlier definitions of hoarding as the excessive accumulation of money, these same papers speculated that the Collyers "had secreted a hoard of money" ever since they first moved to Harlem in 1909, and that police would discover "the millions that the Collyers were reputed to have hidden in the house."[41]

Amidst these anecdotes about their cash hoarding were unconfirmed reports about their fantastic things, a material opulence thought to best their outstanding personal savings. In 1942, a journalist conjectured that "the tales of what the sheriff will find when he finally gains entrance to the old house rival a thrilling mystery novel. Behind the dust-covered windows, the stories go, will be found a house full of antique furniture and rare books." Local newspaper headlines likewise hyperbolized: "Neighbors Say Old House Has Grand Piano in Each Room." Such exaggerated accounts of spectacular things were in keeping with depictions of the Collyers as Old Society hailing from the neighborhood of Murray Hill, and a few treated the brownstone's facade of disorganization as precisely that—a cover-up of their interior riches. After detailing "the neighborhood, mainly inhabited by Negroes, in which the Collyer Brothers, members of an old New York family," lived, one correspondent suggested that "others said he would find, behind the outward appearance of filth and squalor, a veritable Arabian Nights of Chinese rugs, cut-glass rarities in antique China closets, thousands of morocco-bound books, and more than one grand piano."[42]

That didn't happen. In the weeks after police discovered their corpses, press representations of filth and squalor—explicitly connected to threatening social fantasies of Harlem's urban disorder—displaced this hearsay of the Collyers' hoarded wealth, and rampant speculation about the elite contents of the house changed course. Following the discovery of Homer's body, crowds gathered in the streets outside the mansion, and newspapers reported on the fascination and repulsion prompted by the items pulled from the mansion (figure 1.3). As these congregations grew in number and as newspapers encouraged their reactions, the Collyers' things shifted status from rarities hoarded in a mansion to

FIGURE 1.3 "Crowd Watching Search of Collyer Mansion," March 24, 1947.
Courtesy of Corbis Images.

trash packed into a decrepit old house: "The interior of the house was an incredibly dirty mass of debris, old newspapers, cartons, broken furniture and all sorts of junk that Langley had lugged in."[43]

As we see from this last quote, the majority of the postmortem descriptions rested on recurring motifs of dirt and debris (and their synonyms: junk, refuse, rubbish, "pot pourri").[44] These depictions, in turn, advanced an emergent narrative that objects of former opulence had degenerated into an "incredibly dirty" mess—a complication to the disorganization thesis. Almost every news outlet shared this unifying tale, and the crowds did as well. Take but two selected quotes. One: "Then Langley—engineer, musician and cultured gentleman who turned his back on the world to create a fantastic debris-filled cosmos—will be buried beside Homer, the onetime admiralty lawyer, who preferred rubbish to riches." Two: "The mountain of rubbish cluttering the second floor" was full of "ingenious piles of rubbish" where "tons of paper and cardboard were interlaced with butts of metal and stone to form a booby trap for unwary intruders." Aided by photographic splashes of the mansion's insides, these narratives of incredible trash displaced narratives of incredible affluence. What emerged was a story that paralleled the brothers' decline into Harlemitis, and one that further set the stage for later depictions of the two men as strange hoarders of junked goods.

The chronicles of 2078, in other words, did not stop there: as visual and rhetorical representations of a riches-to-rubbish narrative cohered, the press sensationalized the descriptions of the Collyers' once-opulent objects (figures 1.4– 1.6). Newspapers played up tropes that centered on the strange accumulation of oddities and shocking curios by referring to "an incredible collection of junk," "stacks of fantastic junk," and "the amazing accumulation of junk and bric-a-brac piled up from floor to ceiling." Citing "More Collyer Curiosa Dug Up," journalists stressed the "new oddities" that police uncovered as pieces of "once handsome Victorian furniture were scattered in disorderly fashion amid indescribable filth," and they imagined the Collyers collecting "newspapers, trash and any portable oddities" on midnight walks before their deaths. Such oddities included not only several grand pianos but any and every piece of minutiae crammed inside the brownstone: "Among the curios were several tickets to the annual excursion of the Sunday School of Trinity Episcopal Church to Glen Island on Sunday, July 8, 1905." Every piece of supposed junk became a remarkable curiosity, and every "dirty" item became a point of interest in this popularized discourse of spectacular debris.

Hence while journalists referred to many of the mansion's materials as worthless (thereby debunking the scads of hidden money myth), the things in

FIGURE 1.4 The Collyers' sitting room, 1947. Courtesy of Corbis Images.

the Collyer house were nevertheless characterized as "fascinating," "amazing," and "incredible," and newspapers delighted in titillating audiences with sensational catalogs of excavated items. Headlines proclaimed a "Weird Yield of Relics" or "Oddities Tossed Out," and papers rattled off lists of objects such as an automobile radiator, coffee grinders, a child's chair, and a horse's jawbone. Also removed from the building were mantel clocks, phonograph records, a wooden cradle filled with bones and skulls, violins, a cello, bottles, hats, revolvers, a 1914 program for the Metropolitan Opera House, elementary school con-

FIGURE 1.5 The Collyers' sitting room, 1947. Courtesy of Corbis Images.

duct reports, sheets of Braille, newspaper bundles, balls of twine, cereal boxes, shelves of books, piles of cartons, a peeling machine, piles of tin cans, pinups of women, and a Ford Model T automobile.

As newspapers recorded these items, discourses of disorganized Harlemitis began to accompany another deviant narrative, that of the queer curio. Traditionally, *curiosa* refer to curiosities or oddities, whereas a *curio* refers to "an object of art, piece of bric-à-brac, etc., valued as a curiosity or rarity; a curiosity; more particularly applied to articles of this kind from China, Japan, and the far East."[45] We see references to these two definitions with the Orientalist Chinese rugs and the cut-glass rarities from antique china closets that some journalists imagined inside the mansion in the late 1930s. By comparison, postmortem references to the Collyer curiosa and their spectacular oddities tied the brothers to another root source of these terms—that of the *curiosity cabinet*. Adjectives used to describe their curios, such as *fantastic*, played on themes inherent in these cabinets, and I briefly condense the centuries-long cultural history of this item, since it aided perceptions of the Collyers as pathologized hoarders of weird debris as much as social disorganization contributed to perceptions of the brothers as pathologized exemplars of personal disorder.

Also referred to as *wonder cabinets*, curiosity cabinets first appeared in fifteenth-century Europe to display the glories of the known world, though by the twentieth century the term could refer to a mantel of bric-a-brac. Originally referred to as *Wunderkammern* (cabinets of wonders) or *Kunstkammern* (cabinets of art objects), curiosity cabinets were, according to Patrick Mauriès, rooms that featured jaw-dropping collections categorized according to *mirabilia* (marvels), *animialia*, and *naturalia*. These two cabinet styles fused into *Kunst- und Wunderkammern* a century later, and exhibitors showcased phenomena as various as seashells, precious stones, stuffed animals, and instances of "nature deformed" oddities.[46] Likewise, these wonder cabinets would sometimes include *Americana*, or exoticized cultural artifacts from the Americas.[47] As we see from one reprint of the Museum of Ole Worm of Copenhagen engraved in 1655, the cabinet's *mirabilia* impressed the viewer upon entrance into the room (figure 1.7). From floor to ceiling, one could behold extraordinary sea creatures, reptiles, and other goods as the wonders of the world were carefully arranged to provoke a sensory overload.

Popular among the elite and taken up by bourgeois collectors, these cabinets possessed three goals: first, "the ability of such collections to dazzle";[48] second, to draw attention to exotic things; and third, to produce "a perfect and completed picture of the world."[49] By the eighteenth century, emphasis on the *mirabilia* component waned as collections of *animalia* and *naturalia* evolved into modern natural history museums.[50] Moving further down the historical timeline, scholars have traced the continuities of these cabinets to spectacular expos of supposedly primitive foreigners at US World's Fairs, and even to curiosity collections of toolboxes featured in mass-produced magazines such as Depression-era *Popular Mechanics*.[51]

This last tidbit of trivia is useful for tracking how discourses of the modern curiosity cabinet and its curios informed representations of the Collyers and their "debris-filled cosmos" in Harlem. By the mid-1930s, wonder cabinets had evolved not just into natural history museums but into affordable pieces of furniture reproduced on "a large-scale mass."[52] Across the late nineteenth- and early twentieth centuries, one update of the cabinet became the mass-produced display case, or what we today refer to today as a *corner curio cabinet*.[53] In 1901, for instance, the Sears, Roebuck catalog distributed an advertisement spread for "Book Racks and Music Stands" that included a "$1.65 Bamboo Corner Cabinet, . . . a Beautiful Corner Cabinet for bric-a-brac or books" (figure 1.8).

FIGURE 1.7 Frontispiece for Ole Worm, *Museum Wormianum*, 1655, engraving.
Courtesy of the University of Bristol Special Collections Library.

These inexpensive corner cabinets were meant to hold personal collections, and
they encouraged the display of marvelous bric-a-brac and oddities such as a
"Star Sea Shell," fortune-telling cards, and Orientalized straw boxes—each for
thirty-three cents (figure 1.9).[54]

As much as we situate the Collyers in the contemporaneous history of social disorganization, then, we see that their riches-to-rubbish curios became
snagged in the centuries-spanning spectacle of the cabinet as a form of elite
and mass-produced wonder—but with some notable deviations. Across early
and later periods of modernity, the cabinet was a tasteful extension of the collector. The Collyers' curios, by contrast, were a dismal failure of discrimination.
Cultivation of a cabinet or a curio collection epitomized order, yet the Collyers'
curios were not spatially well organized: workers found "tons of junk mixed
indiscriminately with valuable belongings in the weird three-story brownstone
mansion." Further, whereas wonder cabinets were limited to a display room
or a corner display case, piles of supposed exotica overtook every inch of the
Harlem brownstone. Marking these distinctions (if not their deeper history),

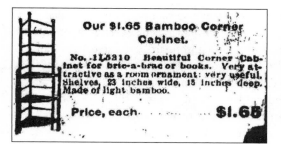

FIGURE 1.8 Enlargement of bamboo corner cabinet advertisement "for bric-a-brac or books." Sears, Roebuck catalog, no. 110 (Spring 1901): 1119. Courtesy of Sears Holdings Archives.

FIGURE 1.9 Curios advertisement. Sears, Roebuck catalog, no. 120 (Spring 1910): 392. Courtesy of Sears Holdings Archives.

newspapers thus represented the Collyer house as a decrepit *Kunst- und Wunderkammer* that was a site of repulsion rather than a scene of refinement. Instead of producing delight, their house became a nightmare scenario of disorganized curios, "an amazing accumulation of junk and bric-a-brac piled up from floor to ceiling." Such descriptions confirm anthropologist James Clifford's observation, in his overview of the modern-day curiosity cabinet, that "the good collector (as opposed to the obsessive, the miser) is tasteful and reflective. Accumulation unfolds in a pedagogical, edifying manner. . . . Indeed a 'proper' relation with objects (rule-governed possession) presupposes a 'savage' or deviant relation (idolatry or erotic fixation)."[55]

This emphasis on misers' "deviant relation" to their strange things is important: it allows us to chart how the Collyers' disorderly curios further pathologized two white men simultaneously cast as abnormal for their relation to black Harlem. As I hypothesized, the Collyers' effects harked back to themes of the wonder cabinet even as they spoiled these tropes with their "amazing rubbish." But their incredible piles of junk also incorporated another definition of accumulated curiosa—one that emerged not in the early modern period but in the later nineteenth century—as deviant objects. Unusual forms of curios, for some, signaled more than oddities such as a stuffed alligator, since *curiosa* also came to refer to a euphemistic description for "erotic or pornographic books" by the 1880s.[56] Newspaper references to "several pin-up girls" found in the mansion confirm this definition of erotic attachment with regard to the brothers' material things, but the case remains that every item pulled out of the house was treated as a perverse curio.[57] Noted reporters: "All sorts of queer objects were removed from the building, including an intricate potato peeler, a nursery refrigerator, a beaded lampshade, a box of boy's tops, and a toy airplane."[58]

Given these intertwined meanings of *curiosa*, and given the brothers' "deviant relation" to their curios, it is clear that the Collyers were not only pathologized by the aberrance of social disorganization: they were also queered by material deviance, the pathologization of the things extracted from their mansion in the early spring of 1947. So often figured by the press as strange, fantastic, filthy, and weird, their curios became a poor reflection on the brothers, and these possessions realized a now-popular conception that "people who hoard appear to find it difficult to define the boundary between 'who they are' and 'what they own.'"[59] Local New York newspapers, I stress, manufactured this boundary confusion by conflating the odd curiosa of the house with the supposedly aberrant personages who inhabited it. As much as the brothers were racialized by Harlemites, then, they were just as much made queer by their weird relics. While such queerness was not entirely unrelated to sexual deviance (Scandura references the Collyers as "two bachelor brothers descended from Pilgrims and dependent on each other in a way more incestuous than fraternal"), I spotlight a perversion associated more with material attachments than with eroticized bodies.[60] Deviant goods became cross-identified with deviant ownership, and thanks to disorganization theories and to the botched disordering of the curiosity cabinet, material oddities became human ones as well.

I rephrase this last claim by returning again to the *New York Sun* letter to the editor: the Collyers' queer things became part of the Collyer condition. As police extracted items, a definition of hoarding as the aberrant accumulation of a person's disorganized things coalesced, and a new definition of the hoarder as a material and mental deviant rather than a mere eccentric began to cohere. This definition, my later chapters will argue, merged with other discourses regarding improper collecting, inappropriate cluttering, and unsuccessful aging. For now I note how integral the Collyers were to advancing hoarding as a popular psychopathology. One nonmedical expert, Coleman O. Parsons of the City College of New York, made the mental illness of the hoarder's object relations explicit in an interview published with the *World-Telegram* in the spring of 1947. A scholar of Scottish literature as well as the author of an unpublished manuscript on hoarders and aberrant misers ("Studies in Eccentricity") now housed at Columbia University, Parsons was invited as expert witness to comment on the Collyers and their deviant things.[61] In a newspaper write-up by Norton Mockridge, the article first identifies Parsons as a member "of the City College English Department, who has made a study of more than 120 misers and eccentrics in the past year and a half." Parsons then offered this diagnosis:

> "In the final judgment, Homer and Langley Collyer will take their place among the great hoarders and recluses of history." He [Parsons] declared that persons who hoard gold or other objects of value exhibit rational behavior, but that the Collyers "who practiced unselective hoarding showed definite irrationality." He compared them with a nineteenth-century French hoarder who accumulated huge stores of butter during a shortage with the expectation of selling at a profit. When the price boom failed to materialize, he stubbornly refused to sell. After his death, the vast cache of rancid butter was found stored away in his home.

Charting a shift in definitions of hoarding as the stockpiling of "gold or other objects of value," Parsons links the Collyer brothers to a novel form of this act, and his assessment marks an epistemic break as his diagnosis moves hoarding from eccentric amassing to pathological pileup. He makes no mention of careful selection in terms of the Collyers' curiosities but instead psychologizes them to find that the brothers engaged in "unselective hoarding," and he connects them to "definite irrationality"—thinly veiled code for the madness of a personal disorganization that we also saw at work in discourses of Harlemitis. Thus, we are back to the Collyer condition on "unfashionable" Fifth Avenue but with an added layer of historical complexity: a messy domestic interior equates with a messy psychology. As the brothers became spectacles of curious material and mental disorganization, their minds, like that of the French hoarder who accumulated tubs of butter, went rancid.

Drawing on older definitions of the curiosity cabinet as well as novel takes on curiosa, late 1940s reports on the Collyers, their decrepit mansion, and their irrational things introduced some of the groundwork for one modern conceptualization of hoarding. In the early 1930s the contents of their house had been a potent scene of material opulence. By 1947, the home was a sorry site of oddity, amazing junk, material decline, and shocking debris—a dynamic process facilitated by sensational reportage, photography, and expert testimony by individuals such as Parsons. But given that dirt and disorder are always in the eye of the beholder, it is useful to remind ourselves that the Collyers may have viewed their things as ordinary (or at least as ingenious traps for would-be burglars). We will never know their final appraisal, but in the eyes of the press and its readerships the brothers were no longer wealthy white eccentrics warding off potential black intruders with their whimsies. They were instead filthy, irrational hoarders of Harlem, given "the bizarre conditions under which the brothers were living." "If the show 'Hoarders' had been around in the 1940s," notes one 2012 *New York Daily News* article, "the eccentric Collyers would have been prime candidates."[62]

The *Daily News* article is not incorrect. The strangest curiosa extracted from the brownstone were not infant skulls but Homer and Langley. As I complicated the grotesque picture of their lives by attending to their seemingly abnormal possessions, it is safe to say that the Collyers' house became a *Kunst- und Wunderkammer* of personal and social disorganization in their much-maligned neighborhood—a horrific cabinet of curious urban disorder. By the time their rotting corpses were removed from their mansion, the Collyers appeared less like gentile throwbacks to the 1880s and more like psychiatric freaks, confirming disability studies scholar Rosemarie Garland Thomson's claim that "eclectic cabinets of curiosities" historically "moved from the freak show stage into the medical theater."[63] As the city mystery of 2078 Fifth Avenue was solved, the Collyers and their "weird relics" became both freakish oddities and psychological maladies—a common understanding of hoarding today as it traverses both scientific literature and popular media.

Within "Harlem's House of Horrors," opulence became rubbish became curiosa became the disturbing specter of irrational hoarding, and the brothers moved from eccentrics into something that began to look like the bizarre accumulating that now informs the modern-day hoarder. This may further explain why media represented their "house of mystery and misery" not as a site of affluent wonder but as a site of domestic terror. Buried side by side in Brooklyn's Cypress Hills Cemetery, the Collyers, of course, had no say in these matters, but the fusion of their botched curiosa with the storied tales of Harlem's disorganization haunts one piece of hoarding's development as a pathological identity in modern America. In the terms laid out by this book's introduction, the object panic of the Collyers sprung from a moral panic over blacks and immigrants. One discourse compounded with the other, and the basis (if not the final touches) for the foundation of Collyer Brothers syndrome—the historical stuff that now houses the idea of chronic disorganization—was laid.

"POSTHUMOUS INFAMY"

As these narratives of Harlemitis and spoiled curiosa coupled, the fallout was immediate and gradual in terms of what would eventually become known as hoarding disorder. Over the decades, subsequent chapters also reveal, interest in the irrational psychology of hoarders accelerated by fits and by starts in news media, fiction, film, and medical literatures. Yet we can say with confidence that the links between pathological accumulation, social disorganization, and the rancid wonder cabinet established by 1947 only grew stronger after the brothers were interred. This final section traces how the Collyers became conflated with mental and material deviance across local, national, and international registers well into the twenty-first century. Surveying a few more postmortem newspaper reports, a 1954 middlebrow novel, a medical journal from 1963, and a 2007 self-help guide, we find that that their legend not only congealed into a singular and cautionary tale of compulsive hoarding and personal disorganization, but also catalyzed a societal pathology whose historical underpinnings would be overwritten by contemporary scientists, clinicians, and pop psychologists alike.

One entrepreneur wanted to turn the mansion into a wonder cabinet of Harlem detritus. Days after searchers found the last brother's body, the article "Collyer House May Be Museum" reported:

> The possibility that the ramshackle Collyer house at 2078 Fifth Avenue may one day become a commercial museum designed to attract visitors interested in the now-solved mystery of the dead Collyer brothers was seen today in the remark of a man who stood gazing at the dilapidated structure as laborers resumed the removal of junk and occasional items of value from the house.
>
> The man declined to identify himself, but told reporters he was considering buying the three-story building with a view to cleaning up the place, converting it into a curio house and charging admission to those who would like

to wander through the old house in which Homer and Langley Collyer lived like hermits amid cobwebs and tons of junk for many years.

Here we see a convergence of the major themes that would enable representations of the Collyers to become a harrowing pathology in midcentury America and the decades thereafter. The article features their "tons of junk" intermixed with "occasional items of value," and it reveals that early modern definitions of *Wunderkammern* were reconfigured into "curio house" as the anonymous man considered transforming the Collyers' possessions into a freak show. Most important for this section's argument, the newspaper account foreshadows how the Collyers became ongoing objects of sensational inquiry for the interested masses in the years following their deaths.

This proposed business venture to renovate the mansion into a tourist site did not pan out (Hubert's Dime Museum and Flea Circus in Times Square did, however, display several items as "freakish attractions" for several years).[64] Then again, it did not have to once the Collyers began to saturate popular imagination as legends of pathological hoarding. One newspaper report testified to this explicitly: "Far greater than the intrinsic value of the items is their appeal to the minds curious about the strange lives of these two brothers, well-educated sons of a doctor, who withdrew from the world and died together in their cluttered home." Likewise, another reporter observed the "publicity which made of the dingy brownstone house a mecca for curiosity seekers" and found that "the public conception of its occupants magnified until the picture assumed legendary proportions." By 1949, this link between the strange brothers and their mythic accumulation assumed such prominence that a journalist could state what must have seemed like the obvious: "The fortune, estimated at anywhere from $100,000 to $250,000 in the feverish days after the emaciated body of blind Homer was found in the one-time Collyer mansion on upper Fifth Avenue, will shrink almost to nothing. . . . The brothers and the fortune are gone. Only the legend lingers on." Moving from filthy-rich eccentrics to deviant hoarders to a possible curio museum to local and soon-to-be national legends, the Collyers became a cautionary tale of dangerous living whose influence extended well beyond the streets of Harlem.

Collyer curiosa became, in fact, the buzz of many cities. As New York reporters puzzled out their mystery, their story resonated with mass audiences across the United States via popular magazines. Replete with several half-page photo spreads, *Life* contributed a piece titled "The Strange Case of the Collyer Brothers" on April 7, 1947. Under the "National Affairs" heading, *Time* published a report on the same day titled "The Shy Men" that distributed the guiding narratives of pathological hoarding for audiences beyond the Big Apple. The article began by noting that "for 38 years, as the great city boiled and throbbed around them, as their house became part of Harlem and Negroes seeped into their neighborhood, they lived in greater and greater seclusion" (the Harlemitis thesis).[65] It detailed that "as the years passed, legends sprang up about the spectral old house. The persistent: it had a fortune" (the hidden-opulence thesis).[66] It then informed readers that "the police found five grand pianos, a library containing thousands of books on law and engineering, ancient toys, old bicycles with rotting tires, obscene photographs, dressmaker's dummies, heaps of coal, and ton after ton of newspapers—the fruit of three decades of hoarding" (the strange curio cabinet meets the aberrant hoarder thesis).[67] A few paragraphs condense links between "Harlem and Negroes," curiosa, and the "decades of hoarding" that I previously summarized. These movements consolidated under the Collyer legend to turn the brothers into a national affair rather than a localized public menace.

Eight years after their deaths, audiences were privy to the fictionalization of their lives with Marcia Davenport's middlebrow best seller *My Brother's Keeper.* Published in 1954 as a Book-of-the-Month Club selection, the novel, like postmortem press reports, merged anxieties of urban social disorganization, material deviance, and the figure of the irrational hoarder into one coherent narrative.[68] Based on the same newspaper accounts that I have traced, *My Brother's Keeper* tells the byzantine story of two wealthy white brothers, Seymour and Randall Holt, and their strange demise—all imagined through the eyes of a banker, Dick Wycherly, who tells readers from the start that "like the rest of the world I first knew of the Holt brothers through the newspapers which made them a sensation" (3). In the novel's opening pages, Wycherly describes "that derelict house crammed from cellar to roof with one hundred and seventy tons of hoarded rubbish" (3); he informs readers that "as everybody knows, the place was a solid impacted block of massed paper and trash, pierced only by those terrifying tunnels" (9); and he tells the tale of the Holts, their hoarding, their overbearing grandmother, and their bizarre love triangle with an Italian opera singer.

Explaining these narrative twists and turns is unnecessary, but I stress that Davenport's book connects the Holt hoarders to a racialized urban disorganization as it substitutes New York City's Chelsea neighborhood for Harlem. Describing their "fetid black hole" full of "stacks and piles of I did not yet know what" (9), the narrator states:

> Nothing on Manhattan Island is more obscenely derelict than the few of those yards that remain, abandoned to filth, trash, rats and the savage stray cats who hunt them; to the ruin wrought by the most wretched type of slum

which seems infinitely uglier and crueler than the vilest railroad tenements of the Lower East Side or dark Harlem. These Chelsea houses were once dignified and beautiful, homes of which gracious people were proud, homes which they loved in much the same way as the children raised in them. (7)

After linking "the Lower East Side" and "dark Harlem" to "obscenely derelict" Chelsea, and disgusted that the neighborhood is now full of "drifting slum-dwellers" and "crazy variegations" (8), Davenport has one of the brothers observe that

Chelsea was turning into a bleak and ugly district, its fine houses one by one degenerating into rooming-houses, its pavements unmended, its trees unreplaced when they died. Many of the neighbors among whom he had grown up had moved away to other parts of the city, eastward and downtown. And here he was, with Randall, condemned to live in the Chelsea house no matter what Chelsea was becoming. (90)

The novel then connects these descriptions of the Holts' filthy slum district to "the strange story" of their hoarding "with its crazy embellishments" (13).

Like *Time* and *Life*, *My Brother's Keeper* implanted the Collyers in the national imaginary as a "harrowing and ghastly" legend (3), but Davenport also made them into an international phenomenon: Dick Wycherly learns of the Holts-cum-Collyers through the press "like the rest of the world" (3), and his reference to the global reach of their legend suggests just how widespread their narrative became by the mid-1950s. A few years after the publication of *My Brother's Keeper*, a northern European medical journal categorized "irrational hoarding" as a psychological aberration connected expressly to the Collyers. In the 1963 study "Collector's Mania," Scandinavian physician Jens Jensen wrote that "a case of collector's mania on a gigantic scale is that of the brothers Collyer. It has only been described in daily press and in 'Time' and 'Life' and in 'True,' never in a medical journal."[69] While his claim was inaccurate given that the US-based *Journal of Chronic Diseases* (now *Journal of Clinical Epidemiology*) published a 1960 article on the Collyers as material deviants, Jensen found that this disease "consists of a compulsory, panic collecting and hoarding of many different objects, useful or useless, but very often things of repulsive, insanitary nature."[70] Confirming Douglas's thesis in *Purity and Danger*, he emphasizes that such "panic collecting and hoarding" is an "offense against public order and cleanliness."[71] He then proceeds to tell the detailed story of the Collyers as exemplars of this odd phenomenon.

These are just a few examples of how the post-1947 Collyer hoarding became further pathologized across literature, science, and reportage. There are more, and their legend remains ongoing. *My Brother's Keeper* went through various soft-cover editions from 1956 until 1982, and the Collyer mystery continued to seep into popular memory as hoarding became further associated with mental aberration and public offense. Stephen King, for instance, would use the Collyer mansion as inspiration for his fictive house of horror in the 1975 vampire novel *'Salem's Lot*, and E. L. Doctorow released a counterfactual novel about the two, *Homer and Langley*, in 2009. To cap off this cultural inundation, in 2004 the journal *American Speech* introduced the noun *Collyer* in its annual list of "New Words" as a "pack rat; a person who collects and stores an unreasonable number of things . . . A pair of New York recluses who achieved posthumous infamy after their bodies were discovered amid more than 100 tons of carefully accumulated debris in 1947."[72]

Thus, "the cases never cease to fascinate," states one *New York Times* reporter in 2003, as "some pass into legend, like the Collyer brothers, 'the hermit hoarders of Harlem,' who in 1947 were buried by the piles of urban junk that filled their four-story Harlem brownstone."[73] Here the "posthumous infamy" of the two brothers continues into the twenty-first century, even as emphases on Harlem disorder and the spoiled curio cabinet that spurred their narrative of irrational hoarding have receded in neurobiological circles—so much so that one of the more popular guides to compulsive hoarding titles itself, with no irony, *Buried in Treasures: Help for Compulsive Acquiring, Saving, and Hoarding*. In the 2007 edition, written by three hoarding disorder advocates, the authors note that "the concept of 'chronic disorganization,' used by professional organizers, is similar in many ways to compulsive hoarding."[74] While the book makes no mention of the Collyer brothers or their syndrome, their disorganized status haunts this text: the cover of *Buried in Treasures* reproduces a cropped 1947 New York newspaper photograph taken from inside the Collyer mansion, reproduced above as figure 1.5. This photograph is never referenced in *Buried in Treasures* nor identified on the back cover. I nevertheless emphasize that in the midst of recent scientific (and pop psychological) claims for the deviant category of the pathological hoarder, the foundational roles that Harlemitis and curiosa played haunt the scientific unconscious of the clinicians and journalists who popularize this condition. *Buried in Treasures* begins by noting that compulsive hoarding is "a potentially serious problem that many doctors and healthcare professionals have never heard of," but I argued that the archive proves otherwise, and the recall of but one repressed genealogy of the modern hoarder has been this chapter's aim.[75] In the wrong place at the right time, the Collyer brothers helped catapult chronic disorganization to a national and eventually international prominence that assumed infamous proportions thanks to newspapers, magazines, popular novels, and online media.

Their things long gone, it feels as if the Collyers' unfortunate legend is not going away anytime soon. When we think about the legions categorized as hoarders in the twenty-first century, we are not always thinking about matter out of mental place. We are thinking about a baleful portrait of Harlem that traces back to a certain fear of migrants in the early to mid-twentieth-century United States. Behind the sad tale of the Collyers is an even sadder story of working-class immigrants and African Americans, and alongside that history is another of modern-day curiosa. At the crossroads of these disparate narratives, the brothers unknowingly enabled dirt and disorder to bypass peculiarity and cohere into an aberrant identity category. When the present-day lot of scientists, social workers, and reporters diagnose their subjects with HD, they bury these materials in the treasures of their research. They reconfirm that hoarding is an inherently corrupt form of material relations, and they reinforce—however unknowingly—what Douglas catalogs as the "social sanctions, contempt, ostracism, gossip, perhaps even police action" that accompany this seemingly disorganized activity (92). Cramped and crushed and created by newspapers back then, Homer and Langley remain overwhelmed by other discursive messes right now.

2

PATHOLOGICAL COLLECTIBLES

Sometime during the spring of 1988—maybe the second week of April?—cookie jars became potentially hazardous objects. Sotheby's auction house in New York City had earlier announced a ten-day estate sale for Andy Warhol's effects that was to run from April 23 to May 3, and a number of observers were alarmed. Warhol had died from complications of gall bladder surgery more than a year before, and he left behind an Upper East Side townhouse filled with possessions that would soon net over twenty-five million dollars for what would become the Andy Warhol Foundation for the Visual Arts. Among the myriad items up for bids were Picasso sketches, pieces of Art Deco furniture, Tiffany silverware, and scores of abstract expressionist paintings. The auction also featured lots of more than seven thousand collectibles that included a Miss Piggy and Kermit the Frog beach towel, a Superman Touch-Tone telephone, and hundreds of cookie jars in different shapes and sizes. These last items drew no small amount of scrutiny laced with no small amount of disdain. Several commentators, it turned out, were distressed by these collectibles in what snowballed into a minor object panic.[1]

Newspapers and magazines alike expressed consternation. One *New York Times* reporter dismissed the auction as "an obsessive shopping spree that lasted several decades," and she homed in on "the cookie jars—everything from a happy Humpty Dumpty to a plump panda" as "the most perplexing purchases" that she encountered while cataloging Warhol's "offbeat Americana."[2] An observer for *Newsweek* derided the event as "the biggest garage sale ever" and expressed shock at "Warhol's vast jumble of objects d'art," particularly "the lower-priced collectibles."[3] Jewelry, she proclaimed with dismay, "was found in cookie tins; a Picasso was stuck in a closet. Another closet was stuffed to the top with stunning Navajo blankets," and it all added up to telltale signs of "Warhol's collecting mania."[4] Reviewing the sale after its completion, *Time* likewise found that "the extent of his hoard had largely been a secret. As compulsive consumers go, he was inconspicuous. . . . Time and again, Andy's kitsch—'collectibles' was Sotheby's more tactful label—fetched upscale prices."[5]

Commentators agreed in other media outlets. *House and Garden* had earlier reproduced color photographs of the townhouse's spruced-up interiors taken by Robert Mapplethorpe, which the magazine accompanied with an essay disparaging "every new mad thing" and Warhol's "essentially nondiscriminatory" possessions.[6] Art and Auction was equally aghast: "Andy Warhol's collection . . . is more the result of his compulsive shopping and hoarding than of any calculated, orderly plan of acquisition."[7] Appalled that Warhol "had masterpieces alongside what would seem to be junk of the most worthless sort," New York inquired less than judiciously: "Is it just a bunch of stuff, or is it invested with a higher meaning? Warhol has been called a hoarder, which suggests he was in the grip of some eccentric or neurotic compulsion to acquire objects" (figure 2.1).[8]

With their references to manic collecting, neurotic objects, and compulsive consumption, these notices approached Warhol's estate as a material perversion (his sexual proclivities for men were never really up for grabs). His acquisitions were a deviation of proper collecting; his refusal to distinguish between containers and luxury goods a sign of mental disorder; his home a secretive cache of material degeneration. As such, his collectibles were often characterized as representing a questionable act of irrational hoarding, another version of the perverse curiosa that we saw in newspaper reports of the Collyers. One article went so far as to diagnose an epidemic of "Warhol fever," the fear that auctioneers and spectators attending the sale might catch the artist's illness in their rush to acquire a bit of Warhol.[9] Collectible cookie jars had become contagious objects of deviance as Andy's stuff became a sensational topic du jour.

Despite this seasonal interest in his possessions, Warhol proves to be one among the many. I begin with this snippet and return to it as one of this chapter's central case studies because it encapsulates anxieties that underpin discussions of his hoarding in the late 1980s as well as those found in numerous accounts of this psychopathology to this day. Given that both treat *excessive accumulation* as a synonym for *pathological collecting*, it seems as if the ever-cascading avalanche of clinical hoarding stories uncannily accords with these media reports. Less than two years after Sotheby's auction, for instance, Jerusalem-based psychiatrist David Greenberg and two of his colleagues published an overview of hoarding in the official journal of the American Society of Clinical Psychopharmacology, titled "Hoarding as a Psychiatric Symptom." The essay began with an extended survey of "normal collecting," a wholesome activity that "involved the collectors in a social world of dealers, artists, historians, art lovers, and other collectors."[10] They then juxtaposed this act to the hoarder's "pathologic behavior," whereby "neurotic patients are unable to part with a variety of useless and valueless objects."[11] In a common formula, later practitioners followed the essay's lead to reiterate that "collecting is a normal phenomenon, in contrast with pathological collecting, or hoarding."[12] Or as DSM-5 states, "Hoarding disorder contrasts with normative collecting behavior."[13] Hence just as we saw in chapter I that HD was typed as chronic disorganization, this diagnosis appears under the rubric of pathological or, alternatively, abnormal collecting.

Never mind that normal collecting has been something of a bugaboo.[14] As they define hoarding behavior as pathological collecting, accounts such as Greenberg's anticipate later medical reports that also invoke tropes of "aberrant collecting behavior" and "abnormal acquisition."[15] Much like the exposés of Warhol's perplexing possessions, these experts stress "the mixing of important with unimportant possessions" as they affirm that hoarded "objects cannot be differentiated or categorized according to their value since all seem at the moment to be 'very important' possessions."[16] Given these descriptive similarities, is there little wonder that Warhol reappears as a prototypical hoarder in several recent accounts? Noting that "some collectors show extreme behaviors that straddle the border between eccentricity and pathology," two HD specialists spotlight the "unusual aspects of Warhol's collecting"—namely, that he "preserved nearly every bit of ephemera that came into his possession."[17]

According to this clinical logic, everything is an aberrant collectible for off-kilter collectors like Warhol. Ergo another example of the hoarder's mental illness: extreme accumulators cannot differentiate between valuables and the valueless as they stash away "characteristic piles of unrelated objects ranging from worthless (e.g., trash) to extremely valuable (e.g., cash)."[18] Yet as each of these select quotes inadvertently suggests, it is not solely the collector who goes deviant. It is as much collected things: that important piece of trash, that worthless hundred-dollar bill, that priceless Muppets towel, that necklace in the cookie tin. Such being the case, we cannot comprehend representations of pathological collectors like Warhol without also considering the starring role that collectibles and their deviations play in the historical development of this material disorder.

Shifting the tenor of hoarding as pathological collecting to hoarding as a nonnormative engagement with collectibles, this chapter argues that individuals typed as hoarders disturb not only the idea of the collection or the activity of normal collecting but also the concept of the normative collectible—a subtle distinction that deepens our appreciation of how one is made, not born, a pack rat. This tweak in nomenclature, we will find, further reflects how hoarders on the American front upset the modern material relations that I began to trace with the previous chapter's emphasis on socially disorganized curiosa.

To support these claims, I first lay out an abbreviated history of collectibles culture (a leisure activity introduced and popularized across post–World War II America) that illuminates how this concept slotted mass-produced goods into select categories of important value. Here I detail the mass publication of

FIGURE 2.1 Frederick Charles, *Warhol's Hoard in Sotheby's Warehouse*, 1988. Published in John Taylor, "Andy's Empire," *New York* 21, no. 8 (1988): 39. Courtesy of FCharles Photography. © Frederick Charles, fcharles.com.

inexpensive reference guides such as *Kovels' Antiques and Collectibles Price Guide* that facilitated the practice of collecting normal stuff for ordinary Americans, and I trace how fears of hoarding agitated this system of classification as they informed clinical and popular takes on pathological collecting. I next return us to Warhol's belongings to substantiate this particular genealogy by looking at Sotheby's auction of his voluminous collectibles and then his *Time Capsules*, a collection of more than six hundred containers filled with over 400,000 personal effects, now housed at the Andy Warhol Museum in Pittsburgh, Pennsylvania.

My discussion of Warhol's objects does a disservice to this brilliant artist, but I am interested in tracing discourses of Warhol-as-hoarder precisely as a reductive distortion. Others before me have written eloquently on Warhol's field-shifting achievements in pop art, experimental film, and gay aesthetics (to name but three arenas of his innovation).[19] While I make passing reference to several of the artist's exhibitions, I am more invested in how Warhol has been misrepresented as a freakish collector by both specialist and nonspecialist discourses since his death, how he has been mischaracterized as a typical hoarder, and what this reveals about the dynamic status of the extreme accumulator in American material cultures. Likewise, while I recognize that Warhol's possessions are in some respects exceptional given the artist's extraordinary wealth and fame, we have nevertheless seen that he currently stands in for an emblematic hoarder, and I believe that he left us with the most exhaustive record to date of the ongoing tension between deviant and normative collectibles. Less about Warhol than about a misguided reception of his things, this chapter handles his goods with critical care in order to showcase how collectibles such as cookie jars continue to play a vital yet woeful role in defining what may or may not count for material life.

NORMAL GOODS

Before I detail how hoarding appeared as the abnormal inverse of collectibles, I establish a brief cultural biography of collectible objects. When the *Newsweek* commentator snickered at Sotheby's auction as "the biggest garage sale ever" and dismissed Warhol's inexpensive collectibles, she unknowingly situated his stuff within a recent social environment for material cultures: the garage sale and its companion piece, the yard sale, which first appeared across the United States in the mid- to late 1960s.[20] While rummage sales existed before the rise of this relatively new marketplace, it was "only over the course of the 1970s [that] the garage sale captured the popular imagination and developed into a mainstream American institution, [and] by the end of the decade, the legitimation and institutionalization of garage sales was firmly established."[21]

I likewise extrapolate from the *Newsweek* quote that whereas practices of collecting have been around for centuries, cultures of inexpensive collectibles have not. According to the *Oxford English Dictionary*, the first citation of collectibles as "things worth collecting, esp. rare, old, or interesting objects (not necessarily valuable or antique)," originated in the United States in 1955.[22] While this definition should not discount the plethora of collectible things available prior to this date—*collectable* (its alternative spelling) as an adjective appears in the later nineteenth century with references to "souvenirs, *objets d'art*, bric-à-brac"— collectibles as a mass-produced phenomenon spiked in post–World War II material cultures.[23]

How did this come to pass, and how does this relate to hoarding? As the OED notes, these midcentury items called collectibles initially distinguished themselves from objects that a few decades earlier had been called antiques. A generation prior, the 1930 Hawley-Smoot Tariff Act formerly classified antiques as any valuable good over one hundred years old. These goods included but were not limited to "works of art (except rugs and carpets made after the year 1700), collections in illustration of the progress of the arts, works in bronze, marble, terra cotta, parian [a type of Grecian marble], pottery, or porcelain, artistic antiquities, and objects of art of ornamental character or educational value which shall have been produced prior to the year 1830."[24]

Collectibles were often contrasted against this official categorization of the antique. According to *Warman's Americana and Collectibles*, a popular price guide launched in 1983, four traits defined a collectible: "The item must have been (1) massed produced and (2) made in the twentieth century. The majority of the items in each category (3) must sell between a few pennies and a hundred dollars and (4) they must have been made in America or collected heavily in America."[25] While the author later notes that "these divisions are artificial and deserve to be broken down," and while many mass-produced collectibles were certainly not forged on American soil, I underscore that the moderately low-cost collectible was differentiated from yet would eventually appear synonymous with the valuable antique.[26] To this day the material kinship between the two announces itself in the ubiquitous yet elastic phrase *antiques and collectibles*.

This is not, however, to overlook that a postwar collectibles culture was made possible by a pre–World War II antiques culture, a wallet-emptying pastime that flourished in the early twentieth century and likewise emphasized the acquisition of Americana. Historian Michael Kammen finds that "the emergence of this passionate preference for Americana occurred swiftly and with remarkably little hesitation between about 1913 and 1923," and just as collectibles culture would be heavily if not exclusively invested in American goods, so too were early antiquing efforts often centered on the collected items from geographic regions such as New England.[27] Journals such as the *Americana Collector* (1925–26) and the *American Collector* (1926–28) often promoted this Americana collecting, or "'antiqueering'" as some informally called it.[28] Aimed at white upper and middle classes, these publications featured advice columns on how to assess and acquire antique items such as rare coins, glassware, hymnals, broadsides, and Revolutionary War propaganda. Coterminous with other collecting enthusiasms, such antiquing invested in "the mythologized New England roots of the newly dubbed primitive imagery," even though the activity expanded beyond this region to encompass non-American objects.[29]

Collectibles culture was the popularization of this elite form of collecting, or what Kammen aptly calls "the democratization of collecting since the 1950s and 1960s."[30] Enabled by the acceleration of postwar consumption, further interest in acquiring collectibles skyrocketed in the decades after World War II. The result was a new leisure activity centered on collecting items that were not necessarily bona fide antiques but were nonetheless desirable objects. One 1973 instruction manual, *How to Hold a Garage Sale*, diagnosed this material spin-off. Penned by American mystery writer James Michael Ullman, the manual notes that "prices of many items traditionally sought by antique buffs have been bid up so high that only the most affluent can now afford them," and it finds that collectibles culture consists primarily of middle-class and lower-middle-class consumers such as "people with collecting instincts but more modest budgets [who] seek new and less expensive things to collect."[31] Acknowledging a "big demand" for "what dealers call 'collectible,'" Ullman then advised that, "generally speaking, the items most in demand by collectors are those no longer being produced which have a touch of 'Americana' about them."[32] A good chunk of post-1945 collectibles culture was, we infer, affordable Americana for the masses, a means of antiquing that bypassed the traditional antique.

That the now-obscure author of this manual sensed a need and a mass market for a cheap how-to guide testifies to the prominence of collectibles culture by the 1970s, and a steady stream of price guidebooks and advice columns propelled this enthusiasm along. One year before the OED flagged the ubiquity of the term *collectibles* in America, a newspaper column appeared in the *Cleveland Press* that proved beneficial to these assessments. Collaboratively written by husband-and-wife team Ralph and Terry Kovel, this question-and-answer column grew to reach audiences in numerous media outlets by the end of the twentieth century, and the Kovels' affiliation with the quickening of post-1945 US collectibles culture is not coincidental (figure 2.2). "Their interest in 'old things,'" Terry Kovel once acknowledged, "seemed to coincide with our country's general postwar awakening."[33] Like earlier journals such as the *Americana Collector* but with a wider readership, the Kovels' half-century of published work facilitated the institutionalization of collectible goods across the United

FIGURE 2.2 Ralph
Kovel and Terry
Kovel in their Ohio
home, ca. 1986.
Courtesy of Kovel
Antiques, Inc.

States—the "normal collecting" later cited by scientists in their efforts to further refine hoarding as a mental disease.

Though crowned "the country's best known authorities on antiques and collectibles" by the late 1980s, the Kovels did not, of course, inaugurate the public's growing hunger for baseball cards, elongated pennies, nutcrackers, and all things Elvis.[34] These pursuits were also stoked by corporations such as the Franklin Mint—begun in 1964 and "a pioneer of the collectibles industry, starting with coins, which the company minted itself, and branching out to include such items as limited edition paintings and books, commemorative plates, figurines, celebrity likeness dolls, jewelry, seasonal giftware, and die-cast model airplanes and automobiles."[35] Newsletters, magazines such as *Hobbies*, competing guides such as *Warman's*, antique dealers and buyers, and more specialized manuals such as *Petretti's Coca-Cola Collectibles Price Guide* likewise played significant roles. Yet the Kovels stood out in this crowded field, and a quick synopsis of their achievements reveals how these two not only familiarized a new domain of material goods for many Americans but also normalized collectibles culture for these postwar consumers.

Self-taught specialists ("we consider ourselves experts on items that were made in the United States from 1750 to yesterday"), the Kovels may not have invented collectibles culture, but they did popularize it.[36] For almost five decades, the pair saturated the nation with their prodigious knowledge via radio, print, television, and the Internet. Two years before their syndicated column appeared, they published *Dictionary of Marks: Pottery and Porcelain, 1650–1850*. This book-length foray into antiques appraisal was followed in 1961 by *A Directory of American Silver, Pewter, and Silver Plate* and in 1965 by *American Country Furniture, 1780–1875*. Expanding beyond traditionally defined antiques in 1967, they released

*Know Your Antiques: How to Recognize and Evaluate Any Antique—Large or Small—*like an Expert, a reference guide that included a later chapter called "Other Collectible Items." The year 1967 also saw the publication of their popular *The Complete Antiques Price List*, a price guide that has seen over forty revised editions and has sold over four million copies as of this writing.

It is difficult to underestimate the cultural contributions of this price guide. Then and now, it served as a gateway into the material and social worlds of mass-produced collecting. As mentioned above, the guide began as a singular *Antiques Price List*, a 436-page inventory of antiques and collectibles prepared using a computer program. The *Price List*'s extensive catalog included no pictures for identification purposes, but it did feature an alphabetized roster of over thirty thousand items that suggested a price and offered a brief description of the object-at-hand. To cite one entry among the hundreds: carnival glass appears as "an inexpensive, pressed, iridescent glass made about 1900 to 1920 (Carnival glass is currently being reproduced). Over 200 different patterns are known."[37] The guide then categorized this collectible by color, pattern, and intended use, just as it listed items such as glass hens, butterflies, ashtrays, piggy banks, and butter dishes. Overall, the Kovels recorded five hundred different variations of carnival glass, with prices ranging from $1 to $225.

By the first decade of the twenty-first century, this *Price List* ballooned into something that could have been called *Know Your Collectibles*. A behemoth of a book at almost eight hundred pages with more than forty-four thousand listed items, *Kovels' Antiques and Collectibles Price Guide* features color images on every page, and it pays equal attention to Ohio Valley cupboards and Little Orphan Annie metal lunchboxes. An online version has been available since 1996 to keep pace with the selling of antiques and collectibles on the website eBay, and the Kovels' website currently catalogs more than 750,000 goods. "The site," one journalist remarked, "tells visitors what is worth saving and what is just junk, answers questions and generally is a fount of information on history and collectibles."[38] In summary, the Kovels' various guides function as one of the nation's more respected resources for a once burgeoning and now booming interest in acquiring collectible things.

How does this concise history of collectibles relate to the widening divide between normal collecting and pathological hoarders? As their best-selling guides recorded the cost of a Mrs. Claus cookie jar, the Kovels accomplished something else: they standardized the collectibles culture that their books evaluated over the decades, and this observation brings us a step closer to understanding how hoarded items began to appear as an offbeat form of collectibles. "A lot of what we do is like biology," Terry contended in a 1980 interview with *Smithsonian* magazine, "devising categories and subcategories for things that have never been categorized before."[39] Her comment suggests that she and her husband imagined themselves as biologists of postwar material culture, and her self-promotion as a Carl Linnaeus of tchotchkes is not that far off the mark. It would not push the historical envelope to say that Kovels' did more than introduce generations of Americans to the possibility of collecting mass-produced goods. These guides also taxonomized material cultures into potentially valuable collectibles by advocating Americana for the masses. As self-ordained specialists in object categorization, Ralph and Terry helped to regulate the monetary value of numerous collectible items ($1 for a carnival glass cup) and contributed to the ongoing social construction of postwar goods as things worth collecting — a construction that was already well under way with the popularity of auction houses, magazines and newsletters devoted to collecting, and flea markets across the nation.

Systematizing mass-produced items into this collectibles culture, the Kovels and their media dynasty thus further instituted the social limits of proper collecting as well as confirmed the definitional confines of a proper collectible. In so doing the two advanced the consumption of collectibles for the better half of the twentieth century, as their price guides determined how such goods were to be valued ("what is worth saving and what is just junk"). Establishing the economic relations of this material world by confirming an estimated market value, they simultaneously regularized the sociability of mass collecting with tips on appreciating your items, preserving your items, showcasing your items, and making scads of money off your items. Hence the two taught consumers how to approach some objects as collectible items and how to envision others as noncollectible. While glimpses into the arbitrariness of this task do pop up — a closing moment of Know Your Antiques informs readers in capital letters that "THERE IS A COLLECTOR FOR ALMOST ANYTHING" — the Kovels nevertheless legitimized, familiarized, and documented a new leisure practice that centered on a new form of material culture.[40] We might go so far as to say that their price guides functioned as object conduct books, since the two "helped create the modern mania for family heirlooms and flea-market finds."[41]

The Kovels and their taxonomies, I mean to say by this last claim, made collectibles a normative part of American material lives, given their attention to "things that have never been categorized before." That said, I do not want the relationship between the couple and collectibles to appear too overdetermined. They were not alone in their achievements, and their price guides were often as much a response to the interests of elite and everyday collectors as they were an incitement. They did nevertheless promote collectibles acquisition as an ordinary cultural practice that was relatively easy on the pocketbook. Matched by competing guides and rival corporations, the two turned collectibles culture into a conventional activity for thousands, and they advanced the historical emergence of an identity category that would become the hoarder's inverse— the *normal collector* implied in works such as *How to Hold a Garage Sale* and cited in scientific documents mentioned in this chapter's introduction. "Our book was written for the average person, not a museum curator," stressed Terry Kovel in 2003, adding that "it was written for people like us who didn't know anything about pottery. You have to remember that 50 years ago collecting was a specialized interest. It was very genteel, now it's very popular. It used to be for the elite, now it's for the common man. Our first price book helped level the playing field."[42]

As we proceed into a discussion of how hoarding perturbed this recent system of objects, we can pocket a few observations from this history of collectibles. First: as much as one couple cataloged postwar material cultures, they also propelled individuals into social roles of average collectorship. Second: the two normalized their readership into the mass cultures of ordinary object relations as the hunt for Snoopy wristwatches became a conventional hobby for many. Third, and most consequential for tracking the social deviance of hoarding: since the early 1950s "America's king and queen of collecting" helped to establish a leisure activity explicitly evoked by psychiatrists such as David Greenberg and implicitly cited by media accounts of Warhol's mad things.[43] This last claim signals the reentry of pathological collecting into my analysis, and the pall that hoarders cast over this now-ubiquitous world of collectible goods.

MATERIAL SUBSTANCE ABUSE

From several vantage points, hoarding appears as the corruption of this collectibles culture sparked by antiqueering and substantiated by individuals such as the Kovels. As much as our contemporary representations of hoarders are beholden to the Collyer brothers and the theme of social disorganization, so too do they rely on the material cultures of antiques and collectibles. Hoarding often turns up as the deviation of this popular pastime: as interest in collectibles instilled itself into the hearts and onto the display shelves of many Americans, threats of pathological collecting haunted the presumed ordinariness of this leisure activity. Fears of excessive accumulation rumbled here and there, and fret over the protocol of normal collecting filtered into cross-disciplinary discussions of pathological collecting as a complement to the irrational hoarding diagnosis inspired by Collyer curiosa. Across different genres from the late 1980s to the present, collectibles culture proved foundational for making sense of the hoarder as an abnormal collector.

The Kovels once again point the way. Though they admit in *Know Your Antiques* that "maybe we should all become junk collectors, or pack rats!," a later pub-

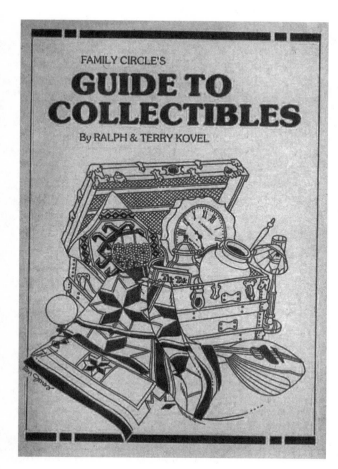

FIGURE 2.3
Ralph Kovel and
Terry Kovel, *Family
Circle's Guide to
Collectibles*, 1987.
Courtesy of Terry
Kovel and Meredith
Corporation.
© 2010 Meredith
Corporation.

lication cautions otherwise.[44] In 1987—one year before Sotheby's auction of Warholiana—the couple released a version of *Family Circle's Guide to Collectibles*, a pullout booklet included at no extra charge for the magazine's consumers (figure 2.3). After introducing what items counted as collectible and informing readers that "the best place to find such collectibles is at shows, flea markets, garage and house sales, auctions, estate sales and resale shops," the Kovels offered advice on acquiring lamps, wicker furniture, Fiesta Ware plates, and other goods.[45] Their general "Tips for Collectors" included the following:

- Check carefully the condition of items you're buying; look for signs of repairs. Broken china and glass are usually of little value. Minor repairs on furniture are usually O.K.

- Never buy anything at an auction that you have not "previewed" (examined closely before the sale).
- Collect, don't hoard. Be sure you have room for the objects you covet.[46]

I see this last bullet point as emblematic, an imperative against excessive accumulation. In keeping with the proper object conduct fostered by the Kovels' price guides, "Tips for Collectors" draws a line between acceptable and unacceptable forms of mass collecting. It also betrays the nagging anxiety that the hoarded item is a debased form of the ordinary collectible, that a person suspected of hoarding is no longer within the acceptable limits of the average collector. Thus it was not exclusively the elite museum curator who troubled collectibles enthusiasts as the affordable leisure activity gained in popularity—it was just as much the endlessly accumulating hoarder.

Numerous medical and popular literatures would voice this injunction to "collect, don't hoard." I have earlier pointed out how several scientific articles characterized hoarding as a perversion of collecting, and we saw examples that referenced aberrant collecting. These clinical citations of normal and deviant objects are now par for the course when it comes to properly identifying hoarders. As one 2005 scientific article in *Brain* remarked after noting that "collecting behaviour is commonplace in the normal population," hoarding "may deviate from the reasonable and acceptable pattern and be directed toward objects that are not only unnecessary for daily life, but are deprived of discernible aesthetic/ emotional and monetary value"—a line toed by DSM-5 as well.[47] The authors then attribute "abnormal collecting" to brain lesions (carnival glass also deserves some due).[48]

Other examples in scientific literatures offer variations on this now-standard rhetoric, but I single out two accounts, both coauthored by David A. Halperin (a psychiatrist once based in New York City) and Jane Glick (a biochemist once based in Philadelphia), that inadvertently historicize pathological collecting even as they insist that hoarding is a psychic aberration. The first article appeared in 2003 in the journal *Addictive Disorders and Their Treatment*. Under a title that parses out distinctions between "collectors, accumulators, [and] hoarders," Halperin and Glick rehearse the common distinction between normal and abnormal collecting. "The collector," they note with a passing nod to chronic disorganization, "ultimately views his collection as presenting a pattern that illuminates each individual object and its relationship to its context. Accumulation and hoarding are less organized pursuits in which the hoarder or accumulator appears to be preoccupied primarily with the quantity or the scale of hoardings rather than the individual objects."[49] Yet after documenting hoarding case studies such as one woman's impassioned attachment to costume jewelry, they find that "the prevalence of auctions of antique materials in New England and elsewhere is evidence that hoarding may be a culturally driven phenomenon rather than simply a syndrome that is the product of individual obsessive and depressive symptoms."[50]

Halperin and Glick do not further historicize this remarkable last claim, but in a 2005 essay they are more explicit about links between hoarding disorder and updated forms of antiqueering. Their comments appear in the fourth edition of the clinical handbook *Substance Abuse*, a compilation that lumps together hoarding, sex addiction, Internet addiction, and eating disorders—problematic conflations that chapter 3 addresses. The article begins by noting distinctions between antiques and collectibles, cites "the ubiquitous catalogs by the Kovels," and contends that "the pursuit of the collectible . . . deserves the interest of the mental health professional."[51] These comments are preceded by the following insight:

> The past two decades have seen the creation of a new sport (according to its participants), a new form of investment (according to its gurus), and a new form of postmodern esthetic (according to a cadre of academics). This new leisure-time activity, which has assumed an overdetermined status as every weekend its acolytes check the Yard Sales columns of newspapers across the country, is simply the accumulation of collectibles.[52]

Here Halperin and Glick take the long view and establish abnormal hoarding as the material inversion of twenty years' worth of collectibles culture—even as they later insist on pathologizing this behavior as an individualized symptom.

Such contradictory glimpses into the historical archives of hoarding are exceptional among the scientific community. From academic journals to local online newsletters, scientists and practitioners more often than not define pathological collecting against ordinary collecting and view the former as a personal symptom removed from the auctions of New England and the web pages of Kovels' price guides. Take one typical case: a 2007 essay, "The Psychology of Collecting," written for the *National Psychologist* begins with the theme of ordinary collecting historicized in the previous section. "Everybody collects something," the author states, "whether it be photographs of a person's vacation, ticket stubs from ballgames, souvenirs of trips, pictures of one's children, athletes' trophies, kids' report cards or those who collect 'junk' (pack-rats) and dispose of it in garage sales." The article then introduces the theme of normative collectibles without calling it such: "On the more formal side of 'collecting,' it does seem that growing up we all collected something we made into a hobby. It could have begun with baseball cards, marbles or stamps. Then it moved on to antique books, Longaberger baskets, state quarters or Atmos clocks." The article next cites "the dark side of 'collecting,' the psychopathological form described as hoarding. The 'abnormality' of the hoarder shows up in those instances where the aberrant behavior interferes with an otherwise 'reasonable life.'" It concludes by conflating pathologized collectibles with pathological collecting: "In extreme instances of aberrant collecting what is one to do? 'Dr. Phil,' the TV mental health guru Philip McGraw, came to Amherst, Ohio to video and 'heal' a Mr. Mishak who had a 10-year accumulation of 'collectibles' that ranged from old cereal boxes, windows, and toothpaste tubes to dead cats."[53] Throughout its narrative arc, the article universalizes differences between average collecting and its unreasonable counterpart. Yet this distinction would not have been possible save for the postwar infrastructure of normative collectibles advanced by the Kovels and their peers.

With its passing mention of Dr. Phil (a celebrity psychologist featured on US television talk shows) the article likewise gestures to the concurrent popularization of hoarding as a deviant form of collectibles culture. Beyond clinical accounts, this idea appears in posts on the Understanding Obsessive Compulsive Hoarding website, where "Antiques and Collectibles gone wrong" are listed under "What Types of Items People Hoard."[54] It crops up in pseudoscientific reports by self-identified experts on informational websites: "Someone who is a 'healthy' collector has the money, time and space to invest in the items they are collecting. . . . Although many hoarders value their possessions, the typical items a hoarder possess do not have monetary value. . . . A hoarder does not show their collectables to others."[55] Like clinical reports, these lay accounts of hoarding similarly situate ordinary collectibles on the side of good health and hoarding behaviors on the side of disease. We could term this split "the psychopathology of the yard sale."

Several scholarly accounts in material culture studies, it should also be said, have critiqued these distinctions. In 1993 Susan Stewart notes that a collection "is dependent upon principles of organization and categorization. As [Jean] Baudrillard has suggested, it is necessary to distinguish between the concept of collection and that of accumulation. . . . Such accumulation is obviously not connected to the culture and the economy in the same way that the collection proper is connected to such structures."[56] She then states that "the insane collection is a collection for its own sake and for its own movement. It refuses the very *system* of objects."[57] Building on Stewart but on a different register, cultural critic Sara Knox likens the hoarder's acquisitions to "morbid collectibles (like protected and endangered species, pornography, and taboo anthropological relics)," and she finds that accumulators "have been seen as having distinct overtones, if not of outright pathology, then of pity and the pathetic."[58] Consumer culture researcher Russell W. Belk concurs. He grounds late modern hoarding within "mass consumption, mass individual collecting, and massive museum collecting," and he finds that "while these behaviors are generally evaluated negatively as aberrant forms of consumerism, collecting is generally evaluated positively."[59] He then denaturalizes the cultural system of collectibles that too many take for granted: "What is considered problematic for the individual is also dependent upon the social milieu in which the collective activity is carried out. Normal and excessive are socially constructed categories. . . . When the collector is inattentive to these rules, he or she may be labeled a manic hoarder or accumulator."[60]

Thus with a promotional baseline established by individuals such as the Kovels starting in the early 1950s, a hodgepodge of antiques specialists, psychotherapists, biochemists, neurobiologists, and talk-show hosts contributed to the present tense of hoarding as an insane collection. When you spot a hoarder these days, bet the house that some out-of-bounds collectibles are within close reach. Hence as much as social disorganization enabled hoarding to cohere as a chronic form of material disorder, so too did collectibles culture enable hoarders to appear as a form of pathological collecting. The gradual invention of the average collector of mass goods established some of the conditions for the hoarder's emergence and produced a normative culture with its own rules and boundaries that individuals could then transgress. Judging from my handful of examples, this was and remains a dynamic process of classifying who gets slotted into the debased category of the material deviant. Any of these signs and symptoms, though, contributes to a diagnosis:

- Deviate from established taxonomic systems of everyday collecting (everything's hot).
- Disconcert postwar categories and subcategories of stuff (everything has monetary value).
- Refuse to cordon off cherished finds throughout your object environment (everything's worth accumulating).
- Insulate yourself from material cultures so that your activities appear to be the photonegative of flea markets, auctions, antique stores, and garden-variety garage sales (everything's worth saving but nothing's worth showing off).

These traits constitute a good chunk of the definitional dilemmas that gravitate around many hoarders since at least the 1980s. They will do so for some time. We now see that many of these culturally ingrained characteristics would leech onto Andy Warhol's effects before, during, and especially after his estate sale. In the same essay where Halperin and Glick define hoarding as a mental perversion of mass-produced collectibles, in fact, they cite Warhol's possessions as a prime example of "pathologic hoarding," given that the artist's "objects were piled in an addictive frenzy."[61] Distressed by his things, the two overlay panicky theories of chronic disorganization with developing theories of abnormal collecting. Recalling chapter 1's investigations, we understand the deeper implications of their findings when they wonder, is "Andy Warhol a hoarder—a Collier [sic] brother with taste?"[62] This is a known-answer question that they were not the first to ask. How Warhol's exemplary estate became ensnarled in these ongoing tensions between normal and pathological collectibles is my next focus.

LOTS OF EVERYTHING

No copy of The Complete Antiques Price List was found among Warhol's many possessions, but to some his things crossed over to the dark side of mass collecting. Posthumous scientific reports attest that his objects signify aberrations of ordinary collecting, suggestive of hoarding. As this chapter's introduction noted, these evaluations were aided in the late 1980s by reports of Warhol's estate sale that represented his collectibles as deviations of mass-produced goods. The artist's possessions thus make for an ideal case study because his archive records the historical processes that advanced this particular component of hoarding disorder.

In many ways Warhol's decades-long zeal for acquisition mirrors the material history of US antiques and collectibles that I have traced. There is no better way to put it: he was an astounding collector. Around the same time that the Kovels launched their empire of goods, the artist began to collect Americana following his move from Pittsburgh to New York City in 1949. Almost three decades later, the Museum of American Folk Art featured his antiques in a 1977 installation titled Andy Warhol's "Folk and Funk." The exhibit's curators noted that "Andy Warhol, the consummate collector, is passionate about all forms of folk art—cigar store Indians, carousel figures, ships' figureheads, weathervanes, whirligigs, decoys, primitive paintings, shop signs, quilts, coverlets, hooked rugs, painted furniture, and pottery."[63] Warhol found many of these materials in secondhand shops in Manhattan—a carryover of earlier antiqueering efforts that were also antiques-queering efforts, as he shared this pastime with several members of his gay male coterie.

What began as his Americana collecting shifted into the acquisition of a remarkable array of artwork from across the centuries, rare furniture pieces, exquisite jewelry, and Native textiles. Desired by a global network of collectors and dealers, these items were far from scattershot. By the time of his death, he had amassed paintings and sketches by Jean-Michel Basquiat, Yves Klein, Jackson Pollock, Robert Rauschenberg, Salvador Dali, Marcel Duchamp, Man Ray,

FIGURE 2.6 Steven Bluttal, *Interior of Andy Warhol's Townhouse at 57 East 66th Street,* 1987. Collection of the Andy Warhol Museum, Pittsburgh.

FIGURE 2.7 Steven Bluttal, *Interior of Andy Warhol's Townhouse at 57 East 66th Street*, 1987. Collection of the Andy Warhol Museum, Pittsburgh.

FIGURE 2.8 Steven Bluttal, *Interior of Andy Warhol's Townhouse at 57 East 66th Street*, 1987. Collection of the Andy Warhol Museum, Pittsburgh.

metal bowls obscure half of the magazine. Despite Sotheby's classifications, it is unclear to me after surveying these selected photographs what items Warhol did or did not consider an antique or a collectible worth saving at the time of his death. Is the Bubbalicious wrapper a collectible? Or the Empire-Monster Robot? Or the cardboard boxes? Or the Wenderoth? The discrepancy between these photographs and those reproduced for the auction reveal the extent to which Warhol's goods throw such questions into relief. Hence if critics have addressed how "the haphazard organization of objects" in some of the artist's earlier installations "can be seen as constituting a disruption of museum space," we also read his self-presentation of domestic things as a disruption of collectibles culture and priceless artwork once they saw daylight.[69] In their original condition and in their later reshuffling, Warhol's possessions muddled the taxonomic systems that the auction house and less elite cultural institutions like the Kovels' price guides tried to protect.

It nevertheless remains the case that Sotheby's cleanup crews and production design teams tried doggedly to counter these disturbances. Some noted this at the time. The lawyer for the Warhol estate, Edward Hayes, did so in *New York* magazine:

> "When I first came here, you couldn't walk into this room—you had to climb over things," Ed Hayes says as he stands in the doorway of the handsomely appointed dining room in Warhol's house. Last fall, Sotheby's cleared it out and, using Warhol's furniture, created a Federal-period room of museum quality. . . . "This is Andy Warhol's paintings and this is Andy Warhol's furniture, but this is not the way Andy Warhol lived. The way the house is now, you don't have a sense of how cluttered it was. These stairs were cluttered with boxes. We found Picassos in the closets. But that was his private life."[70]

What was sorted for Sotheby's was welter for Hayes, who went on to describe what he saw as the strangeness of these indiscriminate collectibles: "When you first came in here, you thought, 'What a weird thing.'"[71]

As I have shown, Sotheby's tried to stamp out much of the weirdness of Warhol's things, and by doing so parts of *Collection* functioned much like scientific articles and price guides that corralled the proper domain of collectibles culture. Written by Warhol's business manager, Frederick W. Hughes, and reprinted at the start of each volume, the catalog's preface confirmed this task as it too staged the normalcy of his acquisitions. Noting that Warhol "was an avid collector," Hughes recalls that "at his house on Lexington Avenue, not far from my own apartment, I found rooms stacked with an extraordinary diversity of objects." He contends that "Andy was an omnivorous observer and recorder of everything, and his collecting habits were, in some ways, an extension of this."[72] He then contradicts sensational depictions of Warhol's collectibles that had begun to appear in the press: "He successfully guarded his privacy and only a very small and select group of friends could guess at the extent of his collections," Hughes insists. "Most were left to form incomplete or distorted impressions of him gleaned from one of several 'public' facets of his highly complex character."[73] Rather than present Warhol's house as an odditorium and his items as a mare's nest, Hughes recasts the artist as a discriminating collector removed from object aberration.

Yet like other testimonials to proper collecting, these endeavors to vanquish material distortion paradoxically enabled other discourses to emerge. As I hinted in my discussion of Warhol's photographed kitchen, attempts to erase the taint of aberrant hoarding were not always victorious. Popular media cast his collectibles as deviant objects, and a few passing observations about Warhol reprinted in *Collection* corroborated this line of thought. One of the artist's collaborators, Rupert Smith, recalled that "Andy's problem of collecting was innate. Perhaps he really should have gone to Collector's Anonymous!"[74] Art historian John Richardson was blunter in his assessment: "The word 'collector' doesn't begin to describe Andy's obsessive—what Freud called anal retentive—hoarding. As a hoarder, he was only surpassed by Picasso (who hung onto old envelopes and cigarette packs) and, of course, the notorious Collyer brothers."[75] Smith's quote mixes boilerplate psychology (Warhol's intrinsic "problem") with contemporary therapeutics as it treats the artist's things as an addiction to stuff—a diagnosis that subsequent scientific accounts would corroborate and that chapter 3 further investigates. Richardson's evaluation reinforces a glib psychoanalysis (Warhol's anality) as well as the collector-hoarder divide as he compares the artist to the legendary Hermit Brothers of Harlem.

Others picked up on this psychopathology once Sotheby's *Collection* hit the bookstore shelves. A February 1988 *Los Angeles Times* article in the newspaper's "Calendar" section stated that "the details of Warhol's hoarding instincts have just been published by Sotheby's (with Abrams) in a six-volume catalogue."[76] Despite the auction's aspiration to a sanitized material normality, then, the publicity surrounding it confirmed Warhol as a fairly manic hoarder. "The auction," one scholar later noted, "established Warhol as an insatiable collector who was interested in everything and could part with nothing."[77] During and after the sale, Warhol's consummate collectibles thus began to take on a mad vibe disseminated throughout media outlets such as *Time*, *Newsweek*, *New York*, *Washington Post*, *New York Times*, and others cited at this chapter's beginning. Appraisals such as "he simply stashed away these tons of junk, like a pack rat" and "about

10,000 objects, which have nothing in common except for having been stored for a few years in Warhol's townhouse" popped up to become a customary account of his things.[78] Ensuing reports of his "feverish hoarding" found that "as soon as Jed [Johnson, one of Warhol's lovers] left, the house overflowed with the detritus of his collecting mania," and later biographers noted that he was "an addictive collector" surrounded by junk rather than a discriminating collector surrounded by well-chosen objects.[79] This reception was only heightened by the fact that Warhol's collections were sometimes highly selective (a piece of art by Edvard Munch) and sometimes completely indiscriminate (a bubblegum wrapper).

Addiction, mania, compulsion, neurosis, hoarding instinct: Sotheby's public distribution of Warhol's goods sidestepped but reinforced the notion that Andy was a Collyer with better taste. Invoking material tenets established by collectibles culture, conversations surrounding the estate as well as the sale itself produced a lasting narrative about the artist's material deviance. Thanks to a steady stream of scientific articles and biographies that standardized the idea of Warhol-as-hoarder, this story of psychopathology achieved the status of biographical fact. Retrospectives recall with little controversy that "what they encountered upon entering Warhol's mid-19th-century town house on Manhattan's Upper East Side—evidence of more than thirty years' worth of obsessive collecting, crammed into two dozen rooms—shocked even the most jaded Sotheby's employees."[80] Because of his many innovations, Warhol made hoarding more famous a mental illness than it already was.

THE ANDY WARHOL STASH, VOL. 2

Warhol's cookie jars were not the only superstars that he gathered about his person, however. Currently sitting in a renovated Pittsburgh warehouse, 612 boxes of his personalia steal a stage set back in 1988. Flipping through *The Andy Warhol Collection*, you come across a few mentions of these boxes, or *Time Capsules*. "Fred Hughes said that for Andy, shopping was part of his job. Actually, when Andy came back each day, he would put everything in a box and mark it 'Time Capsule' with the date," volume 3 informs readers. "The Time Capsule would then be sealed and stored. I still can't figure out how Andy decided to collect what he did."[81] Another volume verifies this account: "To Andy in his role of recording angel, every last scrap of rubbish had validity by virtue of being memorabilia—*Zeitgeist* minutiae. Towards the end of his life he had even contemplated packaging some of this material into metal-edged boxes *à la Beuys* [German performance artist Joseph Beuys] and putting them on the block 'as is.' 'Warhol's time-bombs,' they were to be called."[82]

Warhol was ambiguous about the status of these things as artwork, personal possessions, or purchasable collectibles, and scholars continue to study his intentions to either sell them "on the block" or forget about them. Nevertheless, these boxes augment the anxieties that attached to Warhol's effects during Sotheby's estate sale, as they disturb normative dictates of US collectibles culture. A follow-up to the auction's mania, the *Time Capsules* likewise garble ideals of postwar collectibles by raising the specter of profligate accumulation—a charge often leveled at other nonstandard collectors and one that further cements Warhol's place in the pantheon of hoarders.

Taken in aggregate, the *Time Capsules* (or TCs) consist of more than five hundred cardboard boxes, forty "drawers in metal filing cabinets," and one footlocker that together hold hundreds of thousands of objects.[83] As we see from figure 2.9, the majority of these containers were everyday cardboard boxes into which Warhol collected his material life. Noting that he included sketches, receipts, correspondence, uneaten food, clothing, pornography, insoles, a nude photograph of Jacqueline Onassis, film, toys, and books in the boxes does not do descriptive justice to the hoard. It is safer to say that Warhol included everything. Reports differ about when the artist first began to save these items, but their contents stretch back to material culture from the late 1930s, or perhaps even earlier, as one box holds some of his mother's possessions.

In the featured photograph we get a glimpse at how wide-ranging the *Time Capsules* contents are. Most of the contents here are from the 1960s, and they are primarily books, magazines, "flower books," and "little white trips books," but one box with unidentified contents in the farthest upper-left hand corner of the image has "'50-'60" written on it in pencil. Warhol did offer a contradictory origin story about why he began to collect these goods in *The Philosophy of Andy Warhol* (1975):

> Tennessee Williams saves everything up in a trunk and then sends it out to a storage place. I started off myself with trunks and the odd pieces of furniture, but then I went around shopping for something better and now I just drop everything into the same-size brown cardboard boxes that have a color patch on the side for the month of the year. . . . I want to throw things right out the window as they're handed to me, but instead I say thank you and drop them into the box-of-the-month. But my other outlook is that I really do want to save things so they can be used again someday.[84]

While these much-remembered, much-forgotten boxes have not been fully inventoried, they currently reside at the Andy Warhol Museum, an institution that has cataloged some of the possessions with over six hundred pages of inventory-in-progress. Notes one commentator in a nod to *The Andy Warhol Collection*: "The

FIGURE 2.9 *Time Capsules* held at the Andy Warhol Museum, Pittsburgh. Courtesy of the Andy Warhol Museum, Pittsburgh.

Sotheby's catalog lists everything in tidy categories, and the neat sequence of distinct artifacts curated by John Smith at The Warhol follows similar lines."[85]

Like portions of Sotheby's estate sale, such accounts gently sidestep any hint of neurotic rubbish as they repudiate the stigma of hoarding that attached to Warhol in the late 1980s. "While it is true that on the surface Warhol's collecting might appear to have been indiscriminate hoarding," writes Smith, "a closer look reveals very specific strategies. Far from a psychological aberration, Warhol's collection may be seen as another form of artistic practice."[86] Smith elsewhere notes that "like the Wunderkammer, or cabinets of curiosity, created by Renaissance noblemen, Warhol's *Time Capsules* identify him not only as an artist of vast and far-ranging interests, but also as a humanist with a desire to catalogue and instill a sense of order to his world."[87] I see validity in such assessments, but note the way such reconsiderations refute hoarding. Others have likewise envisioned these accumulated collections as a rational rather than insane act of average collecting, and it is the framing of Warhol's effects within the bounds of appropriate or inappropriate collecting that interests me.

Some have, in fact, taken a more severe line on this collection that regrettably reduces the *Time Capsules* to an aberrant stash. Highlighting "the layers of disorder," one scholar noted on the occasion of the museum's 1994 opening that the "chaotic clutter of numerous shopping bags, steamer trunks, and assorted piles, make up a significant part of the archival collection of the Andy Warhol Museum."[88] A more recent review found that the collection reveals Warhol as "the accumulator, the hoarder of ephemera."[89] And Australia-based art critic Robert Nelson wrote a critique that could have passed peer review at *Journal of Anxiety Disorders*: "But just because of the almost indiscriminate amassing of printed matter, the contents provide a slice of Warhol's psychopathology."[90] Nelson insists that "if you guard things so scrupulously that you put them into cold storage, you cross over into another kind of psychopathology," and he summarizes his evaluation as follows: "the pompous cardboard boxes aren't simply coffins for the experience of each Sunday afternoon: they're an eerie batch of forlorn messages, made useless over time, which transcend to perversity."[91]

As one of these quotes attests, the perverted hoarding supposedly typified by Warhol's *Time Capsules* also marks the artist as a deviant accumulator. Accumulation and hoarding are often mentioned together in HD discourses, and we have seen instances of their overlap before. Halperin and Glick conflate distinctions between the accumulator and the hoarder as they chart the psychopathology of collectibles culture, and Russell Belk finds that when someone collects inappropriately she will be stamped a "manic hoarder or accumulator." Pointing up slippages between these two identity categories, I note how this figure of the accumulator as much as that of the hoarder becomes synonymous with the excessive acquisition of socially unsanctioned collectibles. Both signal the disorganization of collected goods in contrast to the supposed sanity of a culturally condoned acquisition. While it remains unclear whether or not Warhol meant his *Times Capsules* as a commentary on collectibles culture, what remains undeniable is that the artist's possessions further disturb the collectibles-noncollectibles divide initially established in the second half of the twentieth century. Writes Jonathan Flatley in his incisive discussion of the *Capsules*: "War-hol acquired not only 'collectible' objects (i.e., things that other people also collected thereby creating a market), but also a whole range of things that no one else pursued."[92] Intentionally or not, Warhol turned the idea of the ordinary collectible—a comic book, a postage stamp, a postcard—inside out when he placed these objects on the same taxonomic plane as a maid's uniform, a mum-mified foot, breath mints, and slices of cake.

Running with Flatley's observation, we get a better sense of why some harm-less collectibles in Pittsburgh as well as millions of other collections across the land might radiate perversity. It is not solely their trespass of the social assump-tions that dictate what counts for an ordinary item worth keeping. In line with Susan Stewart's remarks on the economic perturbation of accumulations, Flat-ley astutely notes that collectors such as Warhol destabilize the market that sup-ports such categorizing efforts. In so doing the artist again ruffles the feathers of that vast grid of price guides, auction catalogs, and garage sales supporting one system of standardized material culture. As *Time Capsules* throw these sys-tems into disarray (are they trash? *mirabilia? bagatelle?*), we see how it might seem crazy that a hoarder's "objects cannot be differentiated or categorized according to their value since all seem at the moment to be 'very important' possessions."[93] Given that hoarders supposedly cannot differentiate between the valuable and the valueless, their accumulations scramble guidelines gener-ated by experts such as the Kovels, specialists at Sotheby's, and the millions of average collectors who agree to the conventions of this pastime. Even if we grant that Warhol's boxes have taken on the aura of prized and priceless museum pieces, his collectibles in particular and hoarded items in general undercut the economic bearings that secure this material culture.

That's not all. By doing so, these accumulated goods simultaneously disturb the shared structures of feeling underpinning everyday objects—the "aesthetic/emotional and monetary value" referenced by scientists in *Brain* or the "average collector" implied in a *Kovels'* guide. Recall the question posed by a *New York* re-porter in this chapter's introduction, one that also applies to the *Time Capsules*: "Is it just a bunch of stuff, or is it invested with a higher meaning?" As much as Warhol's posthumous things trouble the normalizing of collectibles, they question the consensual cultural significance of these material goods, of how they *feel special* to a social group of collectors. Given the original definition of collectibles as things worthy of collecting, hoarders appear to disregard both affective and socioeconomic worth as they gather about themselves things that do not, Flatley stresses, usually count as collectible goods. This is but one rea-son why extreme accumulation can seem like an extreme act of material mis-conduct. As they refuse to distinguish between the cultural worth of a rotten piece of cake and a McCoy cookie jar, they unnerve the economic and emotional value regimes that the collectibles market depends upon.[94] In a material culture committed to discerning what counts as an important or an unimportant possession, those typed as hoarders render unstable shared distinctions between the worthless and the priceless, the valuable and the valueless. Is it worth saving or is it junk? This central question becomes moot once everything is felt to be a once-in-a-lifetime find.

By turning their backs on this self-policing world of collectible goods, these collectors appear delusional, their accumulated items cast as objects of intense collective disapproval and equally intense fascination. Despite Warhol's professed nonchalance about his possessions—"I say thank you and drop them into the box-of-the-month"—reams of analysis have been published that attempt to psychologize why he collected these things. These inquiries aid scholars in their understanding of his pioneering aesthetics, yet I grow wary when they turn the artist into a case history. Moralizing attempts to decipher the intention of Warhol's material culture seem to complement the ink spilled on other accumulators across scientific journals, middlebrow magazines, price guides, and online chat forums. Tally up these commentaries, and pathological collecting looks less like a personal syndrome and more like a culturally driven mania.

There is another way to state this last point about the freak shows of compulsive hoarding: like the Collyer brothers who preceded him, Warhol continues to incite debate about the correct role of stuff in our everyday material lives. He left us, notes Simon Watney one year after Sotheby's auction, with "a collection which draws attention to collecting, both as an instinct and a taxonomical system."[95] For Andy, everything "had validity": he had the gall to treat every piece of minutiae like a cherished collectible to be tossed away. In an object world where the collection of ordinary things indexes one's material normalcy, such improper acts continue to throw off collectibles culture. When the accumulations of a life start to look like a lifetime of accumulations, insanity is right around the corner. While Warhol's preserved archives may be unique conversation pieces in the deep history of modern US material culture, the surveillance and the obsession that surrounds his belongings are not. At the end of the day, all hoarders are ticking time bombs.

WORTHLESS PERSONS

Warhol fever is now epidemic. Though his object world sits quiet in a mid-Atlantic museum, his boxes speak to the multitude of other offbeat collections. Much like Andy's things, these innumerable possessions also suffer from charges aimed at those who collect too much and keep too much and in too unreasonable a fashion. With property arousing equal parts inquiry and ire, their owners find themselves in fishbowls of negative attention, unreason, and, quite often, madness. That alone can be unconscionable. Yet what distresses me most about these unwise collections is how the questionable value of objecthood becomes inseparable from the questionable value of personhood. What keeps me up at night is how the destabilization of economic, aesthetic, affective, and cultural worth messes with personal merit as well. As they step outside collectibles culture, cling tenaciously to their queer Americana, and improperly stage showpieces for no one special to see, hoarders depart from ideals of average materiality confirmed by the auction gavel and the garage sale. When they make these missteps only to find themselves deranged in the head, their material neuroses transform into personal ones: pathological collections become pathological livelihoods. The more priceless they consider their things, the more they depreciate in social value.

An extended example to support this final claim about Warholian hoarders: on a 2009 blog that has since been removed, Sandra Felton, a self-identified expert on housekeeping, posted her admonition "Andy Warhol, Hoarder or Historian?":

> When Andy Warhol died 22 years ago, he left behind 610 boxes filled with trash and treasures. Only 19 have been opened and cataloged. He had his reasons. He called the boxes time capsules. Some were "collections." They would be valuable some day, he mused. They reflected the times for history, he said. . . . And on and on his reasons supported his obsessions. But his home became a warehouse. He had to pay for extra storage. All in all he dedicated a great deal of his life to the acquisition of unproductive stuff. Those of us who have walked anywhere close to this way of life ourselves or have watched others know the emptiness of its promises. Wonderful personhood becomes buried under worthless possessions. Andy Warhol made his choices. Fortunately we can make ours as well, warned by Andy Warhol's negative example.[96]

Felton's damning take on the philosophy of Andy Warhol is, in some circles, a pervasive creed; her commentary reminds us yet again of Stanley Cohen's observations on folk devils. Like many, she sees his collectibles as a warning sign for those tempted by "this way of life," and her remarks likewise link hoarding back to Foucault's discussion of the dangerous individual. Felton also counsels against the social costs of amassment, and she cautions that the emptiness of your overstuffed room will overtake the fullness of your being as worthless objects end up in the homes of worthless persons. A wonderful material life slowly slips away as soon as you fill up your floors with antiques and collectibles gone very wrong.

I question this zealous assessment of the hoarder's devalued social value—the emphatic certainty of their lives' supposed emptiness—even as I am happy to admit that some "abnormal" collectors, like some "normal" collectors, acquire some objects in order to feel some things. While I dedicated this chapter to a genealogy of US collectibles and various receptions of Warhol's exemplary goods, I have been mindful of those for whom he now stands as a negative example. I have made good on museum studies scholar Susan M. Pearce's claim that "'unacceptable' collectors, among other things, are making important assertions about the 'ordinary' material world and our relationship to it, which we ignore to our detriment."[97] I mapped how one facet of this world came into being across post-1945 America, and I traced how price guides, substance abuse handbooks, scientific journals, auction catalogs, home interior photographs, middlebrow magazines, and museum installations realize one framework of hoarding as an ignominious form of collecting. Together these sites complement the bad stuff that began with the Collyers. A focus on Warhol's accumulations again brings things up to speed, so to speak, as we covered several decades' worth of material deviance. Perhaps we can now see a kitchen full of cookie jars in a less harsh light.

CLUTTEROLOGY

On February 19, 2007, a retired junior high mathematics teacher met up with one of the world's foremost specialists in the psychological study of hoarding to host a teleclass titled "Overcoming Hoarding Tendencies." During one engaged hour, Sandra Felton and Randy O. Frost addressed "how to get out of this problem."[1] One made mention of the Collyer brothers at the start, and a lively discussion followed that addressed self-motivation, the pride of a clean house, the "confusion" of a hoarded one, and how to remove clutter from your personal living space. The instructors then offered pointers to stave off hoarding and answered queries by callers. Recorded onto compact disc, the class was made available for purchase as part of a "Packrat Package" on Felton's website, www.messies.com, or, as it is also called, Messies Anonymous. "Designed to help you overcome the packrat syndrome," this package included a copy of Felton's *I've Got to Get Rid of This Stuff! Strategies for Overcoming Hoarding (The Packrat Syndrome)*, a pamphlet that teaches customers how to "learn how to move through indecision and fear and begin clearing the house of clutter."[2]

Frost and Felton at first seem like two ships passing in the night. At the least they appear strange bedfellows. As noted earlier, Frost is a psychologist who teaches at a small liberal arts college in New England. He specializes in the study of individuals suffering from perfectionism, obsessive-compulsive disorder, and hoarding disorder. Felton is half a world away. Based in her southern Florida home, she is an evangelical Christian and a self-identified professional organizer, an individual who specializes in the organization and cleanup of supposedly disheveled spaces in general and the unkempt home in particular. She often writes under the trademarked pen name The Organizer Lady, and she believes that part of the Lord's divine plan is a clean house. Many of her decades' worth of housekeeping guides have been released by Revell Books, one of the primary publishers of religious literature in the United States.[3]

Despite these incongruities, attentive listeners would have discovered that the two shared much in common. Both agreed that hoarding is a troublesome condition that calls for prevention and treatment. Both were happy to promote recent books that tackle pack rat syndrome. And both implicitly believed that everyday household objects are decisive factors in the ongoing depiction of hoarding as an object panic as they rebuke the inappropriate presence of clutter in the home. As a self-identified recovering "Messie" (someone lax in domestic orderliness), Felton reminisced that while her house was "cluttered," it was "hard to stay living in that cluttered situation." Frost concurred. He told listeners that one effective technique for turning his clients into ex-hoarders involves asking them to first "visualize the room being cluttered" and then "how they want the room to be what an ideal room would be like." Together this couple presented an idealized vision of the normal home, and their team-teaching reflects the close interactions between scientific experts and professional organizers in discourses of tracking and eradicating symptomatic pack rats across the United States and beyond.

We historically restate my last claim: Frost and Felton's teleclass linked abnormal psychology to home economics in an inspired update of what was once called *scientific housekeeping*, the early twentieth-century promotion of social, personal, and material hygiene that advocated efficiency, cleanliness, and material orderliness in the home. Hence while their exchange received little press at its time of release, a cultural document such as "Overcoming Hoarding Tendencies" helps us understand how hoarding anxieties graft onto houses and home possessions as much as onto persons like Warhol and neighborhoods like Harlem. The teleclass illustrates how present-day scientific definitions of hoarding habitually conceptualize a symptom of the disease as an aberration of domestic material culture, or what we shorthand as clutter.

This is not to neglect the fact that what goes by hoarding can also occur in what DSM-5 lists as "vehicles, yards, the workplace, and friends' and relatives' houses."[4] It is to underscore that as much as they borrow from postwar collectibles culture or theories of social disorganization, specialists and nonspecialists alike frequently use a rhetoric of cluttered *housekeeping* to diagnose the presumed abnormality of the hoarder within her lived environment. Psychologists cite "clutter that precludes activities for which living spaces were designed" as a key symptom, and reference to "unsanitary conditions" accompanies this classification.[5] Such experts postulate "clutter as a defining characteristic" and list telltale signs of material illness such as an "inability to complete necessary activities due to clutter (cooking, paying bills, etc.), distress over not providing a 'proper' home environment for children, embarrassment or withdrawal from social relationships due to clutter, inability to invite others into the home, and inability to work because of the clutter."[6] "In cases where . . . clutter prevents the normal use of space for basic activities," an untidy home is an immediate red flag, and these definitions are not the observation of a select few.[7] They can be found in DSM-5's diagnostic, which lists "the accumulation of possessions that congest and clutter active living areas" as a giveaway of this disease.[8]

The recorded teleclass likewise reveals the crucial role that professional organizers such as Felton played in advancing more popular definitions of hoarding as "clutter gone wild."[9] DSM-5's definition of hoarding disorder continues: "If living areas are uncluttered, it is only because of the interventions of third parties (e.g., family members, cleaners, authorities)."[10] By "authorities," this designation perhaps references law enforcement and task forces, but the vague parenthetical nods to other self-authorized experts such as the professional organizer who also contribute to hoarding's popularization over the decades. Organizer guides to clutter reduction often inform scientific diagnostic toolkits, and while titles such as Judith Kolberg's *What Every Professional Organizer Needs to Know about Hoarding* (2008) and Felton's *Winning the Clutter War* ([2005] 2010) may not reference hoarding disorder as such, these texts nonetheless influenced the pathologization of what has elsewhere been called compulsive clutter disorder, messy house syndrome, hoard and clutter syndrome, clutterers syndrome, and clutter addiction.

"Overcoming Hoarding Tendencies" thus points us to a *pas de deux* between scientific accounts of improper housekeeping and more popular accounts such as Felton's that have proved as integral to hoarding's standardization as Collyer Brothers syndrome or pathological collecting. Yet in their mutual agreement that hoarding is clutter is hoarding, some questions remain unanswered: Who, exactly, defines clutter as the antithesis of normal household object use? How did this shared idea about irregular household goods originate? When did a dirty home become a sign of madness? Though clutter—"the seemingly disordered, unkempt array of objects that are found around the home"—can often be a chore to pin down, these objects have a cultural biography that answers such questions.[11]

Charting this history, this third chapter surveys the critical role played by the professional home organizer in advancing HD. It argues that organizers such as Felton assisted in the standardization of hoarding as abnormal untidiness thanks to their concerted efforts to straighten up the pack rat's home, and it contends that as much as we cannot understand insane collecting without comprehending the emergence of the average collector, we cannot appreciate the messy hoarder without attending to the shipshape organizer and her commitments to tidy household decor. While previous genealogies focused on how hoarding crystallized as a mental illness that went by the names of chronic disorganization and aberrant collecting, this one turns to messy house syndrome and its various nomenclatures to examine those who diagnosed this identity category amidst their fervid attempts to clean it up. Starting with preliminary historical alignments between clutter and deviance and ending with the institutionalization of professional organizers influenced by Felton's writings, the chapter explores the symbiosis between those who organize homes into ordinariness and those who turn them into lunacy. The former contributed to a now-pervasive belief that extreme accumulators are as much extremely crazy clutter bugs.

BAD HOUSEKEEPING

It looks as if the professional organizer—like a box of Hamburger Helper—was one of *those* inventions of the 1970s, but a deeper, if forgotten, cultural history is at work. One of the more prominent mentions of this job first appeared in a perplexed September 2, 1974, edition of the *New York Times*. With the headline "It's Her Business to Take the Distressing Disarray out of People's Lives," the article spotlighted the career's novelty ("a hard concept to grasp") and focused on the human-interest story of Stephanie Winston, founder of the Organizing Principle, soon-to-be author of the 1978 manual *Getting Organized: The Easy Way to Put Your Life in Order*, and as of this writing organizational advisor for the multinational workplace supplies company Office Depot.[12] It also detailed Winston's services: "she'll arrange jumbled files, books and financial records, devise efficient use of space in closets, cabinets and other storage areas, and plan personal and household budgets."[13] Nearly half a decade later, the *Los Angeles Times* published a similar news story, "Professional Organizer Cuts Clutter." Profiling Winston and her occupation, the article noted that she aids "those of us who lead cluttered lives amid precarious piles of pipes, stuffed closets, jumbled desktops, [and] accumulated possessions."[14] It then suggested that the trade had picked up some steam: "Since those early days, she has doubled her fee and spawned a flattering group of imitators, the new breed of professional organizers."[15]

This "new breed" of clutter specialist would expand in number by the late 1990s. By the early twenty-first century, clutter specialists manage hundreds of small businesses with company names such as Simply Organized Life, Goodbye Clutter, A Place for Everything, the Clutter Fairy, An Orderly Life, Sane Spaces, Divine Order, and Clutter Rehab. Winston remains an acknowledged pioneer of the profession; Felton praises her guide as a "classic"; and the 2006 revised edition of *Getting Organized* cites its author as "the founder of professional organizing."[16] But later iterations of her line of work move beyond efficiency into the murkier waters of pathology. As they emphasize the mental illness of a household packed with accumulated goods, a central task for many professional organizers these days is to identify and extract aberrant clutter from a hoarder's home. Working alongside medical professionals, "organizers not only transfer skills and help create organizational systems, they also help motivate their clients [i.e., hoarders] to carry out the de-clutter work."[17] Present-day organizers thus specialize in neologism when they clean up the proverbial mess of hoarding disorder. *Declutter* does not yet appear in the *Oxford English Diction-*

ary nor in the *American Heritage Dictionary*, but the verb closely ties organizers to hoarding discourses as these professionals elsewhere refer to themselves as clutter busters and clutterologists—self-appointed experts in the eradication of deviant home possessions.

While *declutter* is an original coinage and hoarding cleanup a relatively recent service industry, this concern with domestic clutter control is timeworn. Though the Organizing Principle indeed influenced later generations of organizers, I am wary of seeing Winston's business as the trade's genesis. Professional organizer may be a new occupation, but many of the job's aims stem from earlier concerns about the social and self-management of household goods, or what I previously cited as scientific housekeeping. With their reference to the abnormal science of domestic things, clutterologists *continue* an ingrained American tradition of policing inanimate matter in the home.

Moving beyond Winston before returning to Felton, the remainder of this section surveys foundational associations between clutter and deviance in American material cultures to find that professional organizers branched from the same family tree as early twentieth-century material reformers. Synthesizing three and a half decades of historical scholarship, I suggest that these reformers established historically resilient protocols for domestic material culture that decluttering organizers such as Felton would tweak for a new age of hoarding prevention and cure.

Commencing in the later nineteenth century, a paradigm shift reoriented many Americans to their personal living spaces. "In 1850," notes historian Suellen Hoy in a questionable but nonetheless telling assertion, "cleanliness in the United States, north and south, rural and urban, stood at Third World levels," and "not until the 1880s and 1890s did the idea become prevalent that running water was a household necessity."[18] Yet by the end of the nineteenth century swaths of US citizenry shifted their organizing principles with an eye toward a dirt-free homestead. For many—and especially for the middle classes—a brave new object world enabled this directive, one that scholars refer to as "the rise of the modern bathroom and kitchen as newly equipped spaces for administering bodily care."[19] Part of this widespread material project consisted of learning to live with once-unfamiliar amenities such as drain traps that blocked the stench of sewer gas, sinks that expelled wastewater, electric lighting that required wiring the house, ventilation systems that allowed for fresher air, and vacuums that sucked up dust and debris.

Steering this revolution in personal and household cleanliness was a slate of "hygiene reformers" who coached Americans into new sanitary regimens.[20] Predominantly but not exclusively middle-class white women, many based their instruction on recent findings in germ theory, a scientific doctrine that focused on hygienic perils feared to linger in household objects.[21] This growing awareness of microbes, it should also be said, proved lucrative, as reformers worked in dialogue with cleaning industries that manufactured and sold products such as soap, toothpaste, and home cleaning supplies.[22]

Often hygiene reformers titled themselves "home economists" who maximized the standards of living mentioned in this book's introduction.[23] The objective-sounding ring of this semiprofessional label signals its debt to concurrent principles of scientific management—the standardization of labor forces furthered by the likes of Frederick Winslow Taylor in his 1911 *The Principles of Scientific Management*. In their efforts to nudge Americans into good housekeeping, home economists produced copious manuals indebted to Taylor that encouraged the orderly appreciation of home possessions.[24] One of the nation's better-known home economists, Christine Frederick, captured this gendered undertaking in *The New Housekeeping: Efficiency Studies in Home Management* (1913). "I learned what the new science of work was accomplishing for the office, the shop, the factory," she informs fellow travelers in house care. "At first it did not occur to me that methods which were applicable to organized industries, like shoe factories, and iron factories, could also be applied to my group of very unorganized activities—the home. Yet the more I studied it, the more possible it seemed."[25]

Yet as they fostered this "science of efficiency," home economists, hygiene reformers, and scientific housekeepers were not wholly scientific.[26] In the midst of discourses on domestic rationalization were expressions of allegiance to Christian cleanliness—an important point to remember when we return to a late modern organizer such as Felton. While many hygienic reformers adhered to secular impulses that supported scientific management, Christian ideals of tidiness were expounded via "the social gospel," "the religious expression of progressivism" that focused on "the moral imperatives of domesticity" by "instructing the recipients of their good will in middle-class domestic propriety."[27] Such class-based emphasis on morally sound hygiene was linked not only to the gender and religion of home economists but to sexuality as well: "public health advocates insisted upon the 'monogamous morality' of respectable domesticity, with its regular households, Christian marriage and morality, and nuclear families."[28] Deliberately or not, many of these advocates built on earlier nineteenth-century traditions established by authors and housekeepers such as evangelical Protestant Catharine Beecher, whose "Christian doctrine informed most domestic-advice manuals" of her period.[29] Merging cleanliness with godliness with modern science, an ironic blend of spirituality and rationalization took hold under the sign of proper house maintenance, but these contradictions were not always of much concern. Some industrialists, it turns out, had little problem vending "the gospel of cleanliness" as they inaugurated institutions such as the Cleanliness Institute in 1927.[30]

To pour these historical ingredients of modern homemaking into the mold of my larger argument: early twentieth-century advocates of godly scientific housekeeping initiated hygiene regimes that called for appropriate forms of material cleanliness—what you should do with your air ducts, your copper pipes, your recently purchased side tables. In so doing they split household object relations into sanitary and unsanitary acts, and this divide gets us closer to the emergence of clutter as one long-standing form of material deviance. Sifting through advice manuals published at this time, one finds reformer concerns over domestic material relations that not only included "washstands, towels, basins and ewers, soap, flesh brushes, [and] tubs" but also addressed *sanitary furnishings* such as carpets, couches, fabrics, curtains, hangings, framed pictures, decorative bric-a-brac, and other materials lying around the home.[31] As much as home economists advocated for the social hygiene reform of persons, so too did they sponsor the hygiene reform of things.

Policing this boundary triggered object panics. As new moralities of cleaning durables emerged alongside new moralities of cleaning bodies, one's home furnishings could become disreputable, and a plethora of reform writings facilitated what historian Nayan Shah terms "normative hygiene."[32] His phrasing is fitting. *Household Hygiene* (1911), for instance, advised readers that "healthful furnishings are those which in material, construction and finish add no injurious particles to the air and allow frequent, thorough and easy cleaning."[33] *Home Sanitation: A Manual for Housekeepers* (1904) emphasized that home furnishings "which destroy comfort and injure health cannot, when judged by this rule, be recognized as truly beautiful. . . . That furnishings may destroy comfort cannot be denied by any woman who has found herself penned in an over-furnished room."[34] *Harper's Bazar* (later retitled *Harper's Bazaar*) also chimed in to proclaim that "lumber and rubbish which cumber our shelves afford admirable lurking-places for germs of disease and a nucleus for dirt and cobwebs."[35]

One word for these unfurnished, unclean, and unhealthy home goods was clutter. As much as some modernized homemakers thrust their families into good material health via sanitary reform, others sickened kin with the faulty use of interior spaces. "So soon as she allows her furnishings to crowd and elbow her in her own home," augurs *Home Sanitation*, "she has reversed the proper relationship."[36] In her 1925 *Everyman's House*, scientific housekeeper and social gospel campaigner Caroline Bartlett Crane shared this sentiment. "Are our houses cluttered with disguised liabilities," she wondered, "rooms we don't effectually use, pictures we don't see (and likely, are not worth seeing), useless furniture and bric-a-brac we haven't the courage to get rid of?"[37] More than two decades earlier,

Charlotte Perkins Gilman agreed in "The Tyranny of Bric-a-Brac," a section of her 1898 polemic *Women and Economics*. The female housekeeper, she laments, "has crowded her limited habitat with unlimited things,—things useful and un-useful, ornamental and unornamental, comfortable and uncomfortable; and the labor of her life is to wait upon these things, to keep them clean."[38] For Gilman, clutter removal "will mean better sanitary conditions in the home, more beauty and less work."[39] While an excessively adorned house was once a bourgeois Victorian given, precarious piles were now marks of unsanitary material life. Susan Strasser, the leading historian of these modern US consumer cultures, concludes succinctly: "Accumulated objects threaten health."[40]

As hygiene reformers manufactured heavily gendered clutter panics, these fears surrounding unlimited things were not unconnected to anxieties about race, ethnicity, and socioeconomic status. "The styles favored in the Progressive period," notes Nancy Tomes, "also represented a conscious reassertion of Anglo-American tastes, a kind of cultural eugenics embraced in response to the 'new immigration.'"[41] Another scholar likewise finds that "vociferous anti-bric-a-brac rhetoric became the rallying cry. . . . These people saw the preponderance of objects and ornament as a class differentiation as well as an ethnic difference."[42] Clutter, interestingly, was sometimes cast as a racially aberrant form of home possessions, the inverse of "ideas of cleanliness, sanitation, and middle-class white material culture."[43] Early twentieth-century cluttered spaces, we conclude, resulted in wayward homebodies who fell outside middle-class (and, on some occasions, white) object conduct. What counted for household disorder suggested other forms of social disorganization discussed in chapter 1's attention to Harlemites, and the eugenics of a wall sconce was not unrelated to disorderly homes thought to shelter non-American and working-class populations.[44]

What bearing does this rich history have on anticlutter professional organizers? First: home economists established a baseline for clean things that subsequent generations honed across gender, racial, and class divides. It is no stretch to claim that scientific housekeepers showed millions how to pick up their rooms as "sanitarian beliefs in the existence of what were termed 'house diseases'" were rooted into American material norms and made ubiquitous.[45] It is also not beyond the pale to claim that these standards have become more exacting in the live-streaming of a clutter-free home life that pulses through the twenty-first century. Walk down the aisle of your neighborhood grocery store and marvel at the shelves that hold Windex glass cleaner, Cascade dishwasher detergent, Endust dusting spray, Lysol disinfectant spray, Weiman cooktop cleaner, Formula 409 antibacterial all-purpose cleaner, and Woolite pet stain and odor remover—to name but six purchased products now under our kitchen sinks. Hence "in the decades since the 1930s, the aesthetic of cleanliness has become the norm in the domestic landscape," one that "reached its peak in the years following World War II."[46] These precursors consequently set the stage for the emergence of professional organizers such as Felton who not only fine-tune the sane use of personal living space but also put a stop to the liabilities of a hoarder's perceived overflow.

Second: hygiene reformers contributed to the novel idea of normal domestic material culture and its inverse. My abridged overview of historical scholarship on modern American housework recaps how clutter originated as a diseased form of bad housekeeping that also went in the guise of unsanitary furnishing and offensive interior decoration. Scientific, religious, or somewhere in the middle, hygiene reformers promulgated the idea of an average household to combat phantom threats of material and moral turpitude, and they upheld one social norm of the ideal housekeeper that professional organizers aspire to when they counteract the disrepute of unsuitable decor.

You hear the not-too-distant echo of a Caroline Bartlett Crane or a Charlotte Perkins Gilman or a Christine Frederick when an organizer like Felton claims that "people of our quality do not live in clutter, do not hurt or embarrass ourselves by living disorderly lives."[47] What present-day clutter busters too often take to be a Platonic ideal is more accurately an unfinished historical process whose standards were initiated decades earlier. When one recent antihoarding essay, "Conquering Clutter," bemoans that we are "hostages to the bric-a-brac that once served us" and casts the professional organizer "as another recent addition to modern life," it may need to rethink this prison house of material modernity.[48] It might reconsider its dependence on once-novel configurations regarding modern household goods.

So should other hoarding specialists when they assume that if you are "drowning under piles of clutter," then "you may be SUFFERING from what is sometimes called Hoard and Clutter Syndrome, Packrat Syndrome, or Compulsive Hoarding."[49] Or that a definition of hoarding syndrome is "When Clutter Goes out of Control."[50] This is one background story to the panic stoked by clutterologists. How organizers such as Felton churned screeds featured in Home Sanitation into Winning the Clutter War and collapsed the distinction between overfurnished rooms and demented headspace is my next concern.

HOLY MESSIES

How did the house disease of clutter become a mental addiction monitored by an industry of organizer experts? This deep history of clutter undergirds the professional organizer trade to function as a backdrop for antihoarding organizers like Felton, who tells us in one of her many housekeeping guides that clutter addicts "fill spaces long after reaching the stylish point. . . . Messies take good, normal activities and seriously overdo them."[51] I present this backstory because it situates organizers like Felton within the aftermath of domestic material culture mandates (the OED's chronological timeline of the entry *pack rat* as "a person who hoards things" itself leaps from 1912 to 1970).[52] While Felton, like Stephanie Winston, was not solely responsible for binding their occupation to hoarding discourses, she nevertheless has had a lasting impact on the popularization of compulsive clutter. Reviewing her prolific organizing oeuvre, these next two sections give us a better sense of the slippery slope that led from clutter as a house disease to clutter as a mental disorder. If early twentieth-century reformers approached clutter as germ-laden home possessions, then organizers like Felton refined improper housekeeping and inappropriate decor into an insane lifestyle, an addiction that the saving grace of the specialist could and should reform.[53]

From one vantage point, it is no coincidence that a professional organizer such as Felton emerges from my survey of clutter panics. More than half a century after the dawn of scientific housekeeping, Felton sounded the keynotes of sanitation reform when she pitched her biography to the *New York Times*. A 1985 newspaper interview identifies Felton as a "50-year-old high school mathematics teacher in Miami," and it discusses her recommendations for a well-organized home.[54] In the midst of these guidelines, Felton confesses: "She's a messie. 'I've always been a messie,' she says. 'My mother, on the other hand, was a cleanie.'"[55] This division between her "cleanie" mother and her "messie" self is of note. Felton's mother, it seems, grew up in the generation of religiously inflected scientific housekeeping standards that her daughter failed to sustain. "Keeping house seemed to come naturally to her," Felton recollects in one of her later works.[56] "My drawers were always neat, my room in order. I functioned in the order she created. She did try to train me, her only daughter. What a discouragement it must have been for her! I took to housekeeping like a cat to water."[57] As she bridges the decades between material hygiene reform and the organizer movements she facilitated, Felton's body of work recompenses for this disappointment: she will become the cleanie her mother wanted her to be.

Felton's eventual triumph as this reformed home manager took decades. She gradually drilled modern principles of good housekeeping into her everyday routines and later urged others to do the same. Her texts often express these accomplishments with religious overtones, as in the following quote that reworks Sri Lankan evangelist Daniel Thambyrajah (D. T.) Niles's 1951 dictum that his faith "is one beggar telling another beggar where to get food": "I am a professional organizer with a master's degree in education, but my main qualification is that I am just one poor beggar telling others where I have found bread."[58] Hence when Felton's work informs readers that "I feared I was doomed to live and die struggling with clutter in my home and disorder in my life," this personal failure, we find, was also a spiritualized one.[59] "For most of Sandra Felton's 24-year marriage, cleanliness wasn't next to godliness, it was next to impossible," states a 1981 *People* magazine article. Asking "Is Your House a Holy Mess?," the piece depicts Felton—the wife of an evangelical Protestant minister—as an exemplar of bad housekeeping surrounded by a cluttered kitchen (figure 3.1).[60]

The remainder of her career has consisted of preaching hard-earned home lessons to other clutterers. From her personal conversion sprang a support group, Messies Anonymous, launched in 1981. Since then Felton has released a flurry of housekeeping guides that address clutter abatement and the liabilities of what would become known as hoarding disorder. In *Winning the Clutter War* she is explicit about the historical through-line that connects her early housekeeping failures to her later attempts to combat pack rat syndrome: "Since the beginning of Messies Anonymous, much has been done to help individuals overcome disorganization. The National Association of Professional Organizers and the National Study Group on Chronic Disorganization have been formed in America. Other professional organizer groups have begun abroad. These offer referrals around the country. Psychologists have turned their attention to the problem, usually focusing on hoarding as an anxiety disorder."[61]

Felton's website supplements these accomplishments when she sells the promise of an average material life via trademarked clutter-abatement products such as the EZ Pocket Organizer and the K.I.S.S. [Keep It Super Simple] Flipper Method (a daily housekeeping guide). The site also includes a treasure trove of housekeeping manuals aimed primarily though not exclusively at married women. Written in the vein of a home economics manual updated for a world of Con-Tact paper, plastic ice trays, and Rubbermaid racks, Felton's bookshelf comprises works such as *The Messies Manual: The Procrastinator's Guide to Good Housekeeping* (1981), *Organizing for Life: Declutter Your Mind to Declutter Your World* (1989), and *Messie No More: Understanding and Overcoming the Roadblocks to Being Organized* (1989), as well as inspirational guides for religious-oriented housekeepers such as *Organizing by the Book: Devotional Ideas from God's Word* (2007). All are mass-market paperbacks that can be ordered online. Fairly formulaic as they walk readers through kitchens and closet space arrangement, they are marked by a tone that is witty at times but earnest when it comes to the cluttered home.

A hybrid genre of home maintenance manual, motivational guide, personal memoir, and inspirational literature, these texts stay on point as they confirm clutter to be a material deviance traced in the previous section, yet they go on to link such presumed disorder to the mental illness of hoarding. In a nod to diagnoses of pathological collecting that chapter 2 tracked and the filthy oddities

FIGURE 3.1 Thomas F. England, photograph of Sandra Felton. Published in Cable Neuhaus, "Is Your House a Holy Mess? Sandra Felton Suggests Ways to Get a Clean Start," *People* 16, no. 7 (August 17, 1981): 75. Courtesy of Thomas F. England.

that chapter 1 mulled over, one work contends that "messies collect too many things, the wrong kind of things, and just junk. They are pack rats."[62] Another describes a cluttered home as soul-deadening: "Each uncontrolled pile of clutter kills a little part of us. A little dies here with an incident of humiliation."[63] Charting "the vicious cycle of messiedom," another text insists that "clutter assaults."[64] On the first page of *I've Got to Get Rid of This Stuff!* Felton even bursts into poetry to plead guilty to the past tense of improper housekeeping that she surmounted:

> I was a packrat,
>   a hoarder,
>   a gatherer,
> or as I preferred to think of it at the time,
>   a frugal and responsible collector.[65]

Like earlier scientific housekeeping manuals, Felton's texts treat clutter as a form of material degeneration. Unlike these previous writings, they often see so-called junk as a symptom of "this 'hoarding disorder.'"[66] They demonstrate a familiarity with evolving psychological discourses of material illness by acknowledging that "among these other categories is what the mental health field calls hoarders."[67]

While some of these excerpts rework ground covered by *Home Sanitation*, Felton's oeuvre never links clutter to working-class immigrants or old-fashioned Victorian decor. It instead accomplishes something historically unprecedented that proves influential to present-day representations of hoarding: it connects the poor mental health of clutter to an improper lifestyle best left behind, an overloaded material mindset that can and should be changed with the help of the organizer. This reference to an aberrant lifestyle marked by misused possessions recurs often in her writings. *I've Got to Get Rid of This Stuff!* eschews "*the pain of the cluttered way of life.*"[68] *Organizing for Life* laments "the disorganized lifestyle."[69] *Organizing by the Book* begs for "freedom from this messy lifestyle" and renounces "the burden of the messy life-style."[70] The texts lead readers to believe that by following these guides, "you are not just fleeing from disorder to order, you are leaving an ugly and hurtful lifestyle for a beautiful and supportive one."[71]

Why these manuals fixate on lifestyles is another historical detour well worth the trip. Given her religious commitments as an evangelical Christian, I wager that Felton uses this term not solely in its more general sense. Though the word *lifestyle* emerged in the later twentieth century to reference "the way in which one lives (or chooses to live) one's life," during the 1970s it also came to refer to social and moral deviation—as in the phrase *the homosexual lifestyle*—that was frequently derided by an emergent New Right in the United States.[72] Alongside their scientific management updates, Felton's antimessy lifestyle aids appear to have reworked the social gospel of early twentieth-century Christian-based cleanliness for a later era that witnessed the rise of the Moral Majority, a conservative coalition of Christian evangelicals whose politics were informed by rhetoric of pro-heterosexual "family values." Her anticlutter advice was, in fact, featured on psychologist and evangelist James Dobson's Focus on the Family (FOF) radio show, a principal media outlet for evolving forms of social and religious conservatism that first aired in 1977. Beginning in the early 1990s, Felton was a guest on Dobson's program, where she contributed "a one-minute daily feature on how to organize your life and reduce household clutter."[73] She also appears as a decluttering expert on FOF's *Home Management for Today's Busy Mom*, "a special two-cassette collection from the national broadcast series" where she tells listeners that "cleanies cannot live in clutter and be happy" and that "we are all made in God's image and God is a God of order and beauty."[74] While she does not denounce homosexuality in her housekeeping manuals, Felton's condemnation of "this messy lifestyle" seems to have translated the dangers that sexual and gender nonconformists purportedly posed to heterosexual family domesticity into the material immorality of extreme cluttering.[75]

My last claim makes more sense when we consider one of Felton's publishing venues, the Fleming H. Revell Company. Describing itself with little exaggeration as "the most significant publisher of evangelical books in North America," this Michigan-based publishing house has released and promoted several of her works.[76] Begun in 1870, Revell gained prominence with the release of evangelist William E. Blackstone's 1878 bestseller *Jesus Is Coming*, and it would later go on to publish New Right and antigay activist Anita Bryant's memoir *Mine Eyes Have Seen the Glory* in 1970.[77] A 1995 promotional guide for the company notes that it "provided a national platform to fundamentalist leaders" and that "two new women authors were successfully introduced in the early 1980s."[78] One of these cited women is Felton, whose affiliation, Revell boasts, resulted in the sale of more than 350,000 copies of *The Messies Manual* alone. The company has publicized her organizing guides alongside evangelical tracts that promote ex-gay movements, antiwomen's studies, and Christian house decorating, and as much as they function as embattled wars against clutter, they also operate as inspirational hymns to devout domestic living. "Many people, both Cleanies and Messies, find that a spiritual dimension in their lives helps moderate their extremes," Felton opines in *Organizing for Life*.[79] With frequent quotations from New and Old Testaments, Felton time and again turns her antihoarding tracts into a domestic mission, a moral crusade to "declutter your mind" as you declutter your lifestyle.

As much as her *Messie* manuals may pull from the terminology of antilifestyle campaigns, her attempts at materials reform also find kinship in the ex-gay literatures published by presses such as Revell and promoted throughout evangelical Christian communities. Starting in the mid-1970s, religious ministries such as Exodus International (founded in 1976 and closed in 2013) attempted to reform members of the "gay lifestyle" into heterosexuals, and in the late 1990s

FOF joined forces with Exodus to advance programs of what was called "sexual reorientation" for lesbian and gay individuals that would convert them into "ex-gays."[80] Felton's organizing guides advocate a *material reorientation* that compares well with these reparative therapies. Though they do not have the same object of focus as an ex-gay program, her writings have similar transformative goals as she attempts to reorient deviant pack rats into ex-hoarders, or those who have turned away from the lifestyle of clutter. Extending her earlier conversion narratives, her more recent texts find that "somewhere, sometimes all of us who live the crazy life of stress and disorder have got to come to the point where we open our eyes and say to ourselves, 'This way of life is insane. I will not continue to live this way no matter what!'"[81] She confesses to the uncleanliness of her former housekeeping ways, and she tells readers, "I had to sacrifice unproductive ways of living to move into the life for which God had put me on the earth."[82] Her promise to reform pack rats is clear: "After the program is over you will be free to live a normal and full life."[83] While this rhetoric is beholden to self-help discourses that appeared in the latter half of the twentieth century, and while indicative of how "ex-identities" pervade late modern Western life narratives, we should not underestimate influential evangelical accounts of sexual and gender deviance.[84] Just as earlier clutter anxieties concerned themselves with racial aberrations and monogamous moralities, so too does one influential organizer appear to borrow from contemporary discourses of sexual normality to secure a case against inappropriate household goods.

Home possessions, for Felton, are more often than not matters of faith. While other professional organizers may not emphasize or entertain these religious components of appropriate housekeeping, their negotiations of clutter as mental and material deviance nevertheless use rhetoric of the abnormal lifestyle as a catalyst for reforming one's material life. "Hoarders are generally unaware of the fact that their lifestyle is a problem or causing a safety hazard to themselves, family, and their animals," notes one Texas-based organizer as she advertises her organizing service, A Helping Hand.[85] Religious-based or not, many organizers advocate for some version of material reorientation on behalf of clutter-laden hoarders. Their final fantasy is that the hoarder shuns her former disorganized lifestyle and embraces that of an average housekeeper in an average family in an uncluttered home with average sanitized furnishings. Their central aim is to restandardize material lives, to turn the clutter bug into an ex-material deviate. This emphasis on the hoarder's lifestyle seems paradoxical when we factor in the supposed neurological origins of HD, but it remains the case that Felton's faith-based manuals blazed some of these orderly trails towards desistance, even as other clutterologists take less sacrosanct routes to arrive at a similar uncluttered way of life.

That Felton's writings reformatted Christian ideals of scientific housekeeping is rich enough. In their attempts at the material reorientation of messy minds, what is equally impressive is how these texts and those of other professional organizers merged this novel idea of clutter as a deviant lifestyle with moralizing discourses of mental addiction to produce "clutter addiction." Through ruminations on the potential insanity of household goods, they perpetuated clutter as an unhealthy codependence on stuff (one of Felton's books, *Messie No More*, alludes to Melody Beattie's 1987 best seller *Codependent No More: How to Stop Controlling Others and Start Caring for Yourself*), and they often cast the aberrant housekeeper as a thing addict. *Organizing for Life* links "the disorganized lifestyle" to "problems of addiction" such as "alcohol and drugs, [and] getting hooked on shopping, eating, gambling, and other activities."[86] *Meditations for Messies: A Guide to Order and Serenity* likewise begins one of its daily reflections with a predominant understanding of alcoholism that first appeared in the 1940s: "the alcoholic suffers from a disease from which he [sic] must have relief."[87] It then applies this thesis to unseemly domestic furnishings: "What about messiness? Is it a disease? From the surface meaning of the word *dis* (not) *ease* (comfortable) it certainly is a disease."[88] Such links between household disorganization and the "disease" of cluttering would become an important component in the psychopathology of hoarding as a degenerate home lifestyle.

This definitional collapse between the material disease of clutter and a dependence on home possessions recurs in Felton's works, and it is clear that her texts imagine hoarders to be addicts as they graft late modern clutter panics onto prevailing discourses of relapse, recovery, and addiction treatment. "Others drink, go on buying binges, overeat, gamble, or whatever. I clutter," her impersonal first-person narrative states in *Meditations*. "I use clutter to comfort myself, to distract myself, to punish myself, to affirm that I am indeed unworthy to live a peaceful and dignified life."[89] Four pages later: "Whether a person is compulsively neat, or in my case, compulsively messy, looking for help through that 'Power greater than ourselves' will bring what the Bible calls temperance, or what Alcoholics Anonymous calls sanity."[90] As these texts religiously identify those who have overcome compulsive clutter as ex-hoarders, Felton's works become a do-it-yourself treatment center for those suffering from the mental addiction of packrattery, or what we with all seriousness might term an unbridled object bender.

On and off the printed page, Felton's other response to this indecorous lifestyle of clutter abuse has been Messies Anonymous (MA), a material addiction recovery group that she chartered in 1981. Almost half a decade later, Messies Anonymous had "more than 6,000 members nationwide," according to one *New*

York Times article that also notes participants in the program receive "a membership card that reads, 'I can find it, dust it, dry it, and put it away in five minutes or less.'"[91] As of this writing, MA prospers. Online groups flourish, and these meetings constitute "a fellowship of those who struggle with clutter and disorder in their lives. . . . Many succeed in this way and find themselves changed and their lives changed from the burden of the messy life-style."[92] The overarching goal of the organization, notes its mission statement, "is a lofty one: a sanely organized and beautiful home (and office) consistently maintained without too much work."[93]

It should be clear from these descriptions that Felton models MA after Alcoholics Anonymous (AA), the recovery program formed in 1935 by Bill Wilson and Robert Holbrook Smith. Now a global phenomenon, AA has been integral to advancing notions of alcoholism as a psychophysiological disease with a support network of face-to-face groups, newsletters (*AA Grapevine: The International Journal of Alcoholics Anonymous*), and a titular program guide (colloquially known as "the Big Book") first released in 1939.[94] Over the years the program has seen spinoffs of comparative recovery groups such as Narcotics Anonymous, Shopaholics Anonymous, Online Gamers Anonymous, Gamblers Anonymous, and Sexual Compulsives Anonymous. With her citations of AA, Felton embeds the aims of Messies Anonymous as well as the decluttering professional organizer within this fairly recent history of addiction treatment (addiction discourses precede the twentieth century, self-help groups do not), and she presents the professional organizer as a material recovery specialist.

Point for point, Felton's myriad texts rehash AA rhetoric as they promote an antihoarding lifestyle program for home life. Given the spiritual overtones of AA's recovery discourse and Felton's own evangelical allegiances, this makes sense.[95] In their claims for clutter therapy, Felton's writings use AA's language of fellowship and "higher power," and like AA they base some of their housekeeping advice on the Serenity Prayer, a short supplication for daily endurance composed by theologian Reinhold Niebuhr. These texts likewise reinterpret AA's influential commitment to sponsorship, a person-to-person mentoring system that emotionally supports those in recovery. *Winning the Clutter War* tells the reader that "if you are living a Messie lifestyle and hating it, you want to make change. Getting a ClutterBuddy, a partner who understands and will support you, can be a tremendous boost. The original support group, Alcoholics Anonymous, was started by two men meeting together to overcome their addiction. Did that ever work out well!"[96]

The cornerstone of Messies Anonymous, its Twelve Steps and Twelve Traditions, almost word-for-word mimics AA's *Twelve Steps and Twelve Traditions*, an appendage to "the Big Book" that was first published in 1953. Felton's works repeat these original principles in *Meditations, Messie No More,* and *Organizing for Life,* and they substitute the core addiction of alcohol in these guidelines with that of clutter. A few selections from the Twelve Steps of Messies Anonymous:

1. We admitted we were powerless over clutter and disorganization—that our lives had become unmanageable.
2. We came to believe that a Power greater than ourselves could restore us to sanity. . . .
12. Having had a spiritual awakening as the result of these steps, we tried to carry this message to others who suffer from disorganization in their lives, and to practice these principles in all our affairs.[97]

And two from the program's Twelve Traditions:

3. The only requirement for membership in an M.A. group is a desire for freedom from clutter and a disorganized lifestyle. Any such group may call itself a Messies Anonymous group provided that, as a group, they have no other affiliation.
5. Each group has but one primary purpose—to help those who desire a sanely organized lifestyle.[98]

Functioning as a program for overcoming hoarding tendencies, these established principles of MA hint at how easily hoarding now appears as a clutter addiction, a compulsive disorder that can be controlled thanks to the efforts of the professional organizer. As clutterologists such as Felton specialized in helping hoarders achieve object sobriety, they further reinforced the now-prevalent notion that hoarding is a mental disease announced by symptoms such as "that pile of papers, that awkward furniture arrangement, that strange storage organization."[99] Transforming inappropriate domestic material culture into an addiction to stuff, organizers reformat what previous reformers characterized as unsanitary furnishings into a pathological dependency on paper, boxes, bric-a-brac, dusty tabletops, and dirty dishes—a discourse that parallels diagnoses of chronic disorganization (chapter 1 above) and links between pathological collecting and substance abuse (chapter 2).

They have been quite successful at this task. Felton's books have sold hundreds of thousands of copies, and the discourses of hoarding as an addictive cluttered lifestyle that she encouraged have been endorsed by others. I'm thinking about nationwide support groups that complement Messies Anonymous such as Clutterers Anonymous (CLA), a similar material addiction recovery group founded in 1989. Other organizing manuals such as *Clutter Busting* also come to mind with their suggestions that "we are junkies to clutter. . . . Clutter is an addiction because we feel uncomfortable when we don't have the feeling anymore."[100] The discourse of an injurious addiction to home possessions has become so widespread that recovery specialists once wary of approaching objects as a form of substance abuse now embrace the theme. Author of *If I Die before I Wake: A Memoir of Drinking and Recovery* and *Clutter Junkie No More*, Barb Rogers tells audiences in a 2010 *Huffington Post* article that "I had no clear understanding that there was such a thing as clutter addiction." But after she personally "watched it happen," she understood that "like alcoholics, drug addicts and over-eaters, clutter addicts use their addiction to avoid reality."[101]

Still others do more of the same in their sustained campaign against a cluttered lifestyle. In *Let Go of Clutter*, organizing expert Harriet Schechter types clutterers as victims of the "Packrat Syndrome" and cites Felton's *When You Live with a Messie*.[102] In his best-selling home organizing guides such as *For Packrats Only*, Don Aslett mentions Messies Anonymous as "at least one organization that has been focusing on helping members overcome clutter and disorganization since the early 1980s."[103] The idea that hoarding is an addiction in need of recovery even makes an appearance in *The Best American Essays 1998*. Under "Notable Essays of 1997," writer Robert Atwan cites Tyler Gore's creative nonfiction essay "Stuff," in which Gore looks aghast at "the knick-knacks, the whatnot, the brick-a-brack of the years" that floods his family's home.[104] "I've begun to think that there must be some sort of syndrome behind our cluttered lifestyle," Gore muses as he details "my family's terrible addiction to objects."[105]

In the words of cultural anthropologist Susan Lepselter, "the disorder of clutter feels like, and discursively becomes, an embodied medical disorder or illness."[106] Informed by religious tenets or not, the writings of organizers such as Felton refined the threat of clutter as an addiction, a symptom of mental illness, rather than a signpost of immigrant deviance or outmoded Victorian design. "What insanity is this?" asks one of the Organizer Lady's meditation guides as it surveys the contents of the disorganized domestic lifestyle.[107] The emphasis here on the unhinged psychic tyranny of bric-a-brac is telling. Clutter busters shore up the insanity characterization as they describe unkempt households as dangerous acquisitions in need of detox. Their assumptions regarding the cluttered lifestyle exerted a lasting influence on scientific representations of hoarding as they continue to stoke anxieties about stuff overload that began more than a century ago.

STANDARDIZED MEASURES

I mentioned that Felton's writings acknowledge developing scientific discourses ("what the mental health field calls hoarders") that dovetailed with diagnoses of pathological collecting and the chronic disorganization of Collyer Brothers syndrome. This final section goes one step further to show how organizer accounts of clutter addiction and messy lifestyles not only confirmed but also contributed to diagnostics advanced by psychologists and social workers alike. While many housekeeping guides to decluttering facilitated this process, Felton's texts once again prove instrumental as popular and more elite discussions incorporated them into chatter over hoarding prevention: this is where *The Messies Manual* crosshatches with *Journal of Clinical Psychology*. Her texts' upbraiding of object dependency informed the institutionalization of decluttering, and many of her ideas now function as components of hoarding diagnoses thanks to the promotional efforts of anticlutter associations such as the Institute for Challenging Disorganization (ICD). After demonstrating how Felton's housekeeping manuals embraced prevailing notions of clutter as deviance and reinterpreted them for a later era of addiction and lifestyle, I look to their cultural entrenchment as professional organizer discourses gradually aligned with the those of scientists to deem hoarding worthy of admission into DSM-5.

Felton herself is one of the best archivists of the organizer's influence across twenty-first-century mental health professions. In *Winning the Clutter War*, she records the international consolidation of anticlutter tenets as Messies Anonymous became a global phenomenon. I quote her narrative account at length:

> In the twenty-plus years since that little group met, the program hammered out there has spread all over the world to English-speaking countries such as Canada, South Africa, Australia, New Zealand, and England. Books in German have become bestsellers, and many German groups have been formed. The word "messie" has entered the German word pool. Books have been translated into Spanish and Dutch, and the Chinese have bought rights to translate and publish. Through newspapers, magazines, radio programs, television, and book distribution, the message of hope has spread to women and men around the world. The program has jumped cultural lines. Cluttering is an equal-opportunity problem and no respecter of social position, intelligence, or any other characteristic.[108]

Much like the Scandinavian doctor who took up the Collyers several years after the deaths of Homer and Langley, Felton charts the dissemination of her approach to insane cluttering beyond the United States. With missionary zeal, she notes that multimedia anticluttering campaigns operate across five continents. What her "message of hope" records is both the universalization and the ongoing standardization of a disorder that exceeds national borders, or what we could call the globalization of the Messie.

As Felton correctly notes, some of her most prominent contributions can be found in German literature, where popular guidebooks translated her writings on Messies and enabled a medicalized diagnosis of *das Messie-Syndrom*. In a 2004 article, "Collecting and Hoarding: A Messy Has No Choice," published in one of Germany's more prestigious medical journals, a team of scientists track a disease that translates into English as "messy house syndrome"; they note that this ailment characterizes those who have an abnormal amount of material in their domestic space and say "the term 'Messy' describes a person who is highly unlikely to keep order."[109] This messy house syndrome, the authors inform readers, was detailed by "American Sandra Felton, [who] described this structure and its dangerous consequences using her own example and fought it with psychological tricks."[110] The researchers then outline the psychopathological nature of cluttered rooms, and under a section on possible therapeutic interventions for messy house syndrome they feature a photograph of a smiling woman surrounded by home possessions who reads a retitled German translation of one of Felton's books, *Im Chaos bin ich Königin: Überlebenstraining im Alltag* (*I'm the Queen of Mess: A Survival Guide for Daily Life*). To this day German-based scientists and nonspecialists continue to refer to abnormal clutterers as Messies. With little hyperbole, we might say that Felton's textbooks introduced one idiom of hoarding in Europe.

Felton's organizing ideas have been just as significant within the United States as they fed into larger systems of professional organizing that work in tandem with scientific diagnoses of HD. Recall Felton's mention in *Winning the Clutter War* that "the National Association of Professional Organizers [NAPO] and the National Study Group on Chronic Disorganization [NSGCD] have been formed in America" following "the beginning of Messies Anonymous."[111] The NSGCD renamed itself the Institute for Challenging Disorganization (ICD) in 2010, and together these two organizations are primary outlets for organizers who espouse cleanliness campaigns that counteract the supposed unhygienic environment of a hoarder's cluttered home. These latter-day cleanliness institutes have extensive certification rituals for legitimizing professional declutterers (a certificate of study in Basic Hoarding Issues, for example), and NAPO has acquired substantial cultural capital as a nonprofit association that sells the promise of a normal domestic life sponsored by household products corporations such as Ziploc, Rubbermaid, Closet Factory, Shelf Genie, and Closet Maid. Listed as an affiliate since 1993, Felton is a member of NAPO's Golden Circle, and the organization nominated her for its Philanthropy Award in 2011. She is also featured on the ICD's "Reading and Resource List for Professional Organizers Working with Chronically Disorganized People," which includes *Messie No More* and *I've Got to Get Rid of This Stuff!* under the respective subject headings "Chronic Disorganization" and "Hoarding."[112]

Felton's acquaintance Judith Kolberg, it turns out, started the Institute for Challenging Disorganization, and Kolberg herself has been elemental to the institutionalization of professional organizer discourses since the late 1980s. In 1989, she launched an organizing business named FileHeads Professional Organizers in Atlanta, and in this southern city she jumpstarted the independent Squall Press that released two of her popular anticlutter manuals—*Conquering Chronic Disorganization* (1999) and *What Every Professional Organizer Needs to Know about Hoarding* (2008). Kolberg once directed the Atlanta Hoarding Task Force, and in 1991 she founded what would become the ICD. Like Felton's own housekeeping guides, Kolberg's antihoarding texts have sold tens of thousands of copies across the globe as they advance the aims of her organization and prominently feature ways to counter messy house syndrome.

Given their intimacy, Felton's various self-help texts about addicted messies and cluttered lifestyles have been a resource for Kolberg's writings and the ICD, which have embraced some of the Organizer Lady's central ideas. Kolberg thanks Felton in her acknowledgments to both books. Felton, in turn, blurbs *What Every Professional Organizer Needs to Know about Hoarding*: "Digging through confusion and distress, Kolberg opens the windows of thought for a fresh look at how hoarders can be helped."[113] Many of Felton's beliefs about clutter course through these texts, minus their religious bent. Kolberg cites Felton's successes as an ex-hoarder; her innovations of Messies Anonymous; the dangers of clutter and "unhealthy surroundings"; and "the inability to comply with the basic obligations of being a responsible homeowner."[114] To cap off these incorporations, her work block quotes Felton's *I've Got to Get Rid of This Stuff!* and cites its promise of "an orderly, satisfying, supportive life-style free of clutter and the drive to collect."[115]

Indebted to Felton's material reorientation programs, Kolberg's texts achieve something equally important as *The Messies Manual* did: they take personalized writings such as Felton's and formalize them into a more legitimated discourse about combating clutter, something more culturally authoritative than a mass-market paperback written by a guest speaker for Focus on the Family. Kolberg's texts often present themselves as empiricist diagnostics for properly identifying hoarders as clutterers, and the end of one of her manuals includes an appendix, "The NSGCD Clutter Hoarding Scale: Official Organizational Assessment Tool." Written in 2002, copyrighted a year later, and subsequently revised into the Clutter-Hoarding Scale (CHS), this document is the standardization of *Messie No More*, and it helps "the industry of organizing to continue to sophisticate, clarify and be credible in its own right."[116] This scale, italicizes Kolberg, "is a *standardized* assessment tool for use by organizers, families, community agencies, social workers, clinicians, and first responders," and this, she believes, is its "single most important aspect."[117] I agree. With no exaggeration she states that "it will be the standard by which hoarding is assessed across a wide range of disciplines."[118] While other assessment scales exist, the scale is a common device for classifying hoarders in the United States, and NAPO's website also makes mentions of it.

Much of the historical dust this chapter has kicked up falls upon this seven-page document. To encapsulate its principal aims: the 2003 version of the CHS equates hoarding with clutter and potentially divides every household into normal and abnormal arrangement and decor. The sliding scale gives organizers diagnostic criteria for properly calibrating the material pathology of a hoarder's home irrespective of gender, class, race, or other identity markers. Like Felton's Messies Anonymous, the scale is an equal-opportunity counter to cluttering hoarders. It presumes an appropriate level of household hygiene, as its diagnoses are "primarily based on the interior of a home" and the levels of "sanitation and cleanliness" that are to be found in it.[119] The scale offers five detailed levels. The first is "normal housekeeping," where "clutter [is] not excessive"—the kind of domestic lifestyle that a home economist such as Christine Frederick would have appreciated. Then things start to go downhill. At Level 2 the household features a "major appliance or regionally appropriate heating, cooling or ventilation device not working for longer than 6 months"; "clutter [that] inhibits use of more than two rooms"; "light pet dander in evidence"; and "limited evidence of housekeeping."[120] At Level 3 the TV is on the front porch and instances of "excessive dust" abound. Bedlam arrives with Levels 4 and 5: "no clean dishes or utensils locatable in the kitchen"; "standing water in basement or room"; and "kitchen and bathroom unusable due to clutter."[121]

By these accounts, I admit, my boyfriend and I are hoarders. The AC flow in our master bedroom is pretty weak; he won't throw away his *Vanity Fairs*; our long-haired cat sheds like crazy; there's this ongoing standoff about who will vacuum the downstairs. Joking aside, the Clutter-Hoarding Scale is sort of like a Kinsey Scale for domestic object perversion. It enables the organizer expert not only to categorize the individual and their material relations as a hoarder or as a nonhoarder, thanks to the observation of household clutter, but also to detail how advanced this material disease has become. At what stage of the clutter addiction is the client? How acute is her pack rat syndrome? Is the domicile's compulsive clutter dire? The various nomenclatures that I have traced thus far fuse into one standardized descriptor—the hoarder's clutter levels—as disreputable acts of domestic object relations reveal the home base of a material deviant as much as an overattachment to goods reveals an abnormal collector.

Enhancing their psychological tricks, scientists have approved and adopted this cultural work that an organizer scale accomplishes for their own identification efforts. Director of the Anxiety Disorders Center at the Institute of Living in Hartford, Connecticut, David Tolin writes the foreword to Kolberg's *What Every*

Professional Organizer Needs to Know about Hoarding. His authorizations of her writing as an adjunct professor of psychiatry at Yale University (he has also appeared on the cable television show *Hoarders*, as mentioned in my introduction) situate the ICD's tight associations between clutter, hoarding, and abnormal interior design within the realm of medical discourse and instrumental authority. In what he takes to be kismet, Tolin alerts readers that "the concept of chronic disorganization emerged from the field of professional organizing around the same time as my colleagues in psychology and psychiatry were noting, with increased interest, a phenomenon they termed *compulsive hoarding*."[122] Introducing hoarding as a mutual discovery in the late twentieth century (and bridging my chapter 1 with chapter 3), Tolin's rhetoric places the findings of the organizer on the same interpretive plane as the findings of the psychopathologist. The intentions of the two sync up as their shared expertise works to sophisticate, clarify, and further legitimate the study of hoarding. "I am particularly hopeful," Tolin adds, "that this work will pave the way toward increased collaboration between organizing and mental health professionals, so that both groups can bring their unique perspectives and skill sets to help those who suffer from this common and debilitating disorder."[123]

His wish has come to pass: organizers and scientific experts are oftentimes interchangeable. Texts such as the 2011 *The Hoarding Handbook: A Guide for Human Service Professionals* no longer desire but presume complementary convergence. Blurbed by Kolberg and Tolin, this antihoarding manual for organizers, social workers, psychologists, and other mental health professionals testifies that "as they accumulate more things and cannot get rid of them, the hallmark feature of hoarding appears in the form of large amounts of *disorganized clutter* in most parts of the home."[124] Contending that "hoarding is a complex problem that manifests as clutter," the professionals who script *The Hoarding Handbook* give detailed advice for assessing the presence of clutter in the home and make reference to the Clutter-Hoarding Scale (57). In an unacknowledged citation of Felton, they find the hoarder's "lifestyle" to be "abnormal, even problematic," given that "a home filled with clutter will tend to reinforce negative core beliefs that the person is inadequate or unworthy" (15). In two toss-away lines that nevertheless offer some of the manual's most important historical insight, the authors state that "professional organizers can be immensely helpful to those who hoard. In fact, *some aspects of the cognitive and behavioral treatment for hoarding are drawn from the practices of professional organizers*" (160; my emphasis). In its own scientific housekeeping way, *The Hoarding Handbook* confirms itself as a Messies manual, and the centuries-spanning work of anti-bric-a-brac material reformers embeds itself into the CBT therapy of hoarders as an integral influence.

My last claim returns us to where this chapter on clutterology began. Flip back to my description of that teleclass hosted by Frost and Felton, "Overcoming Hoarding Tendencies." A CBT advocate himself, Frost has also acknowledged the Clutter-Hoarding Scale in his hoarding diagnoses. He and his co-author cite the NSGCD ratings in a 2011 *Journal of Clinical Psychology* article, and they find that "although no psychometric data exist for this scale, clinicians may encounter cases involving professional organizers and knowledge of this scale may be useful."[125] In *Buried in Treasures*, a text discussed in chapter 1, he and his colleagues Gail Steketee and David Tolin also mention that "some of what we do in treatment is borrowed from the work of professional organizers."[126] I belabor their important point: current research on hoarding done in the name of cognitive science and CBT borrows from the cultural work of clutter-free housekeepers such as Felton and, by historical association, scientific housekeepers such as Christine Frederick. The dominant discourse of hoarding disorder is just as much a residual discourse of scientific housekeeping. As it becomes difficult these days to differentiate between professional organizer manuals and professional scientific documents, we might say that the writings of Frost and his fellow hoarding specialists were informed by Felton's texts and those that came decades before. Like other mental health practitioners who tackle the manufactured problem of hoarding, they too are clutterologists.

Given consultations between these two camps, it appears that professional organizers and the mental health field engineered a feedback loop of cultural legitimization. Professional organizers authorize themselves with associations such as NAPO and the Institute for Challenging Disorganization. Associations are authorized by experts such as Tolin, Frost, and others. Organizers such as Felton and Kolberg recommend these scientists. What falls by the wayside is the messy history that led to their knowledge about this supposedly objective scale. New Right mass-market paperbacks, antilifestyle initiatives of the 1970s, social hygiene promotions of the 1910s and 1920s, the globalization of addiction recovery, an evangelical publishing house, an immigrant's doily: these objects reduce down to a script that perpetuates clutter as a sure sign of hoarding. When the popular science of antiaccumulation forgoes its dependence on its early twentieth-century forebears, we should recall that the hoarder's brain dates back to eugenicist wall sconces now rusting away in someone's attic.

As with previous chapters, I situated my claims for clutterology outside neurons and within a larger social playing field of material relations — here the hygiene management of household objects in twentieth- and twenty-first-century America. After detailing how hoarders materialized thanks to collectibles and curio cabinets, I used this space to analyze the professional organizer, and I traced the pivotal role played by this late modern update of the scientific housekeeper. Placing organizers under the same scrutiny as they place hoarders, I contended that long-standing fears over knickknacks and paper piles contributed to the object panic that goes under the name *hoarding* as much as the yard sales of chapter 2 or the urban disorder of chapter 1. Approaching compulsive clutter as a new cycle of such panic, I argued that professional organizers and their literatures are as important as medical discourses in legitimizing one aspect of hoarding as a psychopathology. Alongside object management, I see this occupation as an instigator of material normalcy: organizers try to reinforce appropriate forms of domestic habitus with their diagnostic tools, DIY manuals, and empirical research data. Through identification and standardization, they regulate domestic material culture in terms of public and private health, sound lifestyle, self-improvement, and sufficient standard of living. This is what Felton deems her "search for normalcy in the area of order in the home."[127]

Many now wave Felton's banner against homewreckers. Her role in the genealogy of material deviance is, in fact, a vital component of the larger story that *The Hoarders* is telling. A retired Christian in southern Florida was as important as the Collyers or the Kovels in contributing to hoarding disorder. If the Hermits of Harlem became a legendary disease, then organizers such as Felton were part of the cleaning cure as they embraced long-standing ideas of clutter as a cultural threat, remixed them for an era of self-help and addiction management, and standardized their assessments with the disciplinary aid of abnormal psychology. The end result was a pervasive idea of hoarding as a messy house whose resident mindset could be cleaned up and treated, one that complements pathological collecting and the presumed disorganization of Homer and Langley.

A folly, however, is that their attempts to eradicate hoarding further excite the disease. In recent years disorderly hoarding and orderly cleaning have gone hand in hand, and organizers play a central role in managing object pathologies as they coach individuals into proper material lives. Borrowing from social hygiene, self-help, and AA, they have built a lucrative enterprise of measurements dedicated to tackling and confirming hoarding in the home as a personal, familial, communal, and even architectural problem. This accomplishment would not have been possible without complementary groundwork set by diseases such as Collyer Brothers syndrome and pathological collecting, even if the fungibility that exists between HD and disorganized clutter seems to have somewhat subsumed the specificity of these nomenclatures. Homer and Langley, as Felton and Frost's class presumed at its start, retroactively appear as clutter bugs whose Harlem brownstone needed better closet space.

Another way to put this last point: once hoarding was gradually treated as a mental pathology, it could also be cured or at least managed by some combo of CBT, self-help, Clutter-Hoarding Scale, and Clutter Rehab. Or, depending on your perspective, mismanaged. What I find interesting is how organizers magnify rather than scale back the societal dangers of hoarding as an insane accrual of household stuff. What appears to be symptom reduction is often symptom intensification, given that the messes they aim to contain are in part those of their own making. I get that pack rats won't make the Parade of Homes, but I hope we better appreciate why they are so often feared to keep such terrible house.

4

OLD RUBBISH

"Big Edie syndrome" does not exist, but it might as well. On October 22, 1971, the Suffolk County Health Department raided Grey Gardens, the East Hampton, New York, mansion that Edith Ewing Bouvier Beale had inhabited with her daughter, Edith Bouvier Beale, since 1952. Shaken by its findings, the department documented a surplus of cats, evidence of semidomesticated raccoons, "a five-foot-high mound of empty cans," furniture in tatters, two impoverished white women.[1] Word soon spread that the seventy-six-year-old "recluse mother" and her fifty-three-year-old daughter—close relatives of Jacqueline Lee Bouvier Kennedy Onassis—faced possible eviction from their once-opulent homestead.[2] Magazines such as the *National Enquirer*, *Paris Match*, and *TV Radio Mirror* as well as newspapers such as *East Hampton Star*, *New York Post*, and *Los Angeles Times* pounced on the story to release sensational photographs of Big Edie, Little Edie, and their home (figures 4.1–4.5). In the summer of 1972, Jacqueline and her husband Aristotle Onassis funded an extensive cleanup for her "recluse kin."[3] Three years later, directors Albert and David Maysles immortalized the Beales in their documentary *Grey Gardens*.[4]

Once known for ties to a former first lady, the Beales are now more renowned for their bonds with rubbish. Years after the release of *Grey Gardens*, Beale and her daughter became fixtures in hoarding's Hall of Fame. Alongside Homer, Langley, and Andy, they are considered two of the most prominent hoarders in America, and they rank high on lists of Five Famous Hoarders or "Famous Squalorees."[5] Across genres such as highbrow journalism, cable television production, theater musical, and Internet website, Big Edie proves infamous for wallowing in filth, her daughter notorious for feeding untamed mammals. More recently, the two were the centerpiece of a successful 2006 musical and a well-received 2009 television film, both of which pathologized the duo's material relations. Describing the hoarding featured in the Broadway show, one reporter notes that "the eccentric Beale pair—the first cousin and aunt of Jacqueline Kennedy Onassis—is a classic example of what has also been called squalor disorder, which especially affects the elderly."[6]

While I do not want this chapter to reduce the Beales into caricatures, given

FIGURE 4.1 Harry Benson, photograph of Grey Gardens' exteriors. *Paris Match* 1185 (January 22, 1972): 16. Courtesy of Photographs @ Harry Benson 1971.

their rich representational histories, and while I do not want to overlook Little Edie, the journalist's diagnostic nod to the elder Beale points to a component of hoarding's makeup that I have yet to address: its intimate ties to the aged.[7] Indeed, the reporter's reference to squalor and the elderly is now a commonplace depiction of hoarders shared by US popular cultures and scientific literatures alike. "The stereotypical hoarder," asserts one professional organizer in an exposé, *The Secret Lives of Hoarders*, is "the overweight, elderly woman, unkempt, dressed in layers of clothes, sitting in front of the TV all day long."[8] Unproductive, fat, disheveled, antisocial, gendered, and emphatically old: this gerontophobic sketch of the aging hoarder-recluse has become as notorious as Edith Ewing, and the two are sometimes mentioned in the same breath. Wonders one spokesperson for the Children of Hoarders support network: "When ordinary people—those who had no personal experience with the disorder thought

FIGURE 4.2 Tom Wargacki, photograph of Edith Bouvier Beale. *TV Radio Mirror* 72, no. 12 (November 1972): 45. Courtesy of Tom Wargacki.

FIGURE 4.3 Harry Benson, photograph of Edith Ewing Bouvier Beale and Edith Bouvier Beale. *Paris Match* 1185 (January 22, 1972): 17. Courtesy of Photographs @ Harry Benson 1971.

about hoarding behavior, maybe they imagined an elderly eccentric, noticeably and indisputably troubled, like Edith Beale in 'Gray [sic] Gardens'?"[9]

Here Big Edie exemplifies elderly hoarding in particular and the compulsive hoarder in general. Descriptions of her and her kind thus direct us to the fourth and last piece of the hoarder's cultural makeup—not just socially disorganized, or abnormally acquisitive, or addicted to clutter, but troubled in old age. I grant from this chapter's outset that hoarding is thought to occur across an individual's life span, yet links between pathological possessions and late-life object relations are pronounced. Like other strains of hoarding we have encountered, hard science again plays a crucial role in this construction. Its literature abounds with a surfeit of creatively titled conditions such as senile squalor syndrome, Diogenes syndrome, syllogomania, senile recluse syndrome, elderly hoarding, late-life hoarding, and late-onset hoarding. *Syllogomania* translates as the hoarding of rubbish, and the medical eponym *Diogenes syndrome* alludes to Diogenes the Cynic (412?–323? BCE), an Athens-based contrarian renowned for living without shame in self-chosen poverty. Hoarding specialists invoke this last disease even as some question the medical term's appositeness. It sometimes appears as a synonym for elderly hoarding; sometimes as a subset of compulsive

FIGURE 4.4
Tom Wargacki,
photograph
of Edith Bou-
vier Beale. *TV
Radio Mirror* 72,
no. 12 (Novem-
ber 1972): 46.
Courtesy of Getty
Images / Tom
Wargacki.

FIGURE 4.5
Tom Wargacki,
photograph of
Edith Ewing
Bouvier Beale.
*TV Radio Mir-
ror* 72, no. 12
(November 1972):
46. Courtesy of
Corbis Images /
Tom Wargacki.

hoarding; sometimes as a stand-in for what Sandra Felton called the hoarding disorder. "Diogenes syndrome," several psychiatrists observe, "has been used to describe a cluster of problems (domestic squalor, hoarding of trash, gross self-neglect, poor personal hygiene, isolation) sometimes associated with late-life hoarding."[10] As of this writing, the International OCD Foundation lists "Hoarding in Older Adulthood" as a "type of hoarding," one that "is a serious psychiatric and community problem."[11] DSM-5 also finds that "hoarding symptoms appear to be almost three times more prevalent in older adults (ages 55–94 years) compared with younger adults (ages 34–44 years)."[12]

Despite definitional debates that surround these scientific nomenclatures, specialists generally agree that several of these diagnoses were created in the "early 1960s."[13] Literature reviews that now characterize individuals such as Edith Beale as late-life hoarders often attribute Diogenes syndrome and syllogomania to two influential studies appearing in prominent British medical journals. British Medical Journal published the first study, "Senile Breakdown in Standards of Personal and Environmental Cleanliness," in 1966. It began with a portrait that bests The Secret Lives of Hoarders: "The usual picture is that of an old woman living alone, though men and married couples suffering from the condition are also found. She, her garments, her possessions, and her house are filthy. She may be verminous and there may be faeces and pools of urine on the floor."[14] Exploring seventy-two cases of senior squalor across gender, the researchers asserted that "senile deterioration" is a mental disease and that the objects of several case studies were "independent, aloof, dominant, obstinate, moody, hoarder, particular, [and] self-satisfied."[15]

Published in a 1975 issue of the London-based Lancet, "Diogenes Syndrome: A Clinical Study of Gross Neglect in Old Age" refined these observations. Here "thirty patients (fourteen male, sixteen female) aged 66–92" and suffering from "domestic disorder" were found to have "dirty, untidy homes and a filthy personal appearance about which they showed no shame. Hoarding of rubbish (syllogomania) was sometimes seen."[16] Researchers emphasized that the majority of these individuals lived alone with "useless items" such as "newspapers, tins, bottles, and rags, often in bundles and stacks," and they found the reasoning behind these collections "obscure" even though experts and, eventually, the general public would embrace their observations across the pond.[17] Like Collyer Brothers syndrome's concern with curiosa or messy house syndrome's anxiety over unsanitary furnishings, squalor syndrome too proves to be a decades-in-the-making object panic—here, the grimy belongings of the self-isolated aged.

While scientific literatures cite these essays, they are but two important moments in the genealogy of shameless self- and object neglect. There are others. Though international conversations about the proper definition of elderly hoarding remain ongoing, the disease's diagnosis relies upon a deeper history of the senile recluse. Whether hoarding in the aged is part of a lifelong illness or the late onset of a psychopathology is uninteresting to me. I instead track discourses that enabled the hoarder-recluse to emerge as a scientific and social concern, and I ask why individuals such as Edith Beale continue to bewilder health departments, clinical psychiatrists, and cable television audiences. How was elderly hoarding figured as a serious issue and the senile recluse a syndrome tied to the disorder of hoarding? Why do anxieties over rubbish hover about seniors who keep to themselves as much as they do clutter bugs or peculiar collectors? If hoarding is a modern phenomenon, then might old-age hoarding be as well? Answering the last question in the affirmative, this closing chapter examines how accounts of deviant hoarding evolved alongside accounts of deviant old age—how one aberrant form of late life (the senile recluse) became inextricable from one aberrant form of object relations (squalor syndrome).

Rather than refining elderly hoarding as either a subset of hoarding disorder or its apotheosis, I trace its debt to modern and late modern accounts of abnormal seniors that cement stereotypes of perverse senility. As much as hoarding functions as a panic about curiosa, clutter, and collectibles, this chapter maintains that it also operates as apprehension over the suspect materials of dirty old men and women such as Edith Ewing Bouvier Beale. To state my case most broadly: rubbish-loving seniors contribute to ongoing trepidation over the appropriate role of objects in the relatively recent invention of "late life." Two corollaries follow from this primary argument. First, twenty-first-century anxieties over elderly hoarding thrive on culturally entrenched yet historically novel discourses of the pathological aged and their departures from socially acceptable forms of late-life material culture. Second, hoarding owes a debt to longstanding discourses of the aged recluse and her seemingly unnatural relationship to geriatric object cultures.

As with previous chapters, eclectic historical back files confirm these theses. A synopsis of the cultural emergence of late life in twentieth-century America reveals how discourses of "successful aging" normalized the material relations of old age. I then turn to representations of the senile recluse that undermined this ideal, as well as the later hoarding discourses beholden to them. Finally I return to what I call the Grey Gardens archive: the 1975 documentary, its 2006 sequel The Beales of Grey Gardens, the 2009 film, and a steady stream of Internet commentary on the Beales. For the most part, this archive confirms cultural formulas of elderly hoarding. Yet we also find choice moments in the two documentaries when their featured squalor scenes undermine the pathologized discourses used to document Big Edie, her daughter, their cats Jerome Jr., Hippie,

Whiskers, Singlefoot, Champion, Zeppo, Little Jimmy, and Tedsy Kennedy, their raccoon Buster, and all the rest.

OPTIMAL OBJECT AGING

It seems self-evident that professional organizers, geriatricians, and hoarding experts assume elderly hoarders to be unfit. But what version of material and mental health do they have in mind when they tackle senile squalor syndrome? When specialists claim that late-life hoarding is "quality of life impairment" or that "hoarding syndrome is associated with older age [and] social dysfunction," they presume that accumulators fail a benchmark of advanced aging.[18] In so doing they make debatable supposals about permissible modes of later material life. This section surveys the cultural model of senility from which pathological hoarders both stem and depart. Before I delve further into the contemporary discourses of hoarding that confirm elder object deviance epitomized by Edith Beale, I overview what I mean by the normative and pathological material relations of aging, which requires a brief historical digression into what other scholars have meant by "the law of normality and pathology as applied to senescence."[19] This first section contends that the normalization of aging overlapped with the normalization of object relations thanks to developments in gerontology and geriatrics. The next section gets dirty and turns to this schema's downfall.

It is striking how hoarding discourses align with modern studies of aging. When *The Secret Lives of Hoarders* suggests that the stereotypical hoarder is an elderly couch potato, it also participates in a wider discussion about who counts as a successful or as an unsuccessful ager. During the same decade that scientific essays on compulsive hoarding proliferated following the 1993 publication of "The Hoarding of Possessions," a widespread concept of the elderly helped to frame this discussion. I refer to rhetoric of successful aging promoted by two US-based researchers, geriatrician John W. Rowe and psychologist Robert L. Kahn. Responsive to increases in life expectancy across Western populations thanks to biomedical advances, Rowe, Kahn, and their fellow investigators oversaw a study on aging funded by the MacArthur Foundation Study of Successful Aging (1984–94) and supported by the National Research Agenda on Aging as well as the National Institute on Aging.[20] In an attempt "to develop the conceptual basis of a 'new gerontology,'" they published their findings in 1998 as *Successful Aging*, a best seller released by Pantheon.[21] In this book the two sold a prototype for old age, "that is, the many factors which permit individuals to continue to function effectively, both physically and mentally, in old age. We emphasized the *positive aspects of aging*—which had been terribly overlooked."[22] While others inside and outside the United States offered comparable guideposts for the elderly during this decade, *Successful Aging* blitzed America with a lifestyle regime for "growing old with good health, strength, and vitality."[23] Over subsequent years *Successful Aging*'s geriatric model notched thousands of citations in specialist publications, and its detractors rightly observe that the publication's framework seeped into everyday understandings of elder self-care. Hoarding, needless to say, was not one of their recommendations for getting on in years.

Yet while *Successful Aging* took an individual's maturation into old age as a given, this aging process is actually a novel invention of modernity, and Rowe and Kahn's reference to "new gerontology" alludes to this history. As numerous social historians, cultural theorists, bioethicists, and public health experts have stressed, late life itself is a concept whose die was cast once the field of geriatrics began to coalesce in America during the first third of the twentieth century.[24] To state the historical case in this broad manner is not, of course, to minimize prior contributions, nor is it to disregard the intellectual labors of those outside the United States. Without question the scientific study of old age had antecedents before this period, and historians acknowledge that non-American thinkers were crucial to the burgeoning discipline. Nineteenth-century Americans, alongside European counterparts such as French neurologist Jean-Martin Charcot, for instance, had previously charted the biological intricacies of aging. Moreover, Russian zoologist Élie Metchnikoff formalized the idea of *gerontology* in *The Nature of Man* ([1903] 1908).[25] But as "the age stratification of American society began to become more complex in the latter half of the nineteenth century," notes historian Howard P. Chudacoff in a claim upheld by his peers, "an increasingly explicit identification of old age as a separate stage of life" emerged that the writings of several early twentieth-century US-based doctors expedited.[26]

Scholars often single out two in particular: Austrian-born Ignatz Leo Nascher, a chief of clinic at New York City's Mount Sinai Hospital, and Massachusetts-based psychologist G. Stanley Hall. Nascher devised the term *geriatrics* in a 1909 article for *New York Medical Journal* and fleshed out this keyword in his 1914 treatise *Geriatrics: The Diseases of Old Age and Their Treatment, Including Physiological Old Age, Home and Institutional Care, and Medico-Legal Relations*. In a dictum that would become common sense for most of us in the twenty-first century, he asserted that "senility is a distinct period of life having general features normal to it and abnormal at other periods of life. It is a physiological entity as much so as the period of childhood."[27] Author of *Adolescence* (1904), Hall outlined a corresponding study of later life in *Senescence: The Last Half of Life* (1922). He likewise insisted that "senescence, like adolescence, has its own feelings, thoughts, and wills, as well as its own physiology, and their regimen is important, as well as that of the body."[28] These claims now seem incontrovertible, but I point out, as others have done so before me, how revolutionary they were for their historical moment. If we take the findings of Nascher and Hall to be axiomatic, we posit that windshield wipers—invented in 1903—are older than senior citizens.

As research into this new portion of the life span advanced, scholars conclude that these works often featured "the aged subject as a problem body," an idea not unfamiliar to later investigations of hoarding.[29] Unlike *Successful Aging*'s emphasis on the affirmative aspects of growing old, many first-wave gerontologists frequently approached senescence as an abnormal end-of-life stage.[30] Historian W. Andrew Achenbaum writes of aging discourses that circulated between the two world wars: "Evidence indicated that old age brought pronounced physical decay, mental decline, unpleasant and sometimes deviant psychological and behavioral traits, economic uselessness, personal isolation, and social segregation," alongside "dissatisfaction, lack of humor, conceit, suspicion, hypercriticism, bitterness, depression, or slovenliness."[31] Nascher's *Geriatrics* secures this claim, particularly when its downer of a preface states that "for all practical purposes the lives of the aged are useless, that they are often a burden to themselves, their family and to the community at large. Their appearance is generally unesthetic, their actions objectionable."[32] The modern invention of late life, we surmise, was simultaneously the modern invention of the aged as an unkempt psychic aberration and a communal drag.

Yet as the discipline of gerontology helped to transform late life into "a mass phenomenon" over the course of the twentieth century, the field attempted to rework some of these initial formulas via "the reconstruction of old age."[33] Though they received no reference in 1998's *Successful Aging*, many in the expanding specialty began to reimagine old age as a high point of one's life rather than its "sometimes deviant" disintegration. The discipline did so by backing what one 1965 text called "successful, or optimal, aging," or what we refer to as a fine quality of geriatric life.[34] With a series of now-obscure titles such as *Aging Successfully* (1946), *Living through the Older Years* (1949), *Processes of Aging* (1963), and *Lives through the Years: Styles of Life and Successful Aging* (1965), post–World War II gerontologists launched the concept of optimal aging that would aid later observers cast material acts such as elder hoarding in a threatening light.

Along the way, these writings unleashed several new personages between their pages: the successful ager, the active retiree, the senior citizen soaking up his or her golden years. Male and female, these individuals were over sixty and loving it. They didn't call it quits upon retirement from the workforce. They were interested in their community and interesting to others. They didn't bore you to tears with repetitive tales of walking to school in seven and a half feet of snow. They got out of the house. They took baths. They smelled fine. In the parlance of the day, they were well adjusted with sensible personal and mental hygiene. The editor of *Living through the Older Years*, for example, departs from earlier representations of late life to stress that "continued growth and creative activity are essential to successful aging," and he informs his readers that "it is hoped that the volume will, indeed, help the entire community to live more successfully throughout the life span."[35]

The aging developments that I have rehearsed have been well documented and well challenged by scholars, but what role did material cultures play in these senescent regimes?[36] For the purposes of tracking how senile squalor syndrome functions as material deviance, my contribution to this cross-disciplinary body of knowledge is to suggest that the gerontologists and geriatricians who naturalized old age also contributed to the invention of what I earlier referred to as a normal late object life. Things, it turns out, were a component of this newfangled idea called a well-lived late life, and this observation gets us a step closer to the specter of elderly hoarding that haunts popular scientific literatures. The repeated emphasis on optimal aging, I mean to say, often implied the optimal use and appreciation of stuff. Proper material relations went hand in hand with proper aging, as the latter was thought to enrich the former.

Two examples support this last claim. In an attempt at "deaging or 'defrosting,' if you wish," Columbia University psychologist George Lawton suggested that successful aging could be achieved through "the various arts and crafts that are appropriate to older people."[37] Author of *Aging Successfully* (a work that the next section examines), Lawton published his advice in *Living through the Older Years*, a book that promoted wholesome object conduct such as average collecting, woodwork, pottery making, model train construction, playing cards, finger puppet shows, and "making plastic jewelry."[38] Half a century later, Rowe and Kahn would also mention in *Successful Aging* that "there are other, nonhuman 'social' bonds that are also quite important" to those trying to avoid caducity.[39] While they specifically reference gardening, we infer that sustained engagement with material culture is a sign of good mental health, that creative and sociable things demonstrate a wholesome late lifestyle.

Not only did appropriate elder object usage signal a normal and invigorating late life; orderly elderly possessions also revealed that an individual had nursed positive material relations across the entirety of her life span. Asking seniors to fill their latter days with belongings to confirm a fit senescence, geriatricians advocated possessions that evidenced a lived life *in toto*. This distinction is a fine one but important to make. As much as some midcentury gerontologists prescribed finger puppets to combat senility, later practitioners of the discipline promoted the acquisition of objects such as keepsakes, heirlooms, well-organized records, and treasured possessions. Like arts and crafts, sufficient accrual of these items—"family trees and genealogy records, photograph albums, scrapbooks, diaries, journals, old letters, keepsakes, mementos, and souvenirs"—testified to a successful aging that anchored the elder in material social relations before his last stage of life as well as during it.[40] Sometimes referred to as *reminiscentia* by specialists, these possessions connected an optimal late life to earlier material bonds, and failure to have a few bits of memorabilia lying around the house signaled something off.[41] By the late 1970s, one geriatrician stated with confidence in *Journal of Aging* that "it was clear that the lack of a cherished possession was associated with a lower life satisfaction than those who had such possessions. This suggests that the lack of such possessions might serve as an indicator of (is symptomatic of) a poor adjustment to old age."[42]

To summarize this section: successful aging discourses produced and proselytized a conventional late material life cycle. Experts in the new discipline of geriatrics issued object conduct guidelines for those categorized as aged, and they instilled cultural tenets about what counts for an appropriate elderly relationship with things. As much as previous chapters revealed how discourses of decluttering or average collectibles signaled an ordinary material life, so too did mentally hygienic postretirement crafts or cherished possessions. This is one historical keyhole through which elderly hoarding starts to look like an impaired standard of living. In a 1987 article, "The Significance of Personal Objects to Older People," a gerontologist noted that treasured things "serve to structure space within the home, may aid in giving meaning to that space, and more important, may act as living embodiments that help support, bolster, or authenticate personal ideological systems." In the same breath he mentioned that "one stereotype of older people is that they hang onto everything they have until they die, an image no doubt fostered by press accounts of elderly recluses and their possessions."[43] I turn now to how optimal object aging deteriorated into piles of reclusive rubbish and heaps of hoarded filth.

"CATS AND FILTH"

In the shadows of this properly aged senior citizen lurked a suspicious other, one who aged uncreatively, who tossed away the scrapbook, who spent too much time alone with stuff, who returned to nineteenth-century standards of personal hygiene. This section tracks how this reclusive figure came to be. I start by noting that intrinsic to developing discourses on normalized late-life object cultures were fears that it would all go south. Despite their promotion of successful aging creeds, later gerontologists never completely shirked earlier models that viewed elders as "antisocial, irrational, irritable, petulant, selfish, depressed, suicidal, or sexually perverse."[44] Ironically, their writings continued these caricatures even as they revised them. While the discipline began to advocate positive material relations, it also instilled guidelines to circumvent inappropriate material behaviors that would enable Big Edie Beales of the world to appear as culturally threatening hoarders. Running alongside discourses of busy-bee retirees surrounded by precious things, we find, were those of the unsocial recluse mired in squalor. What goes by the syndrome of elderly hoarding sprang from the marbling of these interdependent discourses.

We better gauge how this imbrication came about by first noting that optimal aging conjured the specter of unsuccessful aging, that fears of the latter streamed through literatures endorsing a well-lived late life. In his 1949 account "Aging Creatively," which I earlier mentioned, George Lawton cautioned that "unsuccessful aging means withdrawal from life. . . . We dwell deep within the dark well of our loneliness and isolation."[45] In the same edited collection where Lawton published this warning, sociologist Ernest Burgess fretted over elderly "maladjustment where a nonadaptive activity is substituted for the desired one."[46] A major player in the Chicago School of Sociology referred to in chapter 1, Burgess found that "this activity represents both social and mental maladjustment. Examples are eccentric behavior, alcoholism, phobias, invalidism, excessive gambling, psychoneuroses, and psychoses."[47] Lawton had earlier offered his own grab bag of psychopathology in *Aging Successfully*: "But, you tell me, what of those old persons who after a lifetime of having been normal, respectable, fine people suddenly become misers, scandalmongers, extremely neglectful of their persons, cantankerous, violators of the moral and legal code? Such behavior is *not* typical of the normal growing-old process, but either of deterioration due to unusual physiological brain changes or to the sudden emergence of emotional disturbances and mental disease."[48]

In the midst of delineating normative aging, Lawton introduces nutcases who wreak havoc on their communities and their persons. Rather than the optimization of late life, there is perverse criminalization. Rather than sound personal hygiene, there is dishevelment. Rather than alert minds, diseased heads. Rather than beneficial social activities such as arts and crafts, scuttlebutt and hoarded wealth. Disseminated across academic and popular print cultures (Lawton thanks *Ladies' Home Journal* magazine for some prior publication), such ideas point to a pervasive anxiety that a typical late life could turn insane on a dime.[49]

Some of this fretting over the gerontological perversion of unsuccessful aging was, as I have hinted, old wine in new bottles. When Lawton references the immoral and illegal acts that lead to a successful ager's downfall, his rhetoric echoes the "deviant psychological and behavioral traits" that early twentieth-century medical expertise saw as one possible stamp of the aged. When he hypothesizes that atypical elder behavior stems from the brain's deterioration, he riffs on a long-standing scientific shibboleth that the aging of gray matter can lead to social deviance. This is what some in the later nineteenth century diagnosed as *senile dementia*.[50]

Take the following character sketch from Allan McLane Hamilton, who introduces himself as "One of the Consulting Physicians to the Insane Asylums of New York City" in his 1883 *A Manual of Medical Jurisprudence*. Hamilton approaches senile dementia as a form of lunacy and defines it as "a senile condition connected with extensive and general arterial deterioration."[51] His highly gendered description of this mental disease is overwrought, yet his rhetoric has startling parallels to twentieth-century discussions of unsuccessful aging:

[The senile dement] is ill tempered and petulant. There is a pitiful lack of concentration which results in restlessness of mind and body. . . . The old man undergoes a moral change as well as an intellectual, and he is amatory, obscene, and fond of telling of the adventures of his youth, and living over again its gallant frivolities. His leer is lascivious, and he goes about with unbuttoned clothing, and is lost to all shame. He is extravagant and prodigal, and buys useless things despite the remonstrances of his friends.[52]

Like Lawton's scandalmongers, these aging males are violators of the legal and moral code. They are cantankerous; they neglect their persons; they betray a "tendency to mental enfeeblement and perversity."[53] Unlike Lawton's mentally diseased elders, however, these aged are cast as shameless sexual deviants, as historian Carole Haber argues. This is one genesis, she rightly observes, of the phrase *dirty old man*, and yet another iteration, I add, of Foucault's dangerous individual.[54]

As scholars such as Haber draw our attention to the unabashed obscenity in Hamilton's description, I must point out that material misconduct also accompanies the sexual dissidence of senile dementia. The old man is pervy not only because of his leer but also because he purchases worthless goods that his nearest and dearest cannot tolerate. His demented use of things supplements his descent into mental, physiological, and sexual debauchery, and we intuit that evolving forms of material deviance in elder adulthood was an enduring concern for research in aging as much as evolving forms of material normalcy. Even prior to the field's institutionalization, physicians interested in the concept of old age associated pathological senility with poor object conduct, and the expansive category of senile mental disease was construed, in part, as an improper relation with personal things. Think of this as one small step for the developing discourses of gerontology and one giant leap for syllogomania. While notable historical differences between demented old men and elderly hoarders exist, there is family resemblance in terms of the questionable acquisition of possessions. The senile dement characterized by Hamilton is by no means a recluse, but themes of slatternly appearance, mental disorder, and inappropriate goods recur throughout unsuccessful-aging discourses and well into the Home Box Office production of *Grey Gardens*.

Subsequent gerontological discourses updated this twinned pathologization of personhood and object relations described in *A Manual of Medical Jurisprudence*. Returning to a tract such as *Aging Successfully*, we find Lawton desexualizing the dirty old senior but retaining an emphasis on material abnormality and personal dishevelment. Alongside his claim that nonnormative elders become "extremely neglectful of their persons" that I cited above, *Aging Successfully* beckons its readers to youthfully "devote ourselves to collecting things," and it then cites "the hoarder, the miser, [and] the string-and-paper bag collector" as "extreme examples of this 'second-childhood' tendency."[55] No further mentions of hoarding appear in this text, but I note that Lawton's reformatted *Manual of Medical Jurisprudence*—written at the dawn of postwar collectibles cultures discussed in chapter 2—nevertheless allows for the hoarder and senile self-squalor to coexist in the same book. Heirs to the demented elders who came before them, Cold War seniors who collect useless papers start to look like extreme accumulators distinct from their successfully aged peers. A binary emerges between the stable retiree and the maladjusted invalid, the normal with their scrapbooks and the perverse with their string.

Aging Successfully was not alone in widening this gap between optimized aging and its botched counterparts. Several other writings of the period likewise contributed to the personage who would become the dysfunctional elder hoarder. Another geriatric text that I referenced, *Lives through the Years*, charted similar territory and segregated its elderly case studies into "most successful agers," "less successful agers," and "least successful agers."[56] Part of the Kansas City Study of Adult Life begun in the early 1950s and a prelude to the MacArthur Foundation Study, the work surveyed the daily activities of more than 150 seniors for over half a decade. *Lives* included numerous examples of normal oldagers between its pages ("Family, Friends, and Fishing") as well as those who did not make the grade ("Hopelessly Confused"). I single out one case history listed under "Cats and Filth" because it anticipates diagnoses of senile squalor syndrome used to define someone such as Edith Beale. Slotting an anonymous seventy-two-year-old woman into the least successful ager category, researchers found that "the respondent presented a picture of slum squalor" but gave no further details about her environment (66). We are told that this nameless woman was a former waitress who had married four times and lived in what the researchers considered to be a "run-down section of the city" (66). She started off with one cat in 1960, but she somehow wound up with seven by 1962. She seemed nonplussed about these pets and her home address. Researchers, however, lamented that "she had no company and said she did not want any. . . . This woman had a very marked style of Living Alone" (68).

In step with other geriatric discourses denouncing elderly self-isolation, *Lives* stigmatized the woman's supposed squalor and her lack of social graces. Her suboptimal life proves inextricable from antisocial tendencies and filthy material surroundings. One compounds the other; as much as pathologized aging was linked to suspect object use, so too was it connected to maladjusted "personal segregation." Hence her "disorganized and demoralized" social withdrawal, researchers believed, put her in a "precarious position" (68). We never learn how this negative example ends up, but the takeaway is clear: this unsuccessful ager represents a "somewhat deviant style," "the exception rather than the rule" (70). In contrast to typical aging, the late life of a Missouri-based elderly woman we know only as "Cats and Filth" becomes a prototype of squalor-ridden reclusion, a dirty old woman complementing earlier discourses of the crusty old man.

If my passing references to slum squalor and disorganized persons recall two other unsuccessful agers—the Collyer brothers—then you are not far off. A 1960 essay, "The Aged Recluse—An Exploratory Study with Particular Reference to Community Responsibility," further realized these tightening connections between mental disease, pathological senility, reclusion, and dirty things. Published in *Journal of Chronic Diseases* and coauthored by Ruth Granick (Bennett) and Frederic D. Zeman, the essay built on press exposés of the Collyers to confirm what the two identified as "senile mental disorder."[57] Both authors were well suited for this diagnostic task. At the time of their essay's publication, Zeman was a gerontologist at New York City's Jewish Home and Hospital who had worked with Nascher at Mount Sinai Hospital. A member of the initial advisory editorial board for the leading academic journal the *Gerontologist*, he was also professionally intimate with other aging experts such as Lawton.[58] Granick was a graduate student at Columbia University whose sociological research focused on solitary senior citizens, and several decades later Columbia University's Center for Geriatrics and Gerontology appointed her its deputy director.[59] Presenting a picture of slum squalor that complemented "Cats and Filth," the two translated press reports of what I earlier cited as the Collyer condition into the mental and material deterioration of the perverted recluse.

From the start of the essay, their findings borrow from articles claiming that Homer and Langley Collyer were "Harlem recluses," "Fifth Ave. recluses," and "brother recluses." I analyzed these reports in chapter 1, and Granick and Zeman adopt newspaper accounts to secure the psychopathology of the elder recluse. Their data consists of "clipping newspaper articles on recluses out of metropolitan papers over the last 17 years," and they use these findings to paint an alarming portrait of "aged behavioral deviants" (640). After number-crunching these articles and detailing the Collyers' biographies, they churn sensational journalism into moralizing science: "The people involved are deviants who are often surrounded by mystery and violence" (639); they betray "behavioral aberrations or deviations from normative expectations" (640); "the living quarters of 37 per cent were described in the press as being in 'shambles,' 'piled with trash,' 'unkempt,' or 'dingy'" (647). Almost half of these recluses are "pack rat[s]" (647), and more than 90 percent are over the age of fifty-six (642). Both writers find that the "aging process" exacerbates these unsanitary collecting tendencies, after they rehearse the discoveries of the Collyers' corpses (651).

Like the case study "Cats and Filth," Homer and Langley function as the exception to normative aging and the rule of thumb when it comes to demented senile material relations. Moreover, the Collyers' individual senile syndrome becomes a prototype. "The story of the Collyers," note Granick and Zeman, "is duplicated many times over in the lives of other recluses" (652), and this cautionary tale cuts across gender as the authors find that "the number of men and women was almost equal" (649). Now a cornerstone of Diogenes syndrome, antisocial aging with trash thus appears as less of a personal preference and more of an "unregulated mental disease" (652), and the fact that Granick and Zeman cull their data from the same newspaper sources that jump-started Collyer Brothers syndrome should not go unremarked. "The Aged Recluse" is where the quickening of hoarding as chronic disorganization intersects with hoarding as senile squalor syndrome. Given that a gerontologist who worked at the same institution as a founder of modern American geriatrics drafted this latter diagnosis, I may modestly claim that the cultural invention of hoarding and the cultural invention of late life are not unconnected.

Hoary paper-bag collectors, grubby heartland divorcées, profligate old consumers, and, once more, two Fifth Avenue hermits: despite their differences, these modern subjects together signal the promise of an optimal late life soiled by the damaged world of goods. In lieu of *reminiscentia*, rubbish. In place of a cherished possession, living spaces riddled with useless items. Establishing normative expectations for successful aging, experts in the study of old age also produced their obverse: the aged recluse surrounded by dinginess. To see one is to see the other, with both bearing witness to the historical emergence of the squaloree. As diagnostic drafts of this personage emerged alongside evolving discourses of pathological collecting, unsanitary furnishing, and Collyer curiosa, it became more and more clear that the recluse was not right in her deteriorating head. She could care less about treasured possessions and rarely cleaned her dwelling. Her clothes were frowsy, her rental home overrun with five too many companionate species. She never said hello to the neighbors. Her golden years amounted to a muddle. People talked and expressed concern at this sad sideshow. She was, some insinuated, an isolated communal threat. While mid-twentieth-century medical jurisprudence made sporadic mention of this dangerous personage, she would soon take center stage as a full blown hoarder-recluse. Enter Edith Ewing Bouvier Beale.

"A GREY GARDENS EFFECT"

This is the historically scenic route that leads us back to Grey Gardens. Suffice it to say that developing stories of the deviant aged recluse established preconditions of historical possibility for later representations of elderly hoarding. Zeman and Granick, for one, were embraced by writing that explored the "abnormal personalities" of trash-collecting isolates, and these latter discourses on insane elders complemented the two British essays on Diogenes syndrome and syllogomania summarized in this chapter's introduction.[60] In a few instances they bled together. A 1992 *Handbook of Mental Health and Aging* published by San Diego-based Academic Press categorizes "the Diogenes or Senile Recluse Syndrome" under a section titled "Psychopathology of Later Life."[61] Another article published in 2001 by a Texas-based scientist notes that "Diogenes syndrome is also referred to as aged recluse."[62] Despite occasional disputes over nomenclature between experts, by the turn of this century a template for mentally unstable late lifers has emerged: senile squalorees "are certainly far from happy, self-sufficient and least of all in search of company. On the contrary they are often described as angry, suspicious, reclusive and buried under an abundance of inanimate objects, dirt and dust."[63]

This diagnostic list has become a refrain that informs academic and popular accounts of elderly hoarding in the early twenty-first century. Scholarly writings in disciplines of social work, abnormal psychology, and even business management have all digested previous gerontological findings that centered on successful and unsuccessful forms of late life.[64] Reformatting these literatures into the mental disorder of extreme rubbish, these experts approach the mentally ill recluse with an aura of common sense. "Consistent with other reports," notes one 2010 article released in *International Journal of Geriatric Psychiatry*, "the majority of older compulsive hoarders in this study demonstrated social impairment and lived alone."[65] The end result is a standardized checklist for senile squalor syndrome that appears across the United States, the United Kingdom, Ireland, Israel, and elsewhere: filth, recalcitrance, solitude, sixty-five-plus.

Much of the above also filters into the popular cultures that contribute to the Grey Gardens archive—the film, the documentaries, and the online discussions of Beale's late life as a paradigmatic hoarder. With this wider historical lens behind us we better comprehend how *The Secret Lives of Hoarders* sees the stereotypical accumulator as an unkempt elderly woman, and how an ordinary person might imagine Edith Beale to be an unsuccessful ager. Geriatric discourses help twenty-first-century commentators make proper sense of the East Hampton curiosity, one who now stands as a case history for squalor syndrome. Like Warhol the perverse collector, she typifies all those other older accumulators out there. The open-access website for the International OCD Foundation, for instance, lists *Grey Gardens* as a hoarding documentary, and Internet references to Beale describe her as a late modern Diogenes attached to domestic trash.[66]

As these last two examples attest (and as we saw earlier with online moralizing over Harlemitis and Sandra Felton's Messies website), web commentary now works alongside more specialized scientific publications to mark subjects as deviant hoarders. In many cases, these lay Internet diagnoses support the findings of their more specialized scientific counterparts. A search query on Google for "edith beale hoarder," to cite one example, turns up several choice finds. You learn that Amy Byrnes, mother of four over in Monmouth County, New Jersey, was channel surfing one night and could not turn off the 1975 documentary. She became "engrossed, and slightly repelled" by "a side dish of crazy," and she got really scared that her closet may have "a Grey Gardens effect."[67] You discover that a member of the Healthline Editorial Team got much more than she or he bargained for at a "church-affiliated community rebuilding project" that was "*Grey Gardens* minus *The Discreet Charm of the Bourgeouis* [sic]."[68] You hit upon Patricia Salber, an online physician-blogger, who treats Diogenes syndrome like a death march: "The consequences can be deadly. To wit, the Collyers and Bouvier Beale" (Big Edie died of pneumonia complications on February 5, 1977).[69] With sometimes breathless rhetoric, all approach genealogies of hoarding as bound to Beale's Diogenes syndrome: "I've seen it before and it's always terrifying. It has a name. It is called Diogenes Syndrome or Squalor Syndrome or Messy House Syndrome."[70]

Beholden to prior geriatric claims even as they erase this historical link, these twenty-first-century fronts of elderly hoarding collectively freeze Edith Beale's late life into that of an addled pack rat. In so doing *Grey Gardens* the documentary retroactively becomes the extended money shot of an insane elder's hoard. Internet commentators allude to the film to shore up their claims for both the facticity and the ubiquity of hoarder-recluses. Presenting a "list of hoarders on stage and screen" as "entertainment," one website states with confidence that "they have been for a long time," and it embeds a YouTube clip of the original trailer to *Grey Gardens*.[71] Filed under "Hoarder Stories, Part 2," it then notes that "the original 1975 documentary by Albert and David Maysles is the definitive peek into the Beale's [sic] life and their horrifically cluttered mansion. Also available: The 2008 sequel, *The Beales of Grey Gardens*, with even more looks at the interior of this falling-down beauty, and a 2009 HBO telepic based on the documentary starring Drew Barrymore."[72]

I return to a closer reading of the documentary in the next section. For now I briefly mention that the diagnosis of Diogenes syndrome informs the HBO production of *Grey Gardens*, which should have been subtitled "Cats and Filth and Jessica Lange." Starring the two-time Academy Award–winning actress as Big Edie and Drew Barrymore as her daughter, the film incorporates numerous references to the original documentary even as its diegesis spans a longer time frame. The documentary was filmed sporadically in the early 1970s, yet the fictive version swings back and forth within the span 1936–78. In several instances, scenes from the original documentary are restaged (and refilmed by the fictionalized Maysles brothers), such as Big Edie conversing with the directors in her upstairs bedroom. In other shots the film drops knowing references to its predecessor across its temporal frame. Big Edie's yellow bathing suit shows up in 1971 rather than 1973 or 1974, and characters repeat lines spoken in the midseventies decades earlier.

As it builds on the original, the HBO production embeds itself and the Maysleses' original version that it incorporates within the social field of twenty-first-century compulsive hoarding discourses. This, I believe, helps viewers envision Edith Beale's mid- to late life as that of an aging hoarder suffering from a chronic bout of Diogenes syndrome. More than halfway through the film, *Grey Gardens* provides a seemingly definitive glimpse into senile squalor: broken window panes, piles of tin cans, moldy ceilings, dingy rooms, unkempt quarters, cats, raccoons. Yet the 2009 film does not attribute the source of this syndrome to both Beales. It instead places the blame for the squalor on Beale the elder, who figures as an early-onset hoarder while her daughter appears to be collateral damage. Abandoned first by her husband Phelan and then by her lover Gould in the 1950s, a distressed Lange/Beale telephones her daughter/Barrymore in New York City while she sits amidst growing piles of cluttered papers and a couple of kittens. She begs Little Edie to return, and in the scene thereafter she informs her prodigal daughter that they should "breed cats" together.[73] Initially put off by these proposals, Barrymore's character goes along but not for the fun of it. In the film's logic, she never breaks away from the older hoarder's dominating psychopathology and becomes one more object inappropriately attached to the prototypical senile recluse. The cable television version of Edith Beale the elder thus confirms *The Secret Lives of Hoarders'* archetype of the unkempt elderly hoarder, and the film exposes the supposed tragedy of syllogomania given Big Edie's unsuccessful aging and the failed promise of her late material life. You begrudgingly understand how a viewer might lump together "the documentary cum Broadway show cum HBO movie."[74]

UNCHERISHED KEEPSAKES

All these recent characterizations of the elder Beale seem unfortunate. One irony of the Grey Gardens archive is that the original documentary resists capturing her as a spectacular piece of geriatric curiosa, or what some later viewers tag as an identifiable elder hoarder. In fact, the 1975 film explicitly counters the modern geriatric discourses that pathologized the unconventional aged. Prior to *Grey Gardens'* release, some local authorities cast Beale (along with her daughter) as demented and portrayed them as unstable isolates drowning in filth. After the Suffolk County Health Department notified the two women that they were a menace to self and others, newspapers and magazines reported on their home's supposed decrepitude. In an in-depth January 1972 *New York* magazine article, "The Secret of Grey Gardens," journalist Gail Sheehy records that "a public nurse said, 'You're sick'" to the daughter of a "76-year-old recluse mother."[75] East Hampton's acting mayor William Abel also chimed in: "The two sweet old things won't move unless they are forcibly moved because, unfortunately, they're not mentally competent."[76]

Visuals reproduced after the October 1971 raid and before a summer of 1972 cleanup aided these psychiatric assessments of "sweet old things." The *East Hampton Star* and *New York Daily News* released exterior photographs of Grey Gardens, and in January 1972 the French weekly *Paris Match* published an exposé that included a teaser headline, "What Tragic Secret Lives with Jackie Onassis' Old Aunt?" This international report also contained an album of three seemingly staged black-and-white interior shots of the Beales taken by celebrity photographer Harry Benson. The *National Enquirer* reprinted one of these photographs, and a double-page spread depicts a robed Beale the elder sitting next to her portrait painted at a much younger age (figure 4.6). At her feet are indiscernible bits of material. To her left are broken windows. The copy below informs readers that "Edith Bouvier Beale, 76 years old, poses near her portrait, that of the young woman that she was forty years ago. . . . Today in the deserted house there is only ruin. Lost in an abandoned garden (see opposite), Jackie's aunt lived as a recluse with her daughter, Edith Bouvier."[77] The phototext rehearses the conventions of elder maladjustment that I have discussed, and a midcentury geriatrician would have had little difficulty slotting Bouvier into the least-successful ager category from this image alone.

The Maysleses, it seems to me, conceived *Grey Gardens* in part as a critique of media that confirmed the deviance of the senile recluse, if not yet the compulsive hoarder. In unpublished production notes for the film (working title: *Portrait*), they challenge the reportage: "Call them recluses for they rarely leave Grey Gardens. But, friends visit and talk on the phone frequently."[78] They then contradict representations of the Beales as incompetent: "Call them eccentrics

FIGURE 4.6 Harry Benson, photograph of Edith Ewing Bouvier Beale. *Paris Match* 1185 (January 22, 1972): 16–17. Courtesy of Photographs @ Harry Benson 1971.

by prevailing standards. . . . Their house inside is far from kept up like large homes usually and they have cats—sometimes 8 or more—and raccoons whom they feed and treat fondly as pets. Yet, today we all know and read about hippies (eccentric?) and commune life where conventional standards are scorned."[79] Approaching the Beales' domestic lives as a counterculture of object relations, the Maysleses question the presumed aberration of the aged recluse by defamiliarizing her habitus. Their film, they propose, uses the Beales to interrogate the "conventional standards" of late modern material relations. (A quick aside: raccoons as domestic pets are not unfathomable. Cultural historian Katherine C. Grier notes that a mail-order company in the late 1950s "not only offered forty-six different breeds of pedigreed puppies but also raccoon cubs, descented baby skunks, mynah birds, and several species of monkeys.")[80]

These expressed intentions became more explicit after the film's September 1975 release, when several well-placed critics faulted the directors for the exploitation that they had tried to offset. The Maysleses filmed *Grey Gardens* in the genre of cinéma vérité or direct cinema, a documentary style that presumably records the unfiltered everyday realities of its subject matter and one that the two utilized in their previous releases *Salesman* (1968) and *Gimme Shelter* (1970). Yet a prominent *New York Times* reviewer attacked the tenets of direct cinema and lambasted the directors for recording the Beales. In "'Grey Gardens': *Cinéma Verité* or Sideshow?" critic Walter Goodman found the "case more noteworthy than the usual recluse-in-messy-old-house story," and he contended that "direct cinema, with all its pretensions to art and high seriousness, has here been reduced to a form of tabloid journalism, not to say a circus sideshow."[81] An overview in *Vogue* magazine agreed with this Beales-as-freaks thesis. It too charged that *Grey Gardens* was "one of the most exploitative, tasteless, and frankly reprehensible films of them all."[82]

The Maysleses' replies to these critiques reveal much about senile squalor discourses that would feed into spectacles of hoarding. In April 1976 the two published a withering response to their critics in the *Times*. Interestingly, their apologia centers on themes of aberrant late life, senile dementia, and elder insanity:

> The darker, unstated but unmistakable, charge was that these women are senile or mentally incompetent. Who is anyone to judge another person unfit for filming? The implications here are chilling, even medieval. Why suggest that Edith Beale at 78 is senile, or that her daughter Edie is not quite all there? The Beales may be eccentric, obsessively individualistic, tormented if you will: and they choose to live in seedy, unorthodox surroundings. But they are not mad.[83]

Here the Maysleses embrace a depathologizing take on the senile recluse. Questioning her mental disorder as much as they question her eccentric reclusion, they turn the tables on moralizing discourses of the "unfit" aged. They remind readers that madness lies in the assessment of the critic, not the renovated bedroom of a Long Island septuagenarian. A subsequent 1986 interview clarified these points. "Then I realised," Albert recollected, "that even making a truthful film, a factual film on old age, will bring the charge of exploitation because people are so sensitive about the issue."[84] One interview question later: "But people who are emotionally immature—who feel insecure about the delicate line, the balance between sanity and insanity, *who feel insecure about getting old*, who feel insecure about rich and poor, of their status, of class status—if they're insecure about all that, then this film becomes very disturbing."[85] Rankling cultural anxieties over socioeconomic status, late life, and mental illness, Maysles interprets *Grey Gardens* in hindsight as a disquieting primer on how to successfully age unsuccessfully. He does not see his film as a textbook case of syllogomania.

I readily concede that no cultural text—particularly a documentary film—is immune from charges of appropriation or voyeurism, but I nevertheless believe that the 1975 film bears out many of the Maysleses' claims. Four select moments from *Grey Gardens* shed light on how the documentary disturbs the evolving discourses of elder insanity that contributed to the popularization of Diogenes syndrome. The first occurs in the film's opening moments. After a brief clip of Beale behind an upstairs banner rail and her daughter worrying that "we'll be raided again by the village of East Hampton," *Grey Gardens* cuts to a montage of pristine mansions that terminates in plant overgrowth covering the Beales' home.[86] This last color image then dissolves into a black-and-white photograph, and viewers find that the Maysleses have filmed a near-identical replica of an earlier newspaper shot that captured Grey Gardens' exteriors. This image, in turn, dissolves into sensational headlines from *East Hampton Star* and *New York Daily News*, a Benson photograph, and a filmed newspaper notice stating that "the Beales are taking part in a motion picture about their life being filmed by David and Albert Maysles ('Salesman,' 'Gimme Shelter')." A black-and-white photograph of the two directors clinches these opening frames. Documenting themselves as part of the Grey Gardens archive, the Maysleses immerse their production in the tales that surround an unsuccessful ager and her daughter, even if they do not confirm them. Given their denials of exploiting senility, it is hard not to read this sequence as another key to understanding the documentary's aims. While their film tracks previous popular discourses of an aged recluse, it literally reframes them from its start. *Grey Gardens* is, in effect, an antiexploitation film that offers an alternative take on sensational representations of old rubbish.

The Maysles brothers confirm this introductory motif when we witness Big Edie's aging body in all of its unkempt, overweight glory. While she sunbathes on her porch, the camera frames her naked back. She wears a white towel around her midriff that leaves her shoulders and cleavage exposed. She is utterly shameless about this state of undress and appears lucid about the social stigma that surrounds geriatric bodies. "Well, I hope—I'm gonna get naked in just a minute, so you better watch out. . . . I haven't got any warts on me. . . . I haven't got any warts on me. . . . I certainly have certain ideas about living a long time. That's what I got ideas about." Beale may be irritable, cantankerous, and ill-tempered throughout *Grey Gardens*, but this does not amount to crazy. Nor does she or the Maysleses treat her person as the epicenter of corporeal or domestic filth. Reading this scene in terms of its fashion politics, film theorist Matthew Tinkcom astutely writes that "Big Edie's presence—bodily and affectively—challenges the claims we might make about eccentricity, mental health, and femininity," and, I would add, senility.[87] Hence later in the film, after her daughter tells her, "Your room is terribly dirty. There's a terrible smell. I can hardly sit here," Big Edie responds, "I love that smell. I thrive on it. Makes me feel good. I'm not ashamed of anything. Where my body is, is a very precious place. It's 'concentrated' ground." One hallmark of elder deviance from *A Manual of Medical Jurisprudence* onward, this lack of shame is not symptomology but what another critic sees as "unembarrassed confidence and stubborn grace."[88] Rooms in supposed shambles, questionable personal hygiene, and negative affective states fail to amount to a discernible senile mental disorder.

This reading applies to Edie's aging things as well. Like the newspaper photograph of Grey Gardens' exterior featured at the film's beginning, the portrait of a young Edith Bouvier Beale displayed in *Paris Match* and the *National Enquirer* also returns in the documentary to play a different role. The painting now lies unhung next to Big Edie's bed, and midway through *Grey Gardens* one of their cats urinates behind it. Edie exclaims with delight that "the cat's going to the bathroom right in back of my portrait." Her daughter corrects her: "God, isn't that awful?" Edie replies: "No, I'm glad he is. I'm glad somebody's doing something they want to do." Similar to their earlier reproduction of Benson's photograph, this filmed portrait signifies on the one published in the weeklies. While it once symbolized cherished possessions gone to seed and Edie's failed senescence given the faded bloom of her youth, the film approaches this emblem of elder *reminiscentia* as an insignificant personal object. It is not, I stress, that Edith is unclear about what is or is not a treasured possession. It is that she couldn't care less about normative elder material relations. In an object culture where "slippage from the accumulation of mementos to the hoarding of meaningless trash . . . is most often considered a sign of mental degeneration among the elderly," Beale establishes her own material standards for an optimal late life.[89]

By doing so, she performs a unique version of *material noncompliance*. This phrase has typically been used within US court systems to impugn inappropriate residential activities such as harboring hazardous waste (landlords cite it in defense of property maintenance). *Noncompliance* also refers to an influential psychodynamic ideal when children refuse to play nice by parental and, by extension, societal standards and lay claim to their particular subjectivity as best they can.[90] I believe that Beale ages this concept and turns a standard feature of rental agreement fine print into late-life praxis. Rather than evidence what a gerontologist would call "lower life satisfaction" or a hoarding expert would term "quality of life impairment," she scorns conventional material standards and stubbornly sidesteps them. This also applies to the documentary as it refutes supposed emblems of senile mental disorder such as "faded pictures, filth and the clutter of their past."[91] Originally conceived as a larger portrait, the film stages a counterexploitation of one elder object world. An unpublished draft version of the Maysleses' *Times* response confirms this last claim. When considering the Beales' "momentos [sic] and memory," the directors write that the two women "have nothing; they only have what is of value to themselves, each other and they thumb their noses at what the rest of us value. That is their strength . . . and 'madness.'"[92]

Lest readers object that I privilege any one item featured in Grey Gardens, I note that the film's unconventional approach to Edie's uncherished keepsakes also applies to her supposed hoard of rubbish. Throughout a good portion of the film, the directors frame her in close-up as she sits, sedentary, in her upstairs bedroom. Yet in the final shot of Beale's body, the camera pans over her mattress to reveal a surplus of plates, blankets, and newspapers and several sleeping cats. It zooms out for a wider shot of her bedroom that pans over empty tissue boxes, a roll of paper towels, fabrics, and her framed portrait. It then cuts to a close-up of a homemade poster-size birthday card from her daughter that reads: "Oct 5th—1973—'Grey Gardens'—At 78 it is true—You can live to be 80 too!" The film does not linger over the stuff that some might consider squalor, and this feels like an ethical gift in contrast to the sensational newspapers referenced at its beginning. Unlike the later HBO production and earlier press portraits, Grey Gardens closes the curtain on an elder sideshow and turns its gaze again to the subject matter of growing old.[93] As it does so, it ends on an annual celebration of a late life that others past and present have denounced as incompetent, mad, creepy, disturbed, unsocial, appalling, and unhygienic.

Granting her daughter's kind wish, Edith Ewing Bouvier Beale did live to see her eightieth year. She died at eighty-one, apparently content with her lot. Her final material life seemed like a full one, if not in the manner often presumed by the current mental diagnosis of extreme clutter. Judging from the examples cited above, it remains difficult for me to conclude that Grey Gardens is a definitive peek into the life of an iconic elder hoarder suffering from Diogenes syndrome. The movie does not show an overstuffed mansion, nor does it record the slow death of a woman suffocating under piles of trash. A lousy example of the hoarding documentary genre, it fails to record Edith Beale as a senile accumulator-recluse. This does not negate the film's later appropriations as a cultural record of squalor disorder. It instead suggests that the film may be more about American culture's ongoing obsession with the social deviance of old age and its attendant material relations. That the film emphasizes the arbitrariness of diagnosing the unsuccessful aged is, without doubt, unsettling, and when scientists, stay-at-home career moms, online doctors, and film geeks cast the documentary as crazy hoarders caught on tape, they would do well to qualify their assessments. In less than two hours of several months' worth of filmed footage, Beale and her daughter slip through the future cracks of a mental diagnosis that envelops them. To paraphrase Little Edie, it is difficult for some hoarding commentators to keep the line between the past and the present.

CONCLUSION: OBJECT OVERGROWTH

In 2006 Maysles Films released *The Beales of Grey Gardens*, a documentary film composed of outtakes from the 1975 original. Minutes before its final credits we find a traumatized Little Edie mulling over recent events behind a screened window. Posted onto YouTube as "Little Edie: On Conformity, East Hampton and Grey Gardens," this scene has become a minor Internet sensation with more than 185,000 hits. To the best of my knowledge, no scientist, social worker, professional organizer, gerontologist, or psychiatrist quotes Edie's words when tackling hoarding disorder. Recorded in the 1970s and uploaded onto the Internet in 2007, the scene speaks to the deep genealogies that contribute to HD. I have tipped my hand on these matters, and so I am happy to give some of my last words to the unmarried, raccoon-feeding, purportedly schizophrenic Little Edie Beale, herself something of an unsuccessful ager when her thoughts were captured on film.

At first blush, her interview with David Maysles has nothing to do with my book. I quote their back-and-forth at some length:

> DAVID MAYSLES: Tell us, what are these plants?
>
> LITTLE EDIE: Trumpet vine. They grew all over the back. They pulled them all down three years ago. They've grown up again. I guess they grow from the ground up. [*Her monologue continues. The camera cuts to two close-ups of trumpet vine blossoms and then back to Edie.*] Eventually everything will grow back. Then they'll rush in, pull it all down again. They do it to everybody. They want everybody to be the same. You can't have anything different. There's great jealousy if you have anything, anything that somebody else—everybody else—hasn't got, you know? Conforming . . .
>
> DM: But you say East Hampton wanted to make you conform?
>
> LE: Well, I think so. I think they did it through this terrible thing of not letting one little flower bloom in this strange place or something. . . . So that's the first thing I heard about what they were doing—to make everything look alike. All places the same. [*The camera again cuts to shots of trumpet vine.*][94]

Neither Beale nor Maysles emphasizes man-made objects in this scene, which screens much like a short nature documentary. Their main concern appears to be the Onassis-funded cleanup of the grounds that included trumpet vine, a perennial also known as trumpet creeper or *Campsis radicans*. A hardy plant that explodes in the summertime with lava-red blossoms, it grows well in the US South and can handle cooler climates such as that of Long Island, New York. Some, like the officials of East Hampton, see it as an invasive weed that must be rooted out, as it was in the summer of 1972 when Grey Gardens faced extensive interior and exterior renovations. Yet when Edie recalls how "they pulled them all down," all you hear is grief in her voice.

As she mourns the cleanup, something curious happens in the closing minutes of *The Beales of Grey Gardens*: quick slippages occur between the vines and then "everything" and then "everybody" and then "anything." When Little Edie talks about these plants, several online viewers have intuited, she is not just talking about trumpet vines. She is also talking about persons such as herself and her mother. She's not the only one. In a diagnosis of homes harboring "the Diogenes syndrome" published as far back as 1981 in the United States, one British expert found that "these houses can always be recognized from the outside by peeling and filthy paintwork, broken windows and unkempt gardens. The squalor inside is usually even worse."[95] Plant overgrowth here becomes indistinguishable from object overgrowth, and someone's grey gardens become a testament to a questionable world of goods. It is a strangely poetic conflation that has done no small amount of harm to those who see a lot of material life and happen to have a lot of things.

To her credit, Edie assails these global systems of material standardization shooting up around her. "They do it to everybody. They want everybody to be the same," she cries. It is unclear who "they" are, but her fury at them is not. "They" could be the Suffolk County Health Department with its threats of eviction. "They" could be reporters eager to catch a glimpse of Jackie's weirdo relatives. "They" could be the nameless crew of knowledge experts who know what's best for an older woman and her middle-aged daughter. What is obvious to Edie is that the vines aren't the takeover; "they" are. A self-trained rubbish theorist, she then takes the particulars of her still-dire situation and applies them to others: "all places the same" also means all things the same. This has come before—post–Great Depression Collyer curiosa, Cold War collectibles gone wild, recluse rubbish in the Me Decade, clutter recovery programs of the 1990s, twenty-first-century diagnoses of HD—and it will come once more. "Then," Edie foreshadows, "they'll rush in, pull it all down again." Pondering the pileup of corrective debris that surrounds her family, Edith Bouvier Beale offers an unsubtle yet poignant critique of the modern psychopathology of material life. She really doesn't want to be fixed. "They" need to respect that.

It sounds odd to close this book with a turn to trumpet vine. But I appreciate the opening that Edie's botanical reimagining gives us, her staunch stance against the encroaching uniformity of stuff. Hers is one instance of material noncompliance in a scientized culture that wants "everybody to be the same." In lieu of making "everything look alike," Beale refuses to reduce the potential biosphere of object diversity into yet another panic over possessions. She instead fantasizes a world where someone can let "one little flower bloom in this strange place."

What goes by hoarding can certainly be harrowing—my childhood terror of the Pack Rat Man attests as much—but it is still important for us to remember that some do allow for stuff to be different, that some find these material lives livable rather than anomalous. I have in mind Warhol's acolytes, the incorrigibles who refuse to clean up after themselves, those who tag the Collyers in delight, the online horticulturalists who transform a YouTube clip into a flourishing greenhouse. "It is [a] movie about flowers, the two most beautiful ones called 'edies,'" posts someone who self-identifies as "sezums."[96] "Like a rare beautiful flower," agrees "BetteDavisMimic," "[who] will only ever be appreciated by a few and understood by even fewer."[97] Another poster, I confess, considers the Beales "loony," and others no doubt agree.[98] This is nothing new at this stage in the diagnostic game, but I have spotlighted a few moments that entertain a different way of thinking about what has come to be known as hoarding disorder. I have not traced those worlds, but they are out there. Like trumpet vine, they continue to thrive in harsh environments.

Having sketched efforts to identify, eradicate, sanitize, and moralize these object worlds, I leave you with a basic premise contrary to the one with which I had to begin: these spaces may not always be completely terrible things. A "terrible thing," to again quote Little Edie, may be the medicalized discourses of hoarding that I made strange across these pages. In 1917 a Russian literary critic called this tried-and-true tactic *ostranenie*, or defamiliarization. Untrained in aesthetic theory, Beale's daughter nevertheless gets at this mode of critique when she calls her personal possessions a flower in a strange place. You can hear Big Edie speaking off screen when Little Edie voices her own version of this criticism, and I find the documentary stirring on this front. In lieu of the freak show of the stereotypical hoarder, the Maysleses once again aim their cameras on the discourses that churn unconventional belongings into fodder for scientific journals, housekeeping guides, blogs, gerontology handbooks, and DSM-5. The directors turn their microphones to those who try to make right the presumed wrongness of someone's personal belongings. Like the Beales, they offer a different take on what can often be a terrible thing.

I have tried, more and less, to do the same with this far from exhaustive book. We all raid Grey Gardens when we pathologize hoarding, so let flora and fauna take back the house in East Hampton. Let trumpet vine grow and raccoons beg for bread. Let Edie soak up her sun, and Homer lie undisturbed next to Langley. Let archivists open Andy's boxes with delight rather than revulsion. Let the other hoards come and go if they please. Look at the peeling paint, the broken windows, the unkempt gardens, the piles and piles not solely with gaping mouths or ogling eyes. Let objects and owners have their quiet, in their peace. It would be nice if these things somehow became less important, more immaterial, not quite so much cause for concern.

NOTE ON METHOD

One of the more frequent questions that people asked me after they heard about the topic of this book—besides whether or not I personally knew any hoarders—was how I culled my archive. My short answer was always "trial and error." Bit by bit, a lead here led to a lead there, one line of inquiry feeding into another after a number of predictable false starts. My guiding principle was to leave no stone unturned. As I wove historical backstories of hoarding disorder in one braided argument, several questions steered my research: What, exactly, are the societal values that make hoarding disreputable? From where do warrants cited by specialists stem? Given that social deviance is thought to lurk in objects, how do we think through the apparent abnormality of these things? Though they are not typically brought into conversation together, three disparate fields of scholarly inquiry—material culture studies, queer studies, and, more implicitly, disability studies—framed my answers. The following paragraphs briefly overview these fields and provide interested readers with suggestions for further reading.

First and foremost, more than three decades of scholarship in material culture studies, or MCS, as some abbreviate it, were instrumental to my analyses. An interdisciplinary field that engages anthropology, art history, literary studies, and American studies (to name but four), material culture studies is principally interested in the cultural definitions of objects. The most prominent formula of this methodological impulse will remain Mary Douglas and Baron Isherwood's 1979 claim in *The World of Goods*: "Instead of supposing that goods are primarily needed for subsistence plus competitive display, let us assume that they are needed for making visible and stable the categories of culture" ([New York: Basic Books, 1979], 59). Sidestepping Marxist readings of commodities as congealed labor and overturning Thorstein Veblen's theory of possessions as conspicuous power plays, Douglas and Isherwood insist that "goods have another important use: they also make and maintain social relationships" (60). Across disciplines, scholars in material culture studies have confirmed Douglas and Isherwood's dictums. Helpful instances include Tim Dant, "Material Civilization: Things and Society," *British Journal of Sociology* 57, no. 2 (2006): 289–308; Dant, *Material Culture in the Social World* (Buckingham, UK: Open University Press, 1999); Stephen Harold Riggins, ed., *The Socialness of Things: Essays on the Socio-semiotics of Objects* (Berlin: Mouton de Gruyter, 1994); Daniel Miller et al., *Shopping, Place, and Identity* (London: Routledge, 1998); Grant McCracken, *Culture and Consumption: New Approaches to the Symbolic Character of Consumer Goods and Activities* (Bloomington: Indiana University Press, 1988); Mihaly Csikszentmihalyi and Eugene Rochberg-Halton, *The Meaning of Things: Domestic Symbols and the Self* (Cambridge: Cambridge University Press, 1981); and Harvey Molotch, *Where Stuff Comes From: How Toasters, Toilets, Cars, Computers, and Many Other Things Come to Be as They Are* (New York: Routledge, 2003).

These works enabled me to better comprehend how hoarded objects rattle social relations and how hoarding often appears to be a culturally bad thing. An offshoot of material culture studies—thing theory—did likewise. Inaugurated by literary and cultural critic Bill Brown, this research program explains, in part, how the materiality of objects dislocates the world of goods. In my treatment, thing theory also asks us to reflect on how and why things and the persons who use them become outlandish, unnatural, or, in the particular case of pathological collecting, supposedly life-threatening. Brown launched this subfield with "Thing Theory," *Critical Inquiry* 28, no. 1 (2001): 1–22, and he has advanced it with essays such as "Object Relations in an Expanded Field," *differences* 17, no. 3 (2006): 88–106. He has been joined by others, including John Frow, "A Pebble, a Camera, a Man Who Turns into a Telegraph Pole," *Critical Inquiry* 28, no. 1 (2001): 270–85; and, especially, John Plotz, "Can the Sofa Speak? A Look at Thing Theory," *Criticism* 47, no. 1 (2005): 109–18. Arjun Appadurai's edited collection *The Social Life of Things: Commodities in Cultural Perspective* (Cambridge: Cambridge University Press, 1986) should be considered a precursor to thing theory, given its introduction's emphasis on how objects go "deviant" as much as they go "normative" (13). Ian Woodward's *Understanding Material Culture* (London: Sage, 2007) can also be considered a complement with its claim that material relations become socially "polluted" or culturally "dangerous" (89).

Alongside thing theorists, other scholars work the edges of material culture studies to discuss how objects potentially sully modern environments. Cultural geographer Tim Edensor's consideration of industrial ruins, for instance, "critically explores the ways in which the material world is normatively ordered" ("Waste Matter: The Debris of Industrial Ruins and the Disordering of the Material World," *Journal of Material Culture* 10, no. 3 [2005]: 311). There he finds that "the materiality of industrial ruins means they are ideally placed to rebuke the normative assignations of objects," and he outlines how "this disordering of a previously regulated space can interrogate normative processes of spatial and material ordering" (314). Edensor examines nonhuman environments to make these claims, but his theories easily apply to extreme accumulators. Analyses in material culture studies that likewise address material disordering include Edensor, *Industrial Ruins: Space, Aesthetics and Materiality* (Oxford: Berg, 2005); Caitlin DeSilvey, "Observed Decay: Telling Stories with Mutable Things," *Journal of Material Culture* 11, no. 3 (2006): 318–38; Judy Attfield, *Wild Things: The Material Culture of Everyday Life* (Oxford: Berg, 2000), on "the prevailing normative sense of order" (153); Victor Buchli, introduction to *The Material Culture Reader*, ed. Buchli (Oxford: Berg, 2002), 1–22; and Julian Stallabrass, *Gargantua: Manufactured Mass Culture* (London: Verso, 1996).

MCS's focus on "normative processes," I was pleased to discover, overlaps with a central interest of queer studies—the roles that perversion and normalization play in our desire for objects of all sorts. An offshoot of lesbian and gay studies, queer studies emerged in the 1990s as scholars sought an interpretive framework that could accommodate a wider array of sexual phenomena beyond those housed under the tent of "lesbian" or "gay." At the same time, the field developed incisive critiques of how social norms inform everyday desires. Principally concerned with matters of sex and sexuality, the field expanded in the decades thereafter to address how sexual norms and their deviations saturate an astonishing range of subject matter: race, religion, gender, class, space, time, nation-state, globalization, and disability.

I gesture to this field's scope in my introduction's citation of Michel Foucault, who is one of its visionaries. In a passage from the first volume of his *History of Sexuality*,

Foucault surveys the widening "world of perversion" that first appeared in the late eighteenth century (*The History of Sexuality*, vol. 1, *An Introduction*, trans. Robert Hurley [New York: Vintage, 1990], 40). He references "children wise beyond their years, precocious little girls, ambiguous schoolboys, dubious servants and educators, cruel or maniacal husbands," and, fundamental for my book, "solitary collectors" (40). That Foucault saw deviant collectors as a modern typology of the dangerous pervert was a telling find for me. Applying his insight to modern American material relations, I was better able to appreciate hoarders as a recent historical addition to what the philosopher referred to as "the numberless family of perverts" under psychiatric and popular review (40).

Making good on this "numberless" headcount, a vein of queer studies has also addressed how social norms structure our desires for material things, and how these desires sometimes stigmatize us as deviant. A good example of this dynamic is Jennifer Terry's observations on "proper objects being sorted from improper objects" in her study of objectùm-sexuality, "a political and cultural formation of people who declare their sexual orientation and love toward objects" ("Loving Objects," *Trans-Humanities* 2, no. 1 [2010]: 61, 34). Other accounts include Sara Ahmed, *Queer Phenomenology: Orientations, Objects, Others* (Durham, NC: Duke University Press, 2006), who ruminates on "queer objects" to consider "the relation between the notion of queer and the disorientation of objects" (91, 160–61); Eve Kosofsky Sedgwick, "Making Things, Practicing Emptiness," in *The Weather in Proust*, ed. Jonathan Goldberg (Durham, NC: Duke University Press, 2011), 69–122; Michael Moon, *Darger's Resources* (Durham, NC: Duke University Press, 2012); Erica Rand, *Barbie's Queer Accessories* (Durham, NC: Duke University Press, 1995); Lucas Hilderbrand, *Inherent Vice: Bootleg Histories of Videotape and Copyright* (Durham, NC: Duke University Press, 2009); Elisa Glick, *Materializing Queer Desire: Oscar Wilde to Andy Warhol* (Albany: SUNY Press, 2009); and Drew Sawyer, "Crisco, or How to Do Queer Theory with Things" (2007), *Thing Theory* (blog), http://www.columbia.edu/ffisf2220/TT2007/web-content/Pages/drew2.html. Together these resources allowed me to further chart the social perversions of everyday material relations as well as how object relations often rely upon a normal-pathological binary.

My observations on the pathology of hoarders and their possessions also found support through disability studies. With its attention to how cultural institutions such as the freak show foster the "need for the containment of 'deviance,'" disability studies matches critiques launched by MCS and queer studies (Sharon L. Snyder and David T. Mitchell, *Cultural Locations of Disability* [Chicago: University of Chicago Press, 2006, 28]). Historically inclined scholars in this field likewise explore how "normalization schemes" are established "to make myriad forms of abnormality visible through the development of disciplines and professions that depend on discovering increasing degrees of human deviance" (7, 23). Given its interest in spectacles of the body and its intricate accounts of intellectual and cognitive disabilities, I found the insights of disability studies foundational for considering supposedly freakish object relations. They let me understand how hoarders and their environments could be presented as culturally specific oddities at the same time that DSM-5 considers this activity a universal mental disorder. Four examples that sparked my thinking on this front included Robert Bogdan, *Freak Show:*

Presenting Human Oddities for Amusement and Profit (Chicago: University of Chicago Press, 1990); Rosemarie Garland Thomson, ed., *Freakery: Cultural Spectacles of the Extraordinary Body* (New York: New York University Press, 1996); Rachel Adams, *Sideshow U.S.A.: Freaks and the American Cultural Imagination* (Chicago: University of Chicago Press, 2001); and Margaret Price, "Defining Mental Disability," in *The Disability Studies Reader*, ed. Lennard J. Davis, 4th ed. (New York: Routledge, 2013), 298–307.

Together these specialized fields—material culture studies, queer studies, and disability studies—created a valuable frame for historically assessing DSM-5 folk devils and the many eccentric accumulators who came before them. It is my wish that cross-disciplinary approaches such as *The Hoarders* prove useful for future research into the diversity of material relations as well as our varied responses to the wide world of goods.

NOTES

Introduction

Parts of this introduction were first published in *Postmodern Culture* 21, no. 2 (2011).

1. Karen Weintraub, "He Makes Study of Hoarding," *Boston Globe*, November 14, 2011, accessed January 17, 2013, http://www.bostonglobe.com/lifestyle/health-wellness/2011/11/14/makes-study-hoarding/7TgQCpRNPM4kOcvBDAGrcK/story.html.

2. Randy Frost, "Clutter Gone Wild," *Smith Alumnae Quarterly* 93, no. 2 (2006–7): 22.

3. Randy Frost, e-mail message, February 28, 2012; cf. Randy O. Frost and Gail Steketee, *Stuff: Compulsive Hoarding and the Meaning of Things* (Boston: Houghton Mifflin Harcourt, 2010), 10.

4. Randy O. Frost and Rachel C. Gross, "The Hoarding of Possessions," *Behaviour Research and Therapy* 31, no. 4 (1993): 367. The APA rephrases this definition as "persistent difficulty discarding or parting with possessions, regardless of their actual value," in American Psychiatric Association, *Diagnostic and Statistical Manual of Mental Disorders*, 5th ed. [DSM-5] (Washington, DC: American Psychiatric Publishing, 2013), 247.

5. Frost and Steketee, *Stuff*, 37.

6. Loïc J. D. Wacquant, "Toward a Social Praxeology: The Structure and Logic of Bourdieu's Sociology," in Pierre Bourdieu and Loïc J. D. Wacquant, *An Invitation to Reflexive Sociology* (Chicago: University of Chicago Press, 1992), 40.

7. The article in reference is David F. Tolin et al., "Neural Mechanisms of Decision Making in Hoarding Disorder," *Archives of General Psychiatry* 69, no. 8 (2012): 832–41. Online citations of this piece include Alan Mozes, "Brain Scans of 'Hoarders' Show Unique Abnormalities," *Yahoo!News*, August 7, 2012, accessed January 17, 2013, now defunct, http://news.yahoo.com/brain-scans-hoarders-show-unique-abnormalities-200907541.html. For criticisms of fMRI, see Kelly A. Joyce, *Magnetic Appeal: MRI and the Myth of Transparency* (Ithaca, NY: Cornell University Press, 2008), and Joseph Dumit, *Picturing Personhood: Brain Scans and Biomedical Identity* (Princeton, NJ: Princeton University Press, 2004).

8. Allan V. Horwitz, *Creating Mental Illness* (Chicago: University of Chicago Press, 2002), 33. Other critiques of DSM discourses include Allan V. Horwitz and Jerome C. Wakefield, *The Loss of Sadness: How Psychiatry Transformed Normal Sorrow into Depressive Disorder* (Oxford: Oxford University Press, 2007); Herb Kutchins and Stuart A. Kirk, *Making Us Crazy: DSM: The Psychiatric Bible and the Creation of Mental Disorders* (New York: Free Press, 1997); Gary Greenberg, *The Book of Woe: The DSM and the Unmaking of Psychiatry* (New York: Blue Rider, 2013), especially his claim that "Hoarding Disorder is another line carved in the sand, a diagnosis that will no doubt be the object of scorn for the leaders of the DSM-6 and DSM-7" (221); and Judith Butler, *Undoing Gender* (New York: Routledge, 2004), 75–101.

9. Yuval Melamed et al., "Hoarding—What Does It Mean?" *Comprehensive Psychiatry* 39, no. 6 (1998): 400, 402.

10. David Mataix-Cols et al., "Hoarding Disorder: A New Diagnosis for DSM-V?" *Depression and Anxiety* 27, no. 6 (2010): 566.

11. David F. Tolin, Randy O. Frost, and Gail Steketee, "An Open Trial of Cognitive-

Behavioral Therapy for Compulsive Hoarding," *Behaviour Research and Therapy* 45, no. 7 (2007): 1462.

12. Mataix-Cols et al., "Hoarding Disorder," 566.

13. V. Holland LaSalle-Ricci et al., "The Hoarding Dimension of OCD: Psychological Comorbidity and the Five-Factor Personality Model," *Behaviour Research and Therapy* 44, no. 10 (2006): 1503.

14. Popular accounts do likewise. One online *Atlantic* article deems hoarding an "unsanitary deviancy" and a paragraph later senses that "it's time for hoarding to take its rightful place as a defined mental disorder" (Lindsay Abrams, "'Hoarders': From a TV Spectacle to a Newly Defined Psychiatric Condition," *Atlantic*, August 10, 2012, accessed January 15, 2013, http://www.theatlantic.com/health/archive/2012/08/hoarders-from-a-tv-spectacle-to-a-newly-defined-psychiatric-condition/260997/).

15. Fabio Gygi, "Hoarding and Disposal in Tokyo," *Material World* (blog), December 19, 2006, accessed November 22, 2010, http://www.materialworldblog.com/2006/12/hoarding-and-disposal-in-tokyo/. Other critical accounts of hoarding as deviance include Marybeth C. Stalp, "Hiding the (Fabric) Stash: Collecting, Hoarding, and Hiding Strategies of Contemporary US Quilters," *Textile* 4, no. 1 (2006): 104–24; Kenneth J. Weiss, "Hoarding, Hermitage, and the Law: Why We Love the Collyer Brothers," *Journal of the American Academy of Psychiatry and the Law* 38, no. 2 (2010): 251–57; Patrick W. Moran, "An Obsession with Plenitude: The Aesthetics of Hoarding in *Finnegans Wake*," *James Joyce Quarterly* 46, no. 2 (2009): 285–304; Neil Maycroft, "Not Moving Things Along: Hoarding, Clutter and Other Ambiguous Matter," *Journal of Consumer Behavior* 8, no. 6 (2009): 354–64, on "material disorder" (361); Susan Lepselter, "The Disorder of Things: Hoarding Narratives in Popular Media," *Anthropological Quarterly* 84, no. 4 (2011): 919–47; Stephanie Foote and Elizabeth Mazzolini, eds., *Histories of the Dustheap: Waste, Material Cultures, Social Justice* (Cambridge, MA: MIT Press, 2012), 254–57, on the "pathology of the individual hoarder" (255); and Jane Bennett, "Powers of the Hoard: Further Notes on Material Agency," in *Animal, Vegetable, Mineral: Ethics and Objects*, ed. Jeffrey Jerome Cohen (Washington, DC: Oliphaunt, 2012), 237–69, who cautions studies of hoarding to "resist the frame of psychopathology" (244).

16. Arnold Arluke, "Inside Animal Hoarding," in Arluke and Celeste Killeen, *Inside Animal Hoarding: The Case of Barbara Erickson and Her 552 Dogs* (West Lafayette, IN: Purdue University Press, 2009), 219, 216. Arluke's sociological account entertains hoarding as a social construct at the same time that it confirms it as a psychiatric disease.

17. Susan M. Pearce, *On Collecting: An Investigation into Collecting in the European Tradition* (London: Routledge, 1995), 194. For more on the pathologization of collecting, see Susan M. Pearce, "The Urge to Collect," in *Interpreting Objects and Collections*, ed. Pearce (London: Routledge, 1994), 157–59; Russell W. Belk, *Collecting in a Consumer Society* (London: Routledge, 1995), who finds with respect to individuals cast as hoarders that "it is doubtful that most of them think of their collecting as truly deviant" (141–42); Leah Dilworth, introduction to *Acts of Possession: Collecting in America*, ed. Dilworth (New Brunswick, NJ: Rutgers University Press, 2003), on how hoarding is capable of "revealing cultural anxi-

eties about commodification, representation, and desire itself" (8); and Sara Knox, "The Serial Killer as Collector," in *Acts of Possession*, 286–302.

18. Franz Lidz, "The Paper Chase," *New York Times*, October 26, 2003, 9.

19. Gail Steketee and Randy Frost, "Compulsive Hoarding: Current Status of the Research," *Clinical Psychology Review* 23, no. 7 (2003): 905.

20. Stanley Cohen, *Folk Devils and Moral Panics: The Creation of the Mods and Rockers* (1972; repr., New York: St. Martin's, 1980), 9; hereafter cited in text.

21. Stanley Cohen, "Moral Panics as Cultural Politics: Introduction to the Third Edition," in Cohen, *Folk Devils and Moral Panics: The Creation of the Mods and Rockers*, Routledge Classics (London: Routledge, 2002), xxvii.

22. Ibid., vii–viii.

23. Ibid., xliii.

24. Mary Douglas, *Purity and Danger: An Analysis of Concepts of Pollution and Taboo*, Routledge Classics (1966; London: Routledge, 2002), 44; hereafter cited in text.

25. Abrams, "Hoarders"; Carina Chocano, "Underneath Every Hoarder Is a Normal Person Waiting to Be Dug Out," *New York Times Magazine*, June 19, 2011, MM52.

26. Michel Foucault, *Abnormal: Lectures at the Collège de France, 1974–1975*, ed. Valerio Marchetti and Antonella Salomoni, trans. Graham Burchell (New York: Picador, 2003), 38.

27. Ibid., 34. See also Mira Engler, *Designing America's Waste Landscapes* (Baltimore: Johns Hopkins University Press, 2004), for an analysis of Foucault's "Heterotopias of Deviation" that "contain and control all social perversions" (35).

28. Ibid., 34.

29. By "object culture," I reference Bill Brown's definition—"the objects through which a culture constitutes itself, which is to say, too, culture as it is objectified in material forms" ("Objects, Others, and Us [The Refabrication of Things]," *Critical Inquiry* 36, no. 2 [2010]: 188).

30. Chocano, "Underneath Every Hoarder," MM52.

31. Ibid.

32. See Ian Woodward, *Understanding Material Culture* (London: Sage, 2007), 167; and Lizabeth A. Cohen, "Embellishing a Life of Labor: An Interpretation of the Material Culture of American Working-Class Homes, 1885–1915," in *Material Culture Studies in America*, ed. Thomas J. Schlereth (Lanham, MD: AltaMira, 1999), 289–305, for more on domestic material culture.

33. "Jennifer and Ron/Jill," August 17, 2009, episode of *Hoarders*, DVD (A&E; Screaming Flea Productions, 2009); all quotations from episode cited in text.

34. Suzanne A. Chabaud, "The Hidden Lives of Children of Hoarders," *Psychiatric Times*, November 10, 2011, accessed July 4, 2013, http://www.psychiatrictimes.com/obsessive-compulsive-disorder/hidden-lives-children-hoarders.

35. Fugen Neziroglu, Jill Slavin, and Katharine Donnelly, "How Compulsive Hoarding Affects Families," *Children of Hoarders*, n.d., accessed July 30, 2013, http://childrenofhoarders.com/wordpress/?page_id=1266.

36. Michel Foucault, *The History of Sexuality*, vol. 1, *An Introduction*, trans. Robert Hurley (New York: Vintage, 1990), 67.

37. Weiss, "Hoarding," discusses some of these diagnoses and finds that "hoarding is usually referred to as compulsive hoarding or syllogomania, thus begging the question of nomenclature" (252).

38. For critical examinations of obsessive-compulsive disorder as a cultural and historical phenomenon, see Lennard J. Davis, *Obsession: A History* (Chicago: University of Chicago Press, 2008); and Jennifer L. Fleissner, "Obsessional Modernity: The 'Institutionalization of Doubt,'" *Critical Inquiry* 34, no. 1 (2007): 106–34. For comparative studies of mental disorders, see Christopher Lane, *Shyness: How Normal Behavior Became a Sickness* (New Haven, CT: Yale University Press, 2007); Jackie Orr, *Panic Diaries: A Genealogy of Panic Disorder* (Durham, NC: Duke University Press, 2006); David Healy, *Mania: A Short History of Bipolar Disorder* (Baltimore: Johns Hopkins University Press, 2011); Emily Martin, *Bipolar Expeditions: Mania and Depression in American Culture* (Princeton, NJ: Princeton University Press, 2007); Ian Hacking, *Rewriting the Soul: Multiple Personality and the Sciences of Memory* (Princeton, NJ: Princeton University Press, 1995); Allan Young, *The Harmony of Illusions: Inventing Post-traumatic Stress Disorder* (Princeton, NJ: Princeton University Press, 1997); and Jonathan M. Metzl, *The Protest Psychosis: How Schizophrenia Became a Black Disease* (Boston: Beacon, 2009). For more on the intricacies of constructivist arguments for mental illness, see Ian Hacking, *The Social Construction of What?* (Cambridge, MA: Harvard University Press, 1999), 100–124.

39. Igor Kopytoff best promotes this phrase via "The Cultural Biography of Things: Commoditization as Process," in *The Social Life of Things: Commodities in Cultural Perspective*, ed. Arjun Appadurai (Cambridge: Cambridge University Press, 1986), 64–91.

40. Craig Calhoun and Richard Sennett, introduction to *Practicing Culture*, ed. Calhoun and Sennett (London: Routledge, 2007), 1.

41. Frost and Steketee, *Stuff*, 62. See also "Hoarders All Over the Globe?" *Hoardhouse Blog*, January 13, 2009, accessed July 31, 2013, http://blog.hoardhouse.com/2009/01/13/hoarders-all-over-the-globe/, on the "deviant use of space and stuff" in European nation-states.

42. Some international accounts of hoarding include Paul B. Fitzgerald, "'The Bowerbird Symptom': A Case of Severe Hoarding of Possessions," *Australian and New Zealand Journal of Psychiatry* 31, no. 4 (1997): 597–600; Peter Subkowski, "On the Psychodynamics of Collecting," *International Journal of Psychoanalysis* 87, no. 2 (2006): 383–401, on "messy syndrome" in Germany (385); and Jen-Ping Hwang et al., "Hoarding Behavior in Dementia: A Preliminary Report," *American Journal of Geriatric Psychiatry* 6, no. 4 (1998): 285–89, whose research is based at Taipei Veterans General Hospital in Taiwan. For a general overview of how US-based mental disorders have become a psycho-empire, see Ethan Watters, *Crazy like Us: The Globalization of the American Psyche* (New York: Free Press, 2010).

43. Harriet Schechter, *Let Go of Clutter* (New York: McGraw-Hill, 2001), 11.

44. Zygmunt Bauman, *Consuming Life* (Cambridge: Polity, 2007), 124. Further analyses of hoarding and consumption studies include Hélène Cherrier and Tresa Ponnor, "A Study of Hoarding Behavior and Attachment to Material Possessions," *Qualitative Market*

Research 13, no. 1 (2010): 8–23; and Don Ross, "Addictive, Impulsive, and Other Counternormative Consumption," in *Handbook of Developments in Consumer Behavior*, ed. Victoria Wells and Gordon Foxall (Northampton, MA: Edward Elgar, 2012), 323–60.

45. A sharp overview of these paradigm shifts is Nikolas Rose and Joelle M. Abi-Rached, *Neuro: The New Brain Sciences and the Management of the Mind* (Princeton, NJ: Princeton University Press, 2013). See, especially, 110–40 for critiques of "neuropsychiatry" (111).

46. A smattering of scientific essays includes Jane N. Nathanson, "Animal Hoarding: Slipping into the Darkness of Comorbid Animal and Self-Neglect," *Journal of Elder Abuse and Neglect* 21, no. 4 (2009): 307–24, that describes its topic as "a deviant behavior" (307); Gary J. Patronek, "Hoarding of Animals: An Under-Recognized Public Health Problem in a Difficult-to-Study Population," *Public Health Reports* 114, no. 1 (1999): 81–87; and Randy O. Frost, Gary Patronek, and Elizabeth Rosenfield, "Comparison of Object and Animal Hoarding," *Depression and Anxiety* 28, no. 10 (2011): 885–91.

47. American Psychiatric Association, DSM-5, 249.

48. Randy O. Frost, Gail Steketee, and David F. Tolin, "Diagnosis and Assessment of Hoarding Disorder," *Annual Review of Clinical Psychology* 8 (2012): 231.

49. Frost and Steketee, *Stuff*, 269. DSM-5 also states a version of this line.

50. Fernand Braudel, *Capitalism and Material Life, 1400–1800*, trans. Miriam Kochan (1967; New York: Harper and Row, 1973), xii.

51. In *Contagious Divides: Epidemics and Race in San Francisco's Chinatown* (Berkeley: University of California Press, 2001), historian Nayan Shah notes that "the concept of the standard of living traveled from economic spheres to cultural and social spheres to become both the aspiration and judgment of lives and social environment" (253).

52. Marina Moskowitz, *Standard of Living: The Measure of the Middle Class in Modern America* (Baltimore: Johns Hopkins University Press, 2004), 7. I take this list from Moskowitz, who overviews the historical invention of "standard of living" as it applies to modern notions of material culture not as "the pinnacle of material life" but as "a high degree of comfort" (11).

53. W. H. Auden, Untitled ("The friends of the born nurse"), in *The English Auden: Poems, Essays and Dramatic Writings, 1927–1939*, ed. Edward Mendelson (London: Faber and Faber, 1977), 51, lines 1–2. Quoted in Adam Philips, *Going Sane: Maps of Happiness* (New York: Fourth Estate, 2005), 189–90.

54. I cull this insight from Jonathan M. Metzl and Anna Kirkland, *Against Health: How Health Became the New Morality* (New York: New York University Press, 2010). See also John Scanlan, *On Garbage* (London: Reaktion, 2005), for readings of "material disorder" (43) whereby "hoarding . . . is considered to be indicative of a general dissoluteness that can extend into a tendency to neglect other important parts of life" (173).

55. William Davies King, *Collections of Nothing* (Chicago: University of Chicago Press, 2008), 160, 91.

56. "Kerrylea/Lauren," September 14, 2009, episode of *Hoarders*, DVD (A&E; Screaming Flea Productions, 2009).

57. "Linda/Todd," January 11, 2010, episode of *Hoarders*, DVD (A&E; Screaming Flea Productions, 2010).

Chapter 1

Unless otherwise noted, all citations from US newspapers regarding the Collyer brothers are from The Collyer Brothers (Homer and Langley): A Collection of Newspaper Clippings, 1937–1962, microform, reel 1 (New York: New York Public Library, 1984). Portions of this chapter were originally published as "Collyer Curiosa: A Brief History of Hoarding," Criticism 53, no. 2 (2011): 159–88.

1. Harold Faber, "Homer Collyer, Harlem Recluse, Found Dead at 70," New York Times, March 22, 1947, 1. See also Fred Penzel, "Langley Collyer: The Mystery Hoarder of Harlem," Western Suffolk Psychological Services (WSPS) website, n.d., accessed June 4, 2011, http://www.wsps.info/index.php?option=com_content&view=article&id=72:langley -collyer-the-mystery-hoarder-of-harlem&catid=0.

2. Randy O. Frost and Gail Steketee, Stuff: Compulsive Hoarding and the Meaning of Things (New York: Houghton Mifflin Harcourt, 2010), 269.

3. Tara Parker-Pope, "A Clutter Too Deep for Mere Bins and Shelves," New York Times, January 1, 2008, F5.

4. Gail Steketee and Randy Frost, "Compulsive Hoarding: Current Status of the Research," Clinical Psychology Review 23, no. 7 (2003): 907.

5. American Psychiatric Association, Diagnostic and Statistical Manual of Mental Disorders, 5th ed. [DSM-5] (Washington, DC: American Psychiatric Publishing, 2013), 248.

6. Dante Alighieri, The Divine Comedy: "The Inferno," "The Purgatorio," and "The Paradiso," trans. John Ciardi (New York: New American Library, 2003), 52, line 56. I note that hoarding experts use this passage to justify the universalism of hoarders. See "From Dante to DSM-V: A Short History of Hoarding," International OCD Foundation (IOCDF)- Hoarding Center website, n.d., accessed June 11, 2011, http://www.ocfoundation.org/ hoarding/dante_to_dsm-v.aspx.

7. Oxford English Dictionary, s.v. "hoarding," accessed January 8, 2010, http://www .oed.com.

8. Penzel, "Langley Collyer."

9. For more on the scientific use of transhistoricism to legitimize mental diseases, see Christopher Lane, Shyness: How Normal Behavior Became a Sickness (New Haven, CT: Yale University Press, 2007), 14–16.

10. Quoted in Jane Collingwood, "The Genetics of Compulsive Hoarding," Psych Central, September 21, 2009, accessed January 15, 2010, http://psychcentral.com/lib/2009/ the-genetics-of-compulsive-hoarding. See also Sanjaya Saxena, "Is Compulsive Hoarding a Genetically and Neurobiologically Discrete Syndrome? Implications for Diagnostic Classification," American Journal of Psychiatry 164, no. 3 (2007): 380–84; and Saxena et al., "Cerebral Glucose Metabolism in Obsessive-Compulsive Hoarding," American Journal of Psychiatry 161, no. 6 (2004): 1038–48.

11. Collingwood, "Genetics of Compulsive Hoarding"; quote attributed to Randy Frost.

12. David F. Tolin et al., "Family Burden of Compulsive Hoarding: Results of an Internet Survey," Behaviour Research and Therapy 46, no. 3 (2008): 335.

13. See but two instances in David Greenberg, "Compulsive Hoarding," American Jour-

nal of Psychotherapy 41, no. 3 (1987): 409–16; and David Greenberg, Eliezer Witztum, and Amihay Levy, "Hoarding as a Psychiatric Symptom," Journal of Clinical Psychiatry 51, no. 10 (1990): 417–21.

14. Ernest Jones, "Anal-Erotic Character Traits" (1918), in Papers on Psycho-analysis, 5th ed. (London: Baillière, Tindall and Cox, 1950), 431.

15. Ibid.

16. Sigmund Freud, "Character and Anal Eroticism" (1908), in The Standard Edition of the Complete Psychological Works of Sigmund Freud, trans. James Strachey, 24 vols. (London: Hogarth, 1959), 9:169.

17. Ibid., 172–73.

18. Mary Douglas, Purity and Danger: An Analysis of Concepts of Pollution and Taboo, Routledge Classics (1966; repr., New York: Routledge, 2002), 44; hereafter cited in text.

19. Jani Scandura, Down in the Dumps: Place, Modernity, American Depression (Durham, NC: Duke University Press, 2008), 165.

20. William James, The Principles of Psychology, vol. 2 (1890; repr., New York: Dover, 1950), 424, 425. James's earlier version of these thoughts appeared as "Some Human Instincts," Popular Science Monthly 31, no. 37 (1887): 666–81.

21. For two examples that elide links between Harlem and the Collyers in their retelling of the brothers' demise, see Franz Lidz, Ghosty Men: The Strange but True Story of the Collyer Brothers, New York's Greatest Hoarders (New York: Bloomsbury, 2003); and Frost and Steketee, Stuff, 1–15.

22. Mik Awake, "Harlemitis," New York Inquirer, November 16, 2006, accessed January 29, 2010, now defunct, http://www.nyinquirer.com/nyinquirer/waste/.

23. For more on these characterizations, see Elizabeth Wilson, The Sphinx in the City: Urban Life, the Control of Disorder, and Women (Berkeley: University of California Press, 1991), 78–82. Necessary counters to this narrative include James Weldon Johnson, who states that Harlem "is not a slum or a fringe" ("The Making of Harlem," Survey Graphic 6, no. 6 [1925]: 635); and Clare Corbould, "Streets, Sounds, and Identity in Interwar Harlem," Journal of Social History 40, no. 4 (2007): 859–94.

24. Robert E. Park, "The Growth of the City: An Introduction to a Research Project," in The City: Suggestions for Investigation of Human Behavior in the Urban Environment, ed. Robert E. Park, Ernest W. Burgess, and Robert D. McKenzie (1925; repr., Chicago: University of Chicago Press, 1984), 54. Exceptions to this urban maladjustment model include David Slight, who finds that "changes called disorganization in one generation are often heralded in the next as steps towards a better arrangement of society" ("Disorganization in the Individual and Society," American Journal of Sociology 42, no. 6 [1937]: 844).

25. Mabel A. Elliott and Francis E. Merrill, Social Disorganization (New York: Harper and Brothers, 1934), 8, 25, 589, 592, 596.

26. E. Franklin Frazier, The Negro Family in the United States, African American Intellectual Heritage (Chicago: University of Chicago Press, 1939), 322. A selection of disorganization proponents in relation to African American urban life in the 1930s and 1940s includes Robert E. L. Faris, Social Disorganization (New York: Ronald, 1948), on high rates of disorganization in "Negro districts" like Harlem (229); Stuart Alfred Queen,

Walter Blaine Bodenhafer, and Ernest Bouldin Harper, *Social Organization and Disorganiza-tion* (New York: Crowell, 1935), on the disorganizing factors of "Negro communities in cities" (243); and Richard Wright, *12 Million Black Voices* (1941; repr., New York: Thunder's Mouth, 1992).

27. Gilbert Osofsky, *Harlem: The Making of a Ghetto—Negro New York, 1890–1930* (New York: Harper and Row, 1963), 150.

28. See, for example, Alexis de Tocqueville, *Democracy in America*, vol. 1, ed. Isaac Kramnick, trans. Henry Reeve (1835; repr., New York: Norton, 2007), on his claim that "the lower orders which inhabit these cities [Philadelphia and New York] constitute a rabble even more formidable than the populace of European towns" (236). By "rabble," de Tocqueville refers to both "freed blacks" and "a multitude of Europeans who have been driven to the shores of the New World by their misfortunes or their misconduct" (236). For more on specious links between Harlem and disorder during the 1930s and 1940s, see Scandura, *Down in the Dumps*, 168–73.

29. William I. Thomas and Florian Znaniecki, *The Polish Peasant in Europe and America: A Classic Work in Immigration History*, ed. Eli Zaretsky (Urbana: University of Illinois Press, 1984), 191; hereafter cited in text.

30. Eli Zaretsky, editor's introduction to ibid., 4.

31. Osofsky, *Harlem*, 127.

32. Ibid., 105.

33. Notes Osofsky: "The most profound change that Harlem experienced in the 1920's was its emergence as a slum. Largely within the space of a single decade Harlem was transformed from a potentially ideal community to a neighborhood with manifold social and economic problems called 'deplorable,' 'unspeakable,' 'incredible'" (135). Osofsky dates this historical emergence to the 1920s, but its representational emergence as a site of disorganization continued well into the 1930s and 1940s.

34. Elliott and Merrill, *Social Disorganization*, 596.

35. Scandura, *Down in the Dumps*, 172.

36. *Quasi-white* references the uneven historical identifications of Irish migrants as whites during the late nineteenth and early twentieth centuries, a process discussed in Matthew Frye Jacobson, *Whiteness of a Different Color: European Immigrants and the Alchemy of Race* (Cambridge, MA: Harvard University Press, 1998), 43–56.

37. *Oxford English Dictionary*, s.v. "condition," accessed February 8, 2010, http://www .oed.com. Foucault antedates this etymology in the span 1860–70 in *Abnormal: Lectures at the Collège de France, 1974–1975*, ed. Valerio Marchetti and Antonella Salomoni (New York: Picador, 2003), 312.

38. Ralph Kramer, "The Conceptual Status of Social Disorganization," *American Jour-nal of Sociology* 48, no. 4 (1943): 470.

39. Quoted in Harold Faber, "Police Fail to Find Collyer in House," *New York Times*, March 25, 1947, 35.

40. Lidz, *Ghosty Men*, 155.

41. Faber, "Homer Collyer, Harlem Recluse," 3.

42. See Thomas W. Kim, "Being Modern: The Circulation of Oriental Objects," *American Quarterly* 58, no. 2 (2006): 379–406, on the early twentieth-century infatuation with consumer objects and curios from Asia, one whose Orientalist "symptoms" operate today (403).

43. Russell Owen, "Something for O. Henry: Story of the Collyers," *New York Times*, March 30, 1947, E10.

44. "Langley Collyer Is Dead, Police Say," *New York Times*, March 27, 1947, 56.

45. *Oxford English Dictionary*, s.v. "curio," accessed February 26, 2010, http://www.oed .com.

46. Patrick Mauriès, *Cabinets of Curiosities* (London: Thames and Hudson, 2002), 111. I borrow my history in this paragraph and the next from Mauriès (50–55). Further accounts of early modern cabinets of curiosity include Steven Mullaney, "Strange Things, Gross Terms, Curious Customs: The Rehearsal of Cultures in the Late Renaissance," *Representations* 3 (1983): 40–67; Russell W. Belk, *Collecting in a Consumer Society* (London: Routledge, 1995); and Umberto Eco, *The Infinity of Lists*, trans. Alastair McEwen (New York: Rizzoli, 2009), 201–9.

47. For more on this *Americana* collecting, see Peter Mason, "From Presentation to Representation: *Americana* in Europe," *Journal of the History of Collections* 6, no. 1 (1994): 1–20.

48. Anthony Alan Shelton, "Cabinets of Transgression: Renaissance Collections and the Incorporation of the New World," in *The Cultures of Collecting*, ed. John Elsner and Roger Cardinal (London: Reaktion, 1994), 199.

49. Ibid., 185. See also Isabel Yaya, "Wonders of America: The Curiosity Cabinet as a Site of Representation and Knowledge," *Journal of the History of Collections* 20, no. 2 (2008): 173–88.

50. For one example of this line of historical thinking, see Joyce Henri Robinson, "An American Cabinet of Curiosities: Thomas Jefferson's 'Indian Hall' at Monticello," in *Acts of Possession: Collecting in America*, ed. Leah Dilworth (New Brunswick, NJ: Rutgers University Press, 2003), 16–41.

51. See Zoe Trodd, "Waste and *Wunderkammern*: Recycling the American Cabinet of Curiosities," *Verb* 4, no. 1 (2006): 1–15, on relationships between wonder cabinets and World's Fairs; and Shirley Teresa Wajda, "'And a Little Child Shall Lead Them': American Children's Cabinets of Curiosities," in *Acts of Possession*, ed. Dilworth, 42–65, on an updated cabinet of curiosities in 1930s *Popular Mechanics* magazine.

52. Mason, "From Presentation to Representation," 7. See also Belk, *Collecting in a Consumer Society*, 10–21, for more on the distribution of the curiosity cabinet into late modern consumer cultures of "familiar everyday consumer goods" (21); Stephen Calloway with Katherine Sorrell, *Obsessions: Collectors and Their Passions* (London: Mitchell Beazley, 2004), 20, 54–57; and Bill Brown, *A Sense of Things: The Object Matter of American Literature* (Chicago: University of Chicago Press, 2004), 87.

53. See Steven M. Gelber, *Hobbies: Leisure and the Culture of Work in America* (New York: Columbia University Press, 1999), on how "household display cabinets" continued col-

lecting practices inherent in curiosity cabinets (65). For a brief overview of modern cabinets as they facilitated "the advancement of culture" (64), see Rémy G. Saisselin, *The Bourgeois and the Bibelot* (New Brunswick, NJ: Rutgers University Press, 1984).

54. For a history of the catalog, see Boris Emmet and John E. Jeuck, *Catalogues and Counters: A History of Sears, Roebuck and Company* (Chicago: University of Chicago Press, 1950).

55. James Clifford, *The Predicament of Culture: Twentieth-Century Ethnography, Literature, and Art* (Cambridge, MA: Harvard University Press, 1988), 219.

56. *Oxford English Dictionary*, s.v. "curiosa," accessed February 29, 2010, http://www.oed.com.

57. Faber, "Police Fail," 27.

58. "Collyer Mansion Yields Junk, Cats," *New York Times*, March 26, 1947, 27.

59. Stephen Kellett et al., "Compulsive Hoarding: An Interpretative Phenomenological Analysis," *Behavioural and Cognitive Psychotherapy* 38, no. 2 (2010): 150.

60. Scandura, *Down in the Dumps*, 163.

61. See Coleman O. Parsons, "Studies in Eccentricity," unpublished ms., n.d., box 7, Coleman O. Parsons Papers, Rare Book and Manuscript Library, Columbia University, New York City.

62. "Inside the Collyer Brownstone: The Story of Harlem's Hermits and Their Hoarding," *New York Daily News*, October 19, 2012, accessed October 31, 2012, http://www.nydailynews.com/new-york/collyer-brothers-brownstone-gallery-1.1187698.

63. Rosemarie Garland Thomson, "Introduction: From Wonder to Error—A Genealogy of Freak Discourse in Modernity," in *Freakery: Cultural Spectacles of the Extraordinary Body*, ed. Garland Thomson (New York: New York University Press, 1996), 2.

64. For an account of this purchase, see "200 Bid Spiritedly for Collyer Items," *New York Times*, June 11, 1947, 54.

65. "The Shy Men," *Time*, April 7, 1947, 28.

66. Ibid.

67. Ibid., 29.

68. All citations of Marcia Davenport can be found in *My Brother's Keeper* (New York: Scribner's, 1954); hereafter cited in text.

69. Jens Jensen, "Collector's Mania," *Acta Psychiatrica Scandinavica* 39, no. 4 (1963): 612.

70. Ibid., 606. We also find references to "the Midas complex"—"adults who are constantly collecting objects, unwilling to relinquish objects, unable to throw them away"—in Emanuel K. Schwartz and Alexander Wolf, "The Quest for Certainty," *Archives of Neurology and Psychiatry* 81, no. 1 (1959): 79. References to hoarding and accumulating as psychic aberrations likewise appear in Henry P. Laughlin, *The Neuroses in Clinical Practice* (Philadelphia: W. B. Saunders, 1956), 198–201; and Richard H. Phillips, "The Accumulator," *Archives of General Psychiatry* 6, no. 6 (1962): 474–77.

71. Jensen, "Collector's Mania," 607.

72. Wayne Glowka et al., "Among the New Words," *American Speech* 79, no. 3 (2004): s.v. "Collyer," 307.

73. Nina Bernstein, "So Much Clutter, So Little Room: Looking inside the Hoarder's Lair," *New York Times*, December 31, 2003, B1.

74. David F. Tolin, Randy O. Frost, and Gail Steketee, *Buried in Treasures: Help for Compulsive Acquiring, Saving, and Hoarding* (New York: Oxford University Press, 2007), 8.

75. Ibid., 3.

Chapter 2

1. A corresponding account of Warhol's estate and its sale can be found in Richard Hellinger, "The Museum Archives," in *The Andy Warhol Museum*, comp. Andy Warhol Museum (New York: Distributed Art, 1994), 195. A corresponding analysis of the auction as "hysterical" can be found in Brenda Danet and Tamar Katriel, "No Two Alike: Play and Aesthetics in Collecting," in *Interpreting Objects and Collecting*, ed. Susan M. Pearce (London: Routledge, 1994), 222.

2. Rita Reif, "Warhol's World on View: Gems and Cookie Jars," *New York Times*, April 15, 1988, C1.

3. Cathleen McGuigan, "The Selling of Andy Warhol," *Newsweek*, April 18, 1988, 60.

4. Ibid., 62.

5. Margot Hornblower, "Garage Sale of the Century," *Time*, May 9, 1988, 90.

6. Steven M. L. Aronson, "Possession Obsession," *House and Garden* 159, no. 12 (1987): 194.

7. Stuart Greenspan, "The Rise and Fall of Warhol Hall," *Art and Auction* 10, no. 9 (1988): 108.

8. John Taylor, "Andy's Empire: Big Money and Big Questions," *New York* 21, no. 8 (1988): 35, 39.

9. Judd Tully, "Warhol Fever at the Auction," *Washington Post*, April 24, 1988, 1.

10. David Greenberg, Eliezer Witztum, and Amihay Levy, "Hoarding as a Psychiatric Symptom," *Journal of Clinical Psychiatry* 51, no. 10 (1990): 417.

11. Ibid. Further mentions of hoarding's relation to the presumed normality of collecting can be found in Randy O. Frost and Rachel C. Gross, "The Hoarding of Possessions," *Behaviour Research and Therapy* 31, no. 4 (1993): 367–81, on "obsessive collecting" (368); and Kenneth J. Weiss, "Hoarding, Hermitage, and the Law: Why We Love the Collyer Brothers," *Journal of the American Academy of Psychiatry and the Law* 38, no. 2 (2010): 251–57, on "ordinary collecting" (252).

12. Yuval Melamed et al., "Hoarding—What Does It Mean?" *Comprehensive Psychiatry* 39, no. 6 (1998): 400. For a similar account, see Ashley E. Nordsletten and David Mataix-Cols, "Hoarding versus Collecting: Where Does Pathology Diverge from Play?" *Clinical Psychology Review* 32, no. 3 (2012): 165–76, on "'normative object relations' . . . characteristic of a large segment of the population" (166).

13. American Psychiatric Association, *Diagnostic and Statistical Manual of Mental Disorders*, 5th ed. [DSM-5] (Washington, DC: American Psychiatric Publishing, 2013), 248.

14. See also Susan M. Pearce, *On Collecting: An Investigation into Collecting in the European Tradition* (London: Routledge, 1995), who finds that "there is a powerful tradition, both

literary and psychological and now of some antiquity, which considered that the process of collecting is abnormal, and that all collectors are necessarily deviants" (194); Brenda Danet and Tamar Katriel, "Glorious Obsessions, Passionate Lovers, and Hidden Treasures: Collecting, Metaphor, and the Romantic Ethic," in *The Socialness of Things: Essays on the Socio-semiotics of Objects*, ed. Stephen Harold Riggins (Berlin: Mouton de Gruyter, 1994), 23–61, on how "collecting may be viewed as untoward, deviant activity" (46); Werner Muensterberger, *Collecting: An Unruly Passion: Psychological Perspectives* (Princeton, NJ: Princeton University Press, 1994); Michael Camille and Adrian Rifkin, eds., *Other Objects of Desire: Collectors and Collecting Queerly* (Oxford: Blackwell, 2001); and Russell W. Belk, *Collecting in a Consumer Society* (London: Routledge, 1995), on "collecting mania" (80–81, 141–45).

15. Randy O. Frost et al., "Excessive Acquisition in Hoarding," *Journal of Anxiety Disorders* 23, no. 5 (2009): 632.

16. Randy O. Frost and Tamara L. Hartl, "A Cognitive-Behavioral Model of Compulsive Hoarding," *Behaviour Research and Therapy* 34, no. 4 (1996): 346.

17. Randy O. Frost and Gail Steketee, *Stuff: Compulsive Hoarding and the Meaning of Things* (New York: Houghton Mifflin Harcourt, 2010), 56, 57.

18. Tamara L. Hartl et al., "Relationships among Compulsive Hoarding, Trauma, and Attention-Deficit/Hyperactivity Disorder," *Behaviour Research and Therapy* 43, no. 2 (2005): 270.

19. The scholarly archive discussing Warhol's gay aesthetics is especially a gift—extraordinary and extensive. Standouts include Jennifer Doyle, Jonathan Flatley, and José Esteban Muñoz, introduction to *Pop Out: Queer Warhol*, ed. Doyle, Flatley, and Muñoz (Durham, NC: Duke University Press, 1996), 1–19; Simon Watney, "Queer Andy," in *Pop Out*, on "an ambition" "to construct a safe space in which everyone and everything is queer" (25); Wayne Koestenbaum, *Andy Warhol* (New York: Viking, 2001); Richard Meyer, *Outlaw Representation: Censorship and Homosexuality in Twentieth-Century American Art* (Oxford: Oxford University Press, 2002), 94–157; and Jonathan Flatley, "Like: Collecting and Collectivity," *October* 132, no. 2 (2010): 71–98, on "new, queer forms of emotional attachment and affiliation" (72).

20. The *OED* cites the first mention of "garage sale" as appearing in a July 1966 issue of the Sacramento-based *Daily Union Family Weekly Magazine* (*Oxford English Dictionary*, s.v. "garage sale," accessed January 29, 2011, http://www.oed.com). The first mention of "yard sale" was in the Michigan-based *Flint Journal* from July 1976 (*Oxford English Dictionary*, s.v. "yard sale," accessed January 29, 2011, http://www.oed.com).

21. Gretchen M. Herrmann and Stephen M. Soiffer, "For Fun and Profit: An Analysis of the American Garage Sale," *Urban Life* 12, no. 4 (1984): 402.

22. *Oxford English Dictionary*, s.v. "collectable," accessed March 29, 2011, http://www.oed.com.

23. Ibid. For an account of collectibles in America prior to this date, see Kenneth W. Goings, *Mammy and Uncle Mose: Black Collectibles and American Stereotyping* (Bloomington: Indiana University Press, 1994). Goings universalizes collectibles as any item or piece of memorabilia worth keeping. I minoritize them as many items made and desired during and after the crest of mass production in the twentieth-century United States. For a theo-

retical consideration of collectibles and material cultures, see Bill Brown, "Reification, Reanimation, and the American Uncanny," *Critical Inquiry* 32, no. 2 (2006): 175–207.

24. "Tariff of 1930 (Hawley-Smoot Tariff)," par. 1811, in *Encyclopedia of Tariffs and Trade in U.S. History*, vol. 3, *The Texts of the Tariffs*, ed. Cynthia Clark Northrup and Elaine C. Prange Turney (Westport, CT: Greenwood, 2003), 654.

25. Harry L. Rinker, introduction to *Warman's Americana and Collectibles*, ed. Rinker (Elkins Park, PA: Warman, 1984), viii.

26. Ibid.

27. Michael Kammen, *Mystic Chords of Memory: The Transformation of Tradition in American Culture* (New York: Vintage, 1991), 313. See also Briann G. Greenfield, *Out of the Attic: Inventing Antiques in Twentieth-Century New England* (Amherst: University of Massachusetts Press, 2009), on "the history of antique collecting and museum display in the first half of the twentieth century, a period that saw the invention of antiques as aesthetic objects and their enshrinement as museum artifacts" (4); Maureen Stanton, *Killer Stuff and Tons of Money: Seeking History and Hidden Gems in Flea-Market America* (New York: Penguin, 2011); and Prasad Boradkar, *Designing Things: A Critical Introduction to the Study of Objects* (Oxford: Berg, 2010), on "collecting cultures" (253).

28. See Kammen, *Mystic Chords*, 323, and see 311 for more on the history of the Americana Collector.

29. Simon J. Bronner, *Grasping Things: Folk Material Culture and Mass Society in America* (Lexington: University Press of Kentucky, 1986), 190.

30. Kammen, *Mystic Chords*, 632. Steven M. Gelber's *Hobbies: Leisure and the Culture of Work in America* (New York: Columbia University Press, 1999) is in general agreement with these developments, though his historical timeline stretches back to the 1930s (297) and 1940s (66).

31. James Michael Ullman, *How to Hold a Garage Sale* (New York: Scribner's, 1973), 27.

32. Ibid.

33. Judy Pennebaker, "Collecting with the Kovels: A Couple Turns Obsession into Successful Business," *Washington Post*, July 14, 1988, H017.

34. Ibid., H015.

35. "The Franklin Mint," in *International Directory of Company Histories*, ed. Jay P. Pederson (Detroit: St. James, 1988), 69:181. See also Belk, *Collecting in a Consumer Society*, 57–59.

36. Connie Nelson, "Collecting's Royal Couple," *Star Tribune* (Minneapolis), November 26, 2003, 5H.

37. Ralph Kovel and Terry Kovel, *The Complete Antiques Price List* (New York: Crown, 1968), 59.

38. Susan Condon Love, "Kovel Helps Readers Tell Treasures from Trash," *Cleveland Plain Dealer*, November 16, 2006, F1.

39. Quoted in Scott Eyman, "Life of Americana's Collectors-in-Chief Is a Bowl of Treasures," *Smithsonian* 11 (1980): 78.

40. Ralph M. Kovel and Terry H. Kovel, *Know Your Antiques: How to Recognize and Evaluate Any Antique—Large or Small—like an Expert* (New York: Crown, 1967), 317.

41. "Price-Guide Pioneer," *Grand Rapids Press*, September 7, 2008, B8.

42. Quoted in Nelson, "Collecting's Royal Couple," 5H.

43. Nelson, "Collecting's Royal Couple," 5H.

44. Kovel and Kovel, *Know Your Antiques*, 318.

45. Ralph M. Kovel and Terry H. Kovel, *Family Circle's Guide to Collectibles* (Mount Morris, IL: Family Circle, 1987), 2.

46. Ibid., 32.

47. Steven W. Anderson, Hanna Damasio, and Antonio R. Damasio, "A Neural Basis for Collecting Behaviour in Humans," *Brain* 128, no. 1 (2005): 201–2. DSM-5 also cites the hoarder's distress over "the aesthetic value of the items" that "most other people would define as useless or of limited value" (American Psychiatric Association, *DSM-5*, 248).

48. Ibid., 202.

49. David A. Halperin and Jane Glick, "Collectors, Accumulators, Hoarders, and Hoarding Perspectives," *Addictive Disorders and Their Treatment* 2, no. 2 (2003): 50.

50. Ibid.

51. David A. Halperin and Jane Glick, "Collecting, Accumulation, and Hoarding: Acquisitions and Their Discontents," in *Substance Abuse: A Comprehensive Textbook*, ed. Joyce H. Lowinson et al., 4th ed. (Philadelphia: Lippincott, Williams, and Wilkins, 2005), 548.

52. Ibid.

53. Mark B. McKinley, "The Psychology of Collecting," *National Psychologist* 16, no. 2 (2007), unpaginated.

54. "What Types of Items People Hoard," *Understanding Obsessive Compulsive Hoarding*, n.d., accessed October 28, 2008, http://understanding_ocd.tripod.com/hoarding1_what1.html.

55. "Collecting versus Hoarding," *Health Guide Info.com*, n.d., accessed June 9, 2011, now defunct, http://www.brighthub.com/mental-health/ocd/articles/101204.aspx#ixzz1D19Z92uB.

56. Susan Stewart, *On Longing: Narratives of the Miniature, the Gigantic, the Souvenir, the Collection* (Durham, NC: Duke University Press, 1993), 153.

57. Ibid., 154.

58. Sara Knox, "The Serial Killer as Collector," in *Acts of Possession*, ed. Leah Dilworth (New Brunswick, NJ: Rutgers University Press, 2003), 297, 287. For another reading of "contemptible collectibles" (7), see Patricia A. Turner, *Ceramic Uncles and Celluloid Mammies: Black Images and Their Influence on Culture* (New York: Anchor, 1994).

59. Belk, *Collecting in a Consumer Society*, 1–2, 141. See also Russell W. Belk et al., "Collectors and Collecting," *Advances in Consumer Research* 15 (1988): 548–53; and Russell W. Belk, "Possessions and the Extended Self," *Journal of Consumer Research* 15, no. 2 (1988): 139–68, on "active collectors as addicts" (155).

60. Ibid., 142–43.

61. Halperin and Glick, "Collecting, Accumulation, and Hoarding," 556.

62. Ibid., 555.

63. Sandra Brant and Elissa Cullman, "Andy Warhol's Folk Art World," in *Andy War-*

hol's "Folk and Funk": September 20, 1977–November 19, 1977, ed. Brant and Cullman (New York: Museum of American Folk Art, 1977), 7.

64. Many of these items are cataloged in "Inventories of Time Capsules" (Pittsburgh: Andy Warhol Museum, 2006). For a reading of Warhol's relationship to collectibles culture, see Matthew Tinkcom, "Kitsch and the Inexpensive," in *Possession Obsession: Andy Warhol and Collecting*, ed. John W. Smith (Pittsburgh: Andy Warhol Museum, 2002), 52, 54.

65. John Richardson, "The Secret Warhol: At Home with the Silver Shadow," *Vanity Fair* 50 (1987): 72; and Brant and Cullman, "Folk Art World," 10. For an earlier account of Warhol's supposed indiscriminate behavior, see Daniel Robbins, "Confessions of a Museum Director," in *Raid the Icebox 1 with Andy Warhol* (Providence: Museum of Art, Rhode Island School of Design, 1969), 8–16.

66. Richardson, "Secret Warhol," 74.

67. Lot 833, "Seven Wrist Watches," in *The Andy Warhol Collection*, vol. 2, *Collectibles, Jewelry, Furniture, Decorations and Paintings* (New York: Sotheby's, 1988), unpaginated.

68. Greenspan, "Rise and Fall of Warhol Hall," 111.

69. Michael Lobel, "Warhol's Closet," *Art Journal* 55, no. 4 (1996): 46. See also Deborah Bright, "Shopping the Leftovers: Warhol's Collecting Strategies in *Raid the Icebox 1*," in *Other Objects of Desire*, ed. Camille and Rifkin, 116–29, on Warhol's "chaotic accumulative storage" (127).

70. Taylor, "Andy's Empire," 34.

71. Ibid., 35.

72. Frederick W. Hughes, preface to *The Andy Warhol Collection*, vol. 1, *Art Nouveau and Art Deco* (New York: Sotheby's, 1988), unpaginated.

73. Ibid.

74. Rupert Smith, "Acquisition and Accumulation," in *The Andy Warhol Collection*, vol. 3, *Jewelry and Watches* (New York: Sotheby's, 1988), unpaginated.

75. John Richardson, "Warhol the Collector," in *The Andy Warhol Collection*, vol. 5, *Americana and European and American Paintings, Drawings and Prints* (New York: Sotheby's, 1988), unpaginated.

76. Suzanne Muchnic, "Rummaging through the Andy Warhol Estate," *Los Angeles Times*, February 21, 1988, K4.

77. Hellinger, "Museum Archives," 195.

78. Melik Kaylan, "The Warhol Collection: Why Selling It Is a Shame," *Connoisseur* 915 (1988): 124; Stuart Klawans, "The Corpse in the Mirror: The Warhol Wake," *Grand Street* 8, no. 2 (1989): 176.

79. Victor Bockris, *Warhol* (New York: Da Capo, 1997), 440, 439; David Bourbon, *Warhol* (New York: Harry N. Abrams, 1989), 351.

80. John W. Smith, "Andy Warhol's Art of Collecting," in *Possession Obsession*, ed. Smith, 14.

81. Smith, "Acquisition and Accumulation."

82. Richardson, "Warhol the Collector."

83. Matt Wrbican, e-mail message, March 13, 2010.

84. Andy Warhol, *The Philosophy of Andy Warhol (From A to B and Back Again)* (San Diego: Harcourt Brace, 1975), 145.

85. Graham Shearing, "The Archive That Got Away: Exploring Andy Warhol's Collecting," *Carnegie* 66, no. 2 (2002): 10.

86. Smith, "Andy Warhol's Art of Collecting," 16.

87. John W. Smith, "Andy Warhol's Time Capsules," in *Andy Warhol's Time Capsule 21,* ed. Andy Warhol Museum (Cologne: DuMont Literatur, 2003), 13.

88. Hellinger, "Museum Archives," 197, 196.

89. Barry Hannegan, "A Place for His Stuff: Time Capsules Hint at Life and Times of Andy Warhol," *Pittsburgh Post-Gazette*, October 23, 2004, B10.

90. Robert Nelson, "When Hoarding Is Art," *The Age* (Melbourne), April 20, 2005, 8.

91. Ibid.

92. Jonathan Flatley, "Liking Things," in *Possession Obsession*, ed. Smith, 9.

93. Randy O. Frost and Tamara L. Hartl, "A Cognitive-Behavioral Model of Compulsive Hoarding," *Behaviour Research and Therapy* 34, no. 4 (1996): 346.

94. This is what anthropologist Igor Kopytoff ("The Cultural Biography of Things: Commoditization as Process," in *The Social Life of Things: Commodities in Cultural Perspective,* ed. Arjun Appadurai [Cambridge: Cambridge University Press, 1986], 64–91) terms "the stamp of collective approval" that guides the appreciation and the pricing of modern goods (81). One of his primary examples for this assessment is the object world that emerges thanks to "new 'collectibles' of the beer can variety" (81). For a comparable theory, see Michael Thompson, *Rubbish Theory: The Creation and Destruction of Value* (Oxford: Oxford University Press, 1979).

95. Simon Watney, "The Warhol Effect," in *The Work of Andy Warhol*, ed. Gary Garrels (Seattle: Bay, 1989), 120.

96. Sandra Felton, "Andy Warhol, Hoarder or Historian?" *The Organizer Lady* (blog), August 22, 2009, accessed July 3, 2011, now defunct, http://organizerlady.com/blog/?p=17.

97. Pearce, *On Collecting*, 196.

Chapter 3

1. Sandra Felton and Randy O. Frost, "The Organizer Lady and Friends Present . . . Overcoming Hoarding Tendencies: A Teleclass by Sandra Felton with Randy O. Frost, Ph.D." © 2007, 2007, CD; all quotations cited in text.

2. "Packrat Package," accessed June 23, 2011, http://messies.com/products/audio_video/packrat_package_1/. The website's offer of this package has been relocated to http://messies.com/index.php/component/content/article?id=26.

3. See, for example, Sandra Felton, *Organizing by the Book: Devotional Ideas from God's Word* (Miami: Five Smooth Stones Communication, 2007), 115.

4. American Psychiatric Association, *Diagnostic and Statistical Manual of Mental Disorders,* 5th ed. [DSM-5] (Washington, DC: American Psychiatric Publishing, 2013), 248.

5. David F. Tolin, "Challenges and Advances in Treating Hoarding," *Journal of Clinical Psychology* 67, no. 5 (2011): 452, 453.

6. Randy O. Frost and Tamara L. Hartl, "A Cognitive-Behavioral Model of Compulsive Hoarding," *Behaviour Research and Therapy* 34, no. 4 (1996): 341, 342.

7. David F. Tolin, Randy O. Frost, and Gail Steketee, "An Open Trial of Cognitive-Behavioral Therapy for Compulsive Hoarding," *Behaviour Research and Therapy* 45, no. 7 (2007): 1462.

8. American Psychiatric Association, DSM-5, 247.

9. Randy Frost, "Clutter Gone Wild," *Smith Alumnae Quarterly* 93, no. 2 (2006–7): 20.

10. American Psychiatric Association, DSM-5, 247.

11. Saulo B. Cwerner and Alan Metcalfe, "Storage and Clutter: Discourses and Practices of Order in the Domestic World," *Journal of Design History* 16, no. 3 (2003): 229. For more on the definitional complexity of clutter, see Judy Attfield, *Wild Things: The Material Culture of Everyday Life* (Oxford: Berg, 2000), 150–53; Neil Maycroft, "Not Moving Things Along: Hoarding, Clutter, and Other Ambiguous Matter," *Journal of Consumer Behavior* 8, no. 6 (2009): 354–64, on the material "breaches of normative functionality" (359); Jane Graves, "Clutter," *Issues in Architecture, Art and Design* 5, no. 2 (1998): 62–69; and Adam Phillips, "Clutter: A Case History," in *Promises, Promises: Essays on Psychoanalysis and Literature* (New York: Basic Books, 2001), 59–71.

12. Enid Nemy, "It's Her Business to Take the Distressing Disarray out of People's Lives," *New York Times*, September 2, 1974, 30.

13. Ibid.

14. Jean M. White, "Professional Organizer Cuts Clutter," *Los Angeles Times*, June 9, 1978, H8.

15. Ibid.

16. Sandra Felton, *Winning the Clutter War* (Grand Rapids, MI: Revell, 2005), 260; "About the Author," in Stephanie Winston with Marnie Winston-Macauley, *Getting Organized: The Easy Way to Put Your Life in Order*, rev. ed. (New York: Warner Books, 2006), 319.

17. Cristina Sorrentino Schmalisch, "Professional Organizers," International OCD Foundation—Hoarding Center website, n.d., accessed October 23, 2011, http://www.ocfoundation.org/hoarding/professional_organizers.aspx.

18. Suellen Hoy, *Chasing Dirt: The American Pursuit of Cleanliness* (New York: Oxford University Press, 1995), 3, 65. See also Adrian Forty, *Objects of Desire: Design and Society since 1750* (1986; London: Thames and Hudson, 2005), whose chronology agrees with these dates (115, 159).

19. Ellen Lupton and J. Abbott Miller, *The Bathroom, the Kitchen, and the Aesthetics of Waste: A Process of Elimination* (Cambridge, MA: MIT List Visual Arts Center, 1992), 1.

20. Ben Campkin and Roise Cox, "Introduction: Materialities and Metaphors of Dirt and Cleanliness," in *Dirt: New Geographies of Cleanliness and Contamination*, ed. Campkin and Cox (London: I. B. Tauris, 2007), 2.

21. See Susan Strasser, *Waste and Want: A Social History of Trash* (New York: Metropolitan Books, 1999), 174; and Nancy Tomes, "Spreading the Germ Theory: Sanitary Science and Home Economics, 1880–1930," in *Women and Health in America*, ed. Judith Walzer Leavitt, 2nd ed. (Madison: University of Wisconsin Press, 1999), 596–99, for more on this historical formation.

22. See Richard L. Bushman and Claudia L. Bushman, "The Early History of Cleanliness in America," *Journal of American History* 74, no. 4 (1988): 1213–38.

23. For social etymologies of the terms *home economics* and *domestic science*, see Emma Seifrit Weigley, "It Might Have Been Euthenics: The Lake Placid Conferences and the Home Economics Movement," *American Quarterly* 26, no. 1 (1974): 79–96; Sarah Stage and Virginia B. Vincenti, eds., *Rethinking Home Economics: Women and the History of a Profession* (Ithaca, NY: Cornell University Press, 1997); and Glenna Matthews, *"Just a Housewife": The Rise and Fall of Domesticity in America* (New York: Oxford University Press, 1987). For more on hygiene reform, see Forty, *Objects of Desire*, 160.

24. Scholarship regarding the scientific management of US housekeeping is vast. A small selection includes Clifford Edward Clark Jr., *The American Family Home, 1800–1960* (Chapel Hill: University of North Carolina Press, 1986), 161; Ian Roderick, "Household Sanitation and the Flow of Domestic Space," *Space and Culture* 1, no. 1 (1997): 105–32; Janice Williams Rutherford, *Selling Mrs. Consumer: Christine Frederick and the Rise of Household Efficiency* (Athens: University of Georgia Press, 2003), 36–45; and Sarah A. Leavitt, *From Catharine Beecher to Martha Stewart: A Cultural History of Domestic Advice* (Chapel Hill: University of North Carolina Press, 2002), 52–53.

25. Christine Frederick, *The New Housekeeping: Efficiency Studies in Home Management* (Garden City, NY: Doubleday, 1916), viii. See also Gavin Lucas, "Disposability and Dispossession in the Twentieth Century," *Journal of Material Culture* 7, no. 1 (2002): 6.

26. Frederick, *New Housekeeping*, 197.

27. Susan Curtis, *A Consuming Faith: The Social Gospel and Modern American Culture* (Columbia: University of Missouri Press, 2001), 2, 62, 69.

28. Nayan Shah, *Contagious Divides: Epidemics and Race in San Francisco's Chinatown* (Berkeley: University of California Press, 2001), 14.

29. Leavitt, *From Catharine Beecher*, 24.

30. Richard J. Callahan, Jr., Kathryn Lofton, and Chad E. Seales, "Allegories of Progress: Industrial Religion in the United States," *Journal of the American Academy of Religion* 78, no. 1 (2010): 26. For more on the Cleanliness Institute, see Hoy, *Chasing Dirt*, 142.

31. Bushman and Bushman, "Cleanliness," 1232.

32. Shah, *Contagious Divides*, 15.

33. S. Maria Elliott, *Household Hygiene* (Chicago: American School of Home Economics, 1911), 152.

34. Ellen H. Richards and Marion Talbot, *Home Sanitation: A Manual for Housekeepers* (Boston: Whitcomb and Barrows, 1904), 52.

35. "Useless Hoarding," *Harper's Bazar* 28, no. 18 (1895): 354.

36. Richards and Talbot, *Home Sanitation*, 54.

37. Caroline Bartlett Crane, *Everyman's House* (Garden City, NY: Doubleday, 1925), 221. For more on Bartlett Crane, see Curtis, *Consuming Faith*, 65–67.

38. Charlotte Perkins Gilman, *Women and Economics: A Study of the Economic Relation between Men and Women as a Factor in Social Evolution* (Boston: Small, Maynard, 1898), 257.

39. Ibid.

40. Strasser, *Waste and Want*, 112.

41. Nancy Tomes, *The Gospel of Germs: Men, Women, and the Microbe in American Life* (Cambridge, MA: Harvard University Press, 1998), 161. See also Susan Strasser, *Never Done: A History of American Housework* (New York: Pantheon, 1982), 206; and Virginia Smith, *Clean: A History of Personal Hygiene and Purity* (Oxford: Oxford University Press, 2007), on Progressive-era "health crusaders" who launched campaigns where "knick-knacks were discouraged" (300).

42. Leavitt, *From Catharine Beecher*, 122. See also Karen Halttunen, "From Parlor to Living Room: Domestic Space, Interior Decoration, and the Culture of Personality," in *Consuming Visions: Accumulation and Display of Goods in America, 1880–1920*, ed. Simon J. Bronner (New York: W. W. Norton, 1989), 157–89, on how "middle-class Americans began to forswear the indiscriminate accumulation of domestic things" (188).

43. Shah, *Contagious Divides*, 113.

44. Indeed, Shah, *Contagious Divides*, finds that "Christian philanthropic work intervened to produce proper nuclear families for Chinatown society, perceived to be socially disordered and populated by social deviants" (111).

45. Tomes, *Gospel of Germs*, 8. Likewise, see Forty, *Objects of Desire*, who claims that "in the 1920s, the pursuit of absolute cleanliness appeared also in the more advanced designs for domestic furniture" (173).

46. Forty, *Objects of Desire*, 156; and Hoy, *Chasing Dirt*, 151.

47. Sandra Felton, *Messies 2* (Old Tappan, NJ: Revell, 1986), 10. Her claims confirm Leavitt, *From Catharine Beecher*, who finds that "domestic advisors of the nineteenth and early twentieth centuries helped shape the curriculum topics, such as sanitation, nutrition, and interior design, that are often still used today" (6).

48. David Dudley, "Conquering Clutter," *AARP* [American Association of Retired Persons] *Magazine* 50, no. 1A (2007): 60, 61.

49. Peggy Hoehne, "Do You Have Hoard and Clutter Syndrome?" *OnlineOrganizing* .com, n.d., accessed January 14, 2012, now defunct, http://www.onlineorganizing.com/ NewslettersArticle.asp?article=449&newsletter=go.

50. Deborah Branscum, "The Hoarding Syndrome: When Clutter Goes out of Control," *Reader's Digest*, March 2007, 169–74.

51. Sandra Felton, *Organizing for Life: Declutter Your Mind to Declutter Your World* (1989; repr., Grand Rapids, MI: Revell, 2007), 64.

52. *Oxford English Dictionary*, s.v. "pack rat," accessed January 28, 2013, http://www .oed.com.

53. Felton, *Organizing by the Book*, 189.

54. "Getting 'Messies' to Clean Up," *New York Times*, December 23, 1985, C18.

55. Ibid.

56. Felton, *Winning the Clutter War*, 29.

57. Ibid.

58. D. T. (Daniel Thambyrajah) Niles, *That They May Have Life* (New York: Harper and Brothers, 1951), 96; Sandra Felton, *Messie No More: Understanding and Overcoming the Roadblocks to Being Organized*, rev. ed. (Grand Rapids, MI: Revell, 2002), 13–14.

59. Felton, *Winning the Clutter War*, 9.

60. Cable Neuhaus, "Is Your House a Holy Mess? Sandra Felton Suggests Ways to Get a Clean Start," *People* 16, no. 7 (1981): 75.

61. Felton, *Winning the Clutter War*, 11.

62. Felton, *Organizing for Life*, 28.

63. Sandra Felton, *Meditations for Messies: A Guide to Order and Serenity* (1992; repr., Miami: Five Smooth Stones Communication, 2003), 77.

64. Sandra Felton, *The Messies Manual: The Procrastinator's Guide to Good Housekeeping* (1981; repr., Old Tappan, NJ: Revell, 1984), 65; Felton, *Meditations for Messies*, 80.

65. Sandra Felton, *I've Got to Get Rid of This Stuff! Strategies for Overcoming Hoarding (The Packrat Syndrome)* (1995; repr., Miami: Five Smooth Stones Communications, 2010), 1.

66. Ibid., 2.

67. Ibid., 3.

68. Felton, *I've Got to Get Rid of This Stuff!* 16.

69. Felton, *Organizing for Life*, 27.

70. Felton, *Organizing by the Book*, 189, 195.

71. Felton, *I've Got to Get Rid of This Stuff!* 13.

72. *Oxford English Dictionary*, s.v. "lifestyle," accessed December 14, 2012, http://www.oed.com. For a historical discussion of the phrase *gay lifestyle* during the 1970s, see Fred Fejes, *Gay Rights and Moral Panic: The Origins of America's Debate on Homosexuality* (New York: Palgrave Macmillan, 2008), 50–51.

73. Rob Boston, "Family Feud," *Church and State* 51, no. 5 (1998): 11.

74. Sandra Felton, "Coping as a Messie," in *Home Management for Today's Busy Mom*, cassette tape (Colorado Springs, CO: Focus on the Family, 1992). See Strasser, *Never Done*, for a brief discussion of historical continuities between "women activists of the New Right" and earlier housekeeping reform efforts (309).

75. See Mark D. Jordan, *Recruiting Young Love: How Christians Talk about Homosexuality* (Chicago: University of Chicago Press, 2011), 129–67, for more on antigay lifestyle discourses of the New Right.

76. Allan Fisher, *Fleming H. Revell Company: The First 125 Years, 1870–1995* (Grand Rapids, MI: Revell, 1995), 7. Scholarly considerations of Revell include Paul C. Gutjahr, "Diversification in American Religious Publishing," in *A History of the Book in America*, vol. 3, *The Industrial Book, 1840–1880*, ed. Scott E. Casper et al. (Chapel Hill: University of North Carolina Press, 2007), 201; and Jan Blodgett, *Protestant Evangelical Literary Culture and Contemporary Society* (Westport, CT: Greenwood, 1997), 40–45.

77. Robert H. Krapohl and Charles H. Lippy, *The Evangelicals: A Historical, Thematic, and Biographical Guide* (Westport, CT: Greenwood, 1999), 292.

78. Fisher, *Fleming H. Revell Company*, 17, 29.

79. Felton, *Organizing for Life*, 67.

80. The most detailed account of Exodus International to date can be found in Lynne Gerber, *Seeking the Straight and Narrow: Weight Loss and Sexual Reorientation in Evangelical America* (Chicago: University of Chicago Press, 2011).

81. Felton, *Organizing for Life*, 200.

82. Ibid., 202.

83. Felton, *I've Got to Get Rid of This Stuff!* 4.

84. See Eva Illouz, *Saving the Modern Soul: Therapy, Emotions, and the Culture of Self-Help* (Berkeley: University of California Press, 2008), 162; and Wendy Simonds, *Women and Self-Help Culture: Reading between the Lines* (New Brunswick, NJ: Rutgers University Press, 1992), on the post–World War II rise of US self-help literatures. For links between "self-improvement literature" and "inspirational literature" over these decades (5), see Micki McGee, *Self-Help, Inc.: Makeover Culture in American Life* (Oxford: Oxford University Press, 2005). On ex-identity formation, see Helen Rose Fuchs Ebaugh, *Becoming an Ex: The Process of Role Exit* (Chicago: University of Chicago Press, 1988).

85. Randi Lyman, "Safety Risks of Hoarding," *A Helping Hand: Professional Organizing Service*, January 30, 2011, accessed January 14, 2012, http://ahelpinghandforyou.blogspot.com/2011/01/safety-risks-of-hoarding.html.

86. Felton, *Organizing for Life*, 62.

87. Felton, *Meditations for Messies*, 62. A typical conceptualization of alcoholism-as-disease appears in E. M. Jellinek, *The Disease Concept of Alcoholism* (New Haven, CT: College and University Press, 1960), which argues that "around 1940 the phrase 'new approach to alcoholism' was coined, and since then this phrase has been heard again and again" throughout examinations of "this deviant behavior" (1).

88. Ibid.

89. Ibid., 106.

90. Ibid., 110.

91. "Getting 'Messies' to Clean Up," C18.

92. Felton, *Meditations for Messies*, 5.

93. Sandra Felton, "Our Mission," Messies Anonymous website, n.d., accessed June 17, 2011, http://www.messies.com/about/. The mission statement has been relocated to http://www.messies.com/index.php/component/content/article?id=17.

94. I'm extracting from histories by Ernest Kurtz, *Not-God: A History of Alcoholics Anonymous* (Center City, MN: Hazelden Education Materials, 1979); and William L. White, *Slaying the Dragon: The History of Addiction Treatment and Recovery in America* (Bloomington, IL: Chestnut Health Systems, 1998). For a discussion of Messies Anonymous, organizer interventions, and clutterholics, see Russell W. Belk, Joon Yong Seo, and Eric Li, "Dirty Little Secret: Home Chaos and Professional Organizers," *Consumption, Markets and Culture* 10, no. 2 (2007): 133–40.

95. On the religious intonations of Alcoholics Anonymous, see Jordan, *Recruiting Young Love*, 158. On links between late twentieth-century evangelicalism and addiction discourses, see Gerber, *Straight and Narrow*, 70–74.

96. Felton, *Winning the Clutter War*, 234.

97. Felton, *Meditations for Messies*, 122.

98. Ibid., 125.

99. Ibid., 107.

100. Brooks Palmer, *Clutter Busting: Letting Go of What's Holding You Back* (Novato, CA: New World Library, 2009), 89.

101. Barb Rogers, "Clutter Addiction," *Huffington Post*, August 4, 2010, accessed Septem-

ber 17, 2011, http://www.huffingtonpost.com/barb-rogers/clutter-addiction_b_667848
.html.

102. Harriet Schechter, *Let Go of Clutter* (New York: McGraw-Hill, 2001), xiv.

103. Don Aslett, *For Packrats Only: How to Clean Up, Clear Out and Dejunk Your Life Forever!* (Pocatello, ID: Marsh Creek, 1991), 177.

104. The citation can be found in Robert Atwan, comp., "Notable Essays of 1997," in *The Best American Essays 1998*, ed. Cynthia Ozick (Boston: Houghton Mifflin, 1998), 257; Tyler Gore, "Stuff," in *Literal Latté: Highlights from Fifteen Years of a Unique "Mind Stimulating" Literary Magazine*, ed. Jenine Gordon Bockman and Jeffrey Michael Bockman (Bloomington: iUniverse, 2008), 95.

105. Gore, "Stuff," 98, 101.

106. Susan Lepselter, "The Disorder of Things: Hoarding Narratives in Popular Media," *Anthropological Quarterly* 84, no. 4 (2011): 926.

107. Felton, *Meditations for Messies*, 15.

108. Felton, *Winning the Clutter War*, 10–11.

109. A. Barocka, D. Seehuber, and D. Schone, "Sammeln und Horten: Ein Messie kann nicht anders" [Collecting and hoarding: A Messie has no choice]," *MMW-Fortschritte der Medizin* 146, no. 45 (2004): 36. Translations by Translation Services USA.

110. Ibid., 36–37.

111. Felton, *Winning the Clutter War*, 11.

112. National Study Group on Chronic Disorganization (presently titled Institute for Challenging Disorganization), *Reading and Resource List for Professional Organizers Working with Chronically Disorganized People*, ed. Randi B. Lyman et al. (St. Louis: National Study Group on Chronic Disorganization, 2008), 10, 11.

113. Sandra Felton, blurb in Judith Kolberg, *What Every Professional Organizer Needs to Know about Hoarding*, 2nd ed. (Decatur, GA: Squall, 2009), iii.

114. Kolberg, *What Every Professional Organizer Needs to Know*, 9, xvi.

115. Judith Kolberg, *Conquering Chronic Disorganization*, 2nd ed. (Decatur, GA: Squall, 2006), 26–27.

116. Kolberg, *Professional Organizer*, xiii.

117. Ibid., 53; her emphasis.

118. Ibid., 54.

119. National Study Group on Chronic Disorganization (presently titled Institute for Challenging Disorganization), "The NSGCD Clutter Hoarding Scale: Official Organizational Assessment Tool" (St. Louis: National Study Group on Chronic Disorganization, 2003), 1.

120. Ibid., 3.

121. Ibid., 4, 5, 6.

122. David F. Tolin, foreword to Kolberg, *Professional Organizer*, vii.

123. Ibid., xii. On April 18, 2013, Tolin delivered the opening keynote address for NAPO's Annual Conference and Organizing Expo in New Orleans, titled "Helping Mainstream Clients Get Unstuck: Lessons from Clinical Psychology."

124. Christiana Bratiotis, Christina Sorrentino Schmalisch, and Gail Steketee, *The*

Hoarding Handbook: A Guide for Human Service Professionals (New York: Oxford University Press, 2011), 4; hereafter cited in text.

125. Randy O. Frost and Veselina Hristova, "Assessment of Hoarding," *Journal of Clinical Psychology* 67, no. 5 (2011): 461.

126. David F. Tolin, Randy O. Frost, and Gail Steketee, *Buried in Treasures: Help for Compulsive Acquiring, Saving, and Hoarding* (New York: Oxford University Press, 2007), 9.

127. Felton, *Organizing for Life*, 9.

Chapter 4

1. Gail Sheehy, "The Secret of Grey Gardens," *New York*, January 10, 1972, 28. See also Jack Graves, "Mother and Daughter Ordered to Clean House or Get Out," *East Hampton Star*, November 25, 1971, 1; and Fred Tuccillo, "Jackie's Recluse Kin Face Eviction," *Los Angeles Times*, March 19, 1972, H5.

2. Sheehy, "Secret of Grey Gardens," 27.

3. Tuccillo, "Jackie's Recluse Kin," H5. See also "Jackie Cleans Up East Hampton Mansion for 2 Kin," *New York Daily News*, July 27, 1972, 32, with an album of photographs on 64–65.

4. While I cite David Maysles and Albert Maysles as *Grey Gardens'* directors, I note that the two shared directing credits with Ellen Hovde and Muffie Meyer.

5. See Jessika Toothman, "5 Famous Hoarding Cases," *TLC Family*, n.d., accessed May 9, 2012, http://tlc.howstuffworks.com/family/5-famous-hoarding-cases.html; and "Famous Squalorees: Edith and Edie Bouvier Beale," *Squalor Survivors*, n.d., accessed May 9, 2012, http://www.squalorsurvivors.com/squalor/famous.shtml#edie.

6. Susan Donaldson James, "Squalor Syndrome: Living Happily among Cats, Fleas and Filth," *ABC News*, January 17, 2007, accessed March 24, 2012, http://abcnews.go.com/Health/story?id=2799460&page=1.

7. In terms of their representational histories, I have in mind gay men who embrace *Grey Gardens* as a cherished site of camp argot, fashion, and inspiration.

8. Matt Paxton with Phaedra Hise, *The Secret Lives of Hoarders: True Stories of Tackling Extreme Clutter* (New York: Perigee, 2011), 15–16.

9. Elizabeth Nelson, "Spreading the Word about COH: On-Line, In-Person, and the Media," Children of Hoarders website, 2008, accessed May 9, 2012, now defunct, http://childrenofhoarders.com/wordpress/?page_id=2604.

10. Catherine R. Ayers et al., "Age at Onset and Clinical Features of Late Life Compulsive Hoarding," *International Journal of Geriatric Psychiatry* 25, no. 2 (2010): 144.

11. Catherine R. Ayers, "Hoarding in Older Adulthood," section in "Types of Hoarding," International OCD Foundation (IOCDF)—Hoarding Center website, 2010, accessed January 5, 2013, www.ocfoundation.org/hoarding/types.aspx.

12. American Psychiatric Association, *Diagnostic and Statistical Manual of Mental Disorders*, 5th ed. [DSM-5] (Washington, DC: American Psychiatric Publishing, 2013), 249.

13. Randy O. Frost and Gail Steketee, *Stuff: Compulsive Hoarding and the Meaning of Things* (New York: Houghton Mifflin Harcourt, 2010), 177.

14. Duncan MacMillan and Patricia Shaw, "Senile Breakdown in Standards of Personal and Environmental Cleanliness," *British Medical Journal* 2, no. 5521 (1966): 1032.

15. Ibid., 1033.

16. A. N. G. Clark, G. D. Mankikar, and Ian Gray, "Diogenes Syndrome: A Clinical Study of Gross Neglect in Old Age," *Lancet* 305, no. 7903 (1975): 366.

17. Ibid., 367, 366.

18. Ayers, "Types of Hoarding"; Sharon M. Valente, "The Hoarding Syndrome," *Home Health Care Nurse* 27, no. 7 (2009): 433.

19. Thomas R. Cole, *The Journey of Life: A Cultural History of Aging in America* (Cambridge: Cambridge University Press, 1992), 194.

20. John W. Rowe and Robert L. Kahn, *Successful Aging* (New York: Pantheon, 1998), xi. I acknowledge this section's debt to—and extend the findings of—Martha B. Holstein and Meredith Minkler, "Self, Society, and the 'New Gerontology,'" *Gerontologist* 43, no. 6 (2003): 787–96, who argue in a piercing critique that "*Successful Aging* is perhaps the single most recognized work in recent gerontology," one whose "normative vision" "has attracted an articulate, popular, and professional following" (787).

21. Rowe and Kahn, *Successful Aging*, xii.

22. Ibid.; their emphasis.

23. Ibid., 23. See comparative texts such as Paul B. Baltes and Karl Ulrich Mayer, eds., *The Berlin Aging Study: Aging from 70 to 100* (Cambridge: Cambridge University Press, 1999), which rests upon a "normative definition of an ideal state" of aging (6); and Paul B. Baltes and Margaret M. Baltes, eds., *Successful Aging: Perspectives from the Behavioral Sciences* (Cambridge: Cambridge University Press, 1990).

24. Useful resources on the emergence of old age in the late nineteenth- and early twentieth-century United States that this section relies upon include W. Andrew Achenbaum, *Crossing Frontiers: Gerontology Emerges as a Science* (Cambridge: Cambridge University Press, 1995); David Hackett Fischer, *Growing Old in America* (Oxford: Oxford University Press, 1978), on "American physicians, who made old age into a special branch of medical science" (188); Carole Haber, *Beyond Sixty-Five: The Dilemma of Old Age in America's Past* (Cambridge: Cambridge University Press, 1983), on "the growing differentiation of the old from the rest of society" (83); Carole Haber, "Geriatrics: A Specialty in Search of Specialists," in *Old Age in a Bureaucratic Society: The Elderly, the Experts, and the State in American History*, ed. David Van Tassel and Peter N. Stearns (New York: Greenwood, 1986), 66–84; Cole, *Journey of Life*, on *geriatrics* and *gerontology* as novel medical terms (195); Stephen Katz, *Disciplining Old Age: The Formation of Gerontological Knowledge* (Charlottesville: University Press of Virginia, 1996), 83–87; Tamara K. Hareven, "Changing Images of Aging and the Social Construction of the Life Course," in *Images of Aging: Cultural Representations of Later Life*, ed. Mike Featherstone and Andrew Wernick (London: Routledge, 1995), 117–31; Bryan S. Green, *Gerontology and the Construction of Old Age* (New York: Aldine de Gruyter, 1993); Margaret Morganroth Gullette, *Aged by Culture* (Chicago: University of Chicago Press, 2004), 17; Andrew Blaikie, *Ageing and Popular Culture* (Cambridge: Cambridge University Press, 1999); and John E. Morley, "A Brief History of Geriatrics," *Journals of Gerontology*, ser. A, 59, no. 11 (2004): 1132–52.

25. Élie Metchnikoff, *The Nature of Man*, ed. P. Chalmers Mitchell (1903; New York: G. P. Putnam's Sons, 1908), 298. For an overview of non-American contributions, see Cole, *Journey of Life*, 195–202.

26. Howard P. Chudacoff, *How Old Are You? Age Consciousness in American Culture* (Princeton, NJ: Princeton University Press, 1989), 5, 54.

27. I. L. Nascher, "Geriatrics," *New York Medical Journal* 90 (1909): 358.

28. G. Stanley Hall, *Senescence: The Last Half of Life* (New York: D. Appleton, 1922), 100.

29. Katz, *Disciplining Old Age*, 89. See also Carroll L. Estes, *The Aging Enterprise: A Critical Examination of Social Policies and Services for the Aged* (San Francisco: Jossey-Bass, 1979), on the "theoretical perceptions of aging as a social problem" (12); and Hackett Fischer, *Growing Old*, who argues that "that stage of life began to be seen as a problem to be solved by the intervention of 'society'" (157).

30. Or as Haber, *Beyond Sixty-Five*, argues, "senility, once merely 'the state of being old,' had been transformed into a pathological condition" (74). This is not to presume a universal creed, however, as some scientists aspired to capture "a 'normal' old age" (Cole, *Journey of Life*, 200).

31. W. Andrew Achenbaum, *Old Age in the New Land: The American Experience since 1790* (Baltimore: Johns Hopkins University Press, 1978), 109, 112.

32. I. L. Nascher, *Geriatrics: The Diseases of Old Age and Their Treatment, Including Physiological Old Age, Home and Institutional Care, and Medico-Legal Relations* (Philadelphia: P. Blakiston's Son, 1914), v.

33. Cole, *Journey of Life*, 223, 225. For more on these dynamic reconstructions of old age in mid-twentieth-century America, see Carole Haber and Brian Gratton, *Old Age and the Search for Security: An American Social History* (Bloomington: Indiana University Press, 1994), 166–67; and Chudacoff, *How Old Are You?* 179.

34. Richard H. Williams and Claudine G. Wirths, *Lives through the Years: Styles of Life and Successful Aging* (New York: Atherton, 1965), 2.

35. Clark Tibbits, introduction to *Living through the Older Years: Proceedings of the Charles A. Fisher Memorial Institute on Aging*, ed. Tibbits (Ann Arbor: University of Michigan Press, 1949), 5. See also Achenbaum, *Crossing Frontiers*, 263; and Cole, *Journey of Life*, on "refurbishing the positive role in the old American dualism of aging" (229).

36. Critiques of successful aging discourses—widespread in the scholarly literature—include Haim Hazan, *Old Age: Constructions and Deconstructions* (Cambridge: Cambridge University Press, 1994), 15; Mike Featherstone and Mike Hepworth, "Images of Positive Aging: A Case Study of *Retirement Choice* Magazine," in *Images of Aging*, 27–46, on "the elaboration of new norms of age-related behavior" (29); Stephen Katz, *Cultural Aging: Life Course, Lifestyle, and Senior Worlds* (Peterborough, ON: Broadview, 2005); Meredith Minkler and Pamela Fadem, "'Successful Aging': A Disability Perspective," *Journal of Disability Policy Studies* 12, no. 4 (2002): 229–35, who note that "*successful aging* was coined more than half a century ago" (23); Cole, *Journey of Life*, 238–39; and, especially, Holstein and Minkler, "Self, Society, and the 'New Gerontology,'" on "the new gerontology's implicit (and thus unacknowledged) normativity" (791) and its "coercive standard" (792).

37. George Lawton, "Aging Creatively," in *Living through the Older Years*, ed. Tibbits, 113, 114.

38. Ibid., 128. For similar examples, see Edward T. Hall, "The Creative Urge in Older People," in *New Goals for Old Age*, ed. George Lawton (New York: Columbia University Press, 1943), 128–31; and Clare de Gruchy, *Creative Old Age* (San Francisco: Old Age Counseling Center, 1946).

39. Rowe and Kahn, *Successful Aging*, 155.

40. N. Laura Kamptner, "Personal Possessions and Their Meanings in Old Age," in *The Social Psychology of Aging*, ed. Shirlynn Spacapan and Stuart Oskamp (Newbury Park, CA: Sage, 1989), 178. Kamptner also lists "old letters, pressed flowers, bronzed baby shoes, journals, diaries, keepsakes, and furniture" in her claim that these things "remind individuals of their ancestors, their own childhoods, and the roots of their personal and cultural origins" (175–76).

41. See, for one, Edmund Sherman, "Reminiscentia: Cherished Objects as Memorabilia in Late-Life Reminiscence," *International Journal of Aging and Human Development* 33, no. 2 (1991): 89–100.

42. Edmund Sherman and Evelyn S. Newman, "The Meaning of Cherished Personal Possessions for the Elderly," *International Journal of Aging and Human Development* 8, no. 2 (1977–78): 191. Scholars in material culture studies can share these claims, as shown in Eugene Rochberg-Halton, "Object Relations, Role Models, and Cultivation of the Self," *Environment and Behavior* 16, no. 3 (1984): 335–68. For a counter to this tendency, see Elizabeth Hallam and Jenny Hockey, *Death, Memory, and Material Culture* (Oxford: Berg, 2001), who trace "material objects that somehow resist and disrupt processes of materialized memory making" (118).

43. Robert L. Rubinstein, "The Significance of Personal Objects to Older People," *Journal of Aging Studies* 1, no. 3 (1987): 231. For an alternate take, see Kathleen Woodward, *Aging and Its Discontents: Freud and Other Fictions* (Bloomington: Indiana University Press, 1991), 137–38.

44. Chudacoff, *How Old Are You?* 58. See also Achenbaum, *Old Age in the New Land*, 147.

45. Lawton, "Aging Creatively," 116. See also Richard H. Williams, "Styles of Life and Successful Aging," in *Processes of Aging: Sociological and Psychological Perspectives*, ed. Williams (New York: Atherton, 1963), on "the limit of unsuccessful aging" (1:336).

46. Ernest W. Burgess, "The Growing Problem of Aging," in *Living through the Older Years*, ed. Tibbits, 18.

47. Ibid.

48. George Lawton, *Aging Successfully* (New York: Columbia University Press, 1946), 15.

49. Ibid., xiii.

50. For detailed discussions of this phenomenon, see Haber, *Beyond Sixty-Five*, 74–75; and Jesse F. Ballenger, *Self, Senility, and Alzheimer's Disease in Modern America: A History* (Baltimore: Johns Hopkins University Press, 2006), whose cultural history of senile dementia notes that "the word *senile* also came to be associated with mental deterioration in par-

ticular. The brain, like the rest of the body, underwent inevitable deterioration with age, and the mental impairments commonly observed in the aged were the result" (18).

51. Allan McLane Hamilton, *A Manual of Medical Jurisprudence, with Special Reference to Diseases and Injuries of the Nervous System* (New York: Bermingham, 1883), 25.

52. Ibid., 28. See also Haber, *Beyond Sixty-Five*, 77–79, who alerted me to this quote's existence in her discussion of senile dementia and "moral perversion" (77).

53. Ibid.

54. See Haber, "Geriatrics," who finds that "the dirty old man had become more than a repulsive stereotype. His portrayal was seemingly based on the findings of clinical research" (78).

55. Lawton, *Aging Successfully*, 23.

56. Williams and Wirths, *Lives through the Years*, 17, 25, 29; hereafter cited in text.

57. Ruth Granick and Frederic D. Zeman, "The Aged Recluse—An Exploratory Study with Particular Reference to Community Responsibility," *Journal of Chronic Diseases* 12, no. 6 (1960): 651; hereafter cited in text.

58. For more on connections between Zeman and Nascher, see Arthur H. Aufses Jr. and Barbara J. Niss, *This House of Noble Deeds: The Mount Sinai Hospital, 1852–2002* (New York: New York University Press, 2002), 207. For more on associations between Zeman and Lawton, see Hyung Wook Park, "Refiguring Old Age: Shaping Scientific Research on Senescence, 1900–1960" (Ph.D. diss., University of Michigan, Ann Arbor, 2009), 303.

59. W. Andrew Achenbaum and Daniel M. Albert survey this career in "Ruth Bennett," in *Profiles in Gerontology: A Biographical Dictionary* (Westport, CT: Greenwood, 1995), 27–29.

60. Felix Post, "Functional Disorders I: Description, Incidence, and Recognition," in *The Psychiatry of Late Life*, ed. Raymond Levy and Post (Oxford: Blackwell Scientific, 1982), 177. In an earlier text (*The Clinical Psychiatry of Late Life* [Oxford: Pergamon, 1965]), Post notes that "in senile recluses, social withdrawal and turning into oneself are most strikingly exemplified. . . . This is another group of elderly persons which has never been studied systematically, but Granick and Zeman [1960] carried out an analysis of newspaper cuttings referring to 105 recluses" (126). In an even earlier piece, he cites "hoarding and collecting rubbish": Felix Post, "Emergencies in General Practice: Senile Confusion," *British Medical Journal* 2, no. 4934 (1955): 315.

61. Peter V. Rabins, "Schizophrenia and Psychotic States," in *Handbook of Mental Health and Aging*, ed. James E. Birren, R. Bruce Sloane, and Gene D. Cohen, 2nd ed. (San Diego: Academic, 1992), 463.

62. Carlos A. Reyes-Ortiz, "Diogenes Syndrome: The Self-Neglect Elderly," *Comprehensive Therapy* 27, no. 2 (2001): 117.

63. E. Cybulska, "Senile Squalor: Plyushkin's not Diogenes' Syndrome," *Psychiatric Bulletin* 22, no. 5 (1998): 319. For a critique of these discourses, see William Lauder, "The Medical Model and Other Constructions of Self-Neglect," *International Journal of Nursing Practice* 5, no. 2 (1999): 58–63.

64. See Gail Steketee, Randy O. Frost, and Hyo-Jin Kim, "Hoarding by Elderly Peo-

ple," *Health and Social Work* 26, no. 3 (2001): 176–84; Norma D. Thomas, "Hoarding: Eccentricity or Pathology: When to Intervene?" *Journal of Gerontological Social Work* 29, no. 1 (1997): 45–55; and Eric Abrahamson and David H. Freedman, *A Perfect Mess: The Hidden Benefits of Disorder* (New York: Back Bay Books, 2007), 274.

65. Ayers et al., "Age at Onset," 148.

66. "Links: Hoarding Documentaries," International OCD Foundation (IOCDF)— Hoarding Center, n.d., accessed January 20, 2013, www.ocfoundation.org/hoarding/ print.aspx?id=704.

67. Amy Byrnes, "The Cluttered Life: Grey Gardens a Cautionary Tale for the Chronically Disorganized Mom," Opinion, *LongBranch Eatontown Patch*, June 30, 2011, accessed March 26, 2012, http://rumson.patch.com/articles/the-cluttered-life-grey-gardens-serves -as-a-cautionary-tale-for-the-chronically-disorganized-mom.

68. Healthline Editorial Team, "Diogenes Syndrome: Living in Extreme Squalor," *Healthline*, n.d., accessed April 10, 2012, http://www.healthline.com/health-blogs/ healthline-connects/diogenes-syndrome-living-extreme-squalor.

69. Patricia Salber, "Diogenes Syndrome: Self-Neglect and Hoarding—Not a Pretty Picture," *The Doctor Weighs In* (blog), September 30, 2007, accessed April 10, 2012, http:// www.thedoctorweighsin.com/diogenes-syndrome-self-neglect-and-hoarding-not-a- pretty-picture/.

70. Healthline Editorial Team, "Diogenes Syndrome."

71. Robrt Pela, "Hoarder Stories, Part 2," *Phoenix New Times*, July 7, 2010, accessed April 10, 2012, http://blogs.phoenixnewtimes.com/jackalope/2010/07/hoard_mentality .php.

72. Ibid.

73. Michael Sucsy, dir., *Grey Gardens*, DVD (Santa Monica, CA: HBO Films, 2009); all quotations from film cited in text.

74. Byrnes, "Cluttered Life."

75. Sheehy, "Grey Gardens," 27.

76. Ibid., 28.

77. "La tante de Jackie Onassis," *Paris Match* 1185 (January 22, 1972): 16. Translation by Denise Cruz.

78. David and Albert Maysles, "PORTRAIT—a Feature Length Documentary Type Film in Progress," in *Grey Gardens*, ed. Rebekah Maysles and Sara Maysles (Philadelphia: Free News Projects, 2009), unpaginated.

79. Ibid.

80. Katherine C. Grier, *Pets in America: A History* (Chapel Hill: University of North Carolina Press, 2006), 259.

81. Walter Goodman, "'Grey Gardens': *Cinéma Verité* or Sideshow?" *New York Times*, February 22, 1976, D15, D19.

82. Charlotte Curtis, "People Are Talking about . . . *Grey Gardens*: Worst-Taste Film Gets Its Draw from a Bouvier Kinship," *Vogue* 165, no. 11 (1975): 192. A brief overview of the Maysleses' oeuvre and its relation to charges of exploitation can be found in Matthew Tinkcom, *Grey Gardens* (London: Palgrave Macmillan, 2011), 16–19.

83. David Maysles and Albert Maysles, "The Maysles Defend Their Film," *New York Times*, April 25, 1976, 79.

84. Jane Castle, "'Doco Direct' et al—Jane Castle Interviews Al Maysles in NYC," *Filmnews* 16, no. 3 (1986): 8.

85. Ibid., 9; emphasis mine.

86. Ellen Hovde, Albert Maysles, David Maysles, and Muffie Meyer, dirs., *Grey Gardens*, DVD (Portrait Films, 1975); all quotations from film cited in text.

87. Tinkcom, *Grey Gardens*, 55. Tinkcom also offers an incisive reading of the Beales and their "hidden poverty" (49).

88. John David Rhodes, "'Concentrated Ground': *Grey Gardens* and the Cinema of the Domestic," *Framework* 47, no. 1 (2006): 100. See also Jonathan B. Vogels, *The Direct Cinema of David and Albert Maysles* (Carbondale: Southern Illinois University Press, 2005), 124–57; and Kenneth J. Robson, "The Crystal Formation: Narrative Structure in 'Grey Gardens,'" *Cinema Journal* 22, no. 2 (1983): 42–53, for more on the 1975 documentary.

89. James Krasner, "Accumulated Lives: Metaphor, Materiality, and the Homes of the Elderly," *Literature and Medicine* 24, no. 2 (2005): 220. See also Krasner, *Home Bodies: Tactile Experience in Domestic Space* (Columbus: Ohio State University Press, 2010), 52–53.

90. See Adam Phillips, *Winnicott* (Cambridge, MA: Harvard University Press, 1988), 70.

91. "Jackie's 'Poor Kin' Live with Cats and Clutter," *Los Angeles Times*, September 26, 1975, 1A.

92. David Maysles and Albert Maysles, "Our Answer to Walter Goodman's Review of GREY GARDENS," in *Grey Gardens*, ed. R. Maysles and S. Maysles, unpaginated.

93. Rhodes, "Concentrated Ground," agrees: the film is "a delicate operation of simultaneously satisfying and frustrating our curiosity as guests and spectators" (92). For a complementary reading, see Marjorie Rosen, "'Grey Gardens'—A Documentary about Dependency," *Ms.* 4, no. 7 (1976): 28–30, on how the filmmakers "consciously restrained themselves from certain kinds of exploitation" (30).

94. "Little Edie: On Conformity, East Hampton and Grey Gardens," YouTube video, 2:47, from the film *The Beales of Grey Gardens*, posted by nickbigd, May 10, 2007, http://www.youtube.com/watch?v=OptEo2NILJc.

95. Anthony Martin, *Problems in Geriatric Medicine* (Philadelphia: F. A. Davis, 1981), 137, 138.

96. sezums, post on "Little Edie."

97. BetteDavisMimic, post on "Little Edie."

98. bennykanny, post on "Little Edie."

INDEX

Page numbers in *italics* indicate photographs.

Hamilton, Allan McLane, *A Manual of Medical Jurisprudence*, 125, 126, 136

Handbook of Mental Health and Aging, A, 129

Harlem: Collyer brothers' attitude toward black residents, 26–27, 28–29, 29; demographic change in, 24, 50; social disorganization as condition, 30, 32–33, 86; unfashionability of, 19, 23, 27–28

"Harlemitis," 4, 23–31, 44, 49, 92, 130

Harper's Bazaar, 91

Hawley-Smoot Tariff Act, 57

Hayes, Edward, 75

hoard and clutter syndrome: home furnishings and, 91–92; pathologization of, 87, 88, 93; professional organizers and, 85–87; as term, 12, 13

Hoarders (TV show), 1, 10–12, 18, 108

hoarding: as addiction, 64–65, 100–111; anal-erotic character and, 22; of animals, 15, 112, 118–19, 126–27, 131, 133; collectibles culture and, 56–64; conformity and, 18, 110, 138–41; consumerism and, 14–15, 18, 66–67, 81, 83, 95; earlier definitions of, 21; family life and, 11–12; as freak show, 14–15, 16, 44, 46, 82, 133–34; Frost's study of, 2, 4, 5, 119; gendering of, 113, 128–30; as greed, 13, 21, 31, 32; as mental illness, 2, 3, 4–5, 11, 19–21, 31, 45, 86, 95–96, 103; moral panic and, 3, 7–8, 110–11; neurological evidence of, 4–5, 6, 31, 99; object panic and, 3, 7–9; pathologizing, 15–17, 21–22, 52, 82–84; reality shows' portrayals of, 1; social deviance and, 2, 5–6, 9, 11, 42–43; as social threat, 5–9, 82–84, 128–29; unselective, 43–44. *See also specific terms*

hoarding disorder (HD): bad housekeeping and, 86, 93; biography of disease, 12–13, 17, 19; contrasted with normal behavior, 52–53; diagnosis viewed as medical breakthrough, 2;

internationalization of, 14, 104–5; legitimization as psychiatric disorder, 1, 10–11, 14, 31; older terms for, 2; prehistory, 3–4, 18, 30–31, 43, 50; problems with diagnosis, 3; shame and, 17; standardization of diagnosis, 2, 19–20, 87, 105; treatments for, 110–11. *See also specific terms*

Hoarding Handbook, The, 108

Hoarding of Animals Research Consortium, 15

"Hoarding of Possessions, The," 2, 4, 5, 119

Hobbies, 59

Home Management for Today's Busy Mom (FOF), 98

Home Sanitation, 91, 93

Horwitz, Allan V., 5

House and Garden, 51–52

Household Hygiene, 91

housekeeping, bad: CBT therapies of, 15; clutter scale and, 107; fears over, 3, 10–12, 94, 102; "house diseases" and, 92–93; recovery from, 94–95

housekeeping, scientific, 89–93; Christians and, 85, 90–91, 94–95, 97–99, 110; clutter scale and, 107; hygiene and, 14; manuals, 90, 91–92, 104; professional organizers as update of, 86, 100; social norms and, 93

Huffington Post, 103

Hughes, Frederick W., 75–76

hygiene and health fears: commercial answers to, 92–93, 95, 105, 110; dirt and disorder, 8, 16–17, 22, 29–30, 86; hoarding and, 2, 5–6, 10–11, 102; race and, 92; sanitary reformers, 89–93, 94, 102, 109–10, 117–18; slums and, 24–25, 29–30, 47–48, 127

immigrants, moral panic over, 7, 25, 50, 92

Institute for Challenging Disorganization (ICD), 104, 105–6, 108, 109